Forty-Four Years, the Life of a Hunter

*Being Reminiscences of Meshach Browning,
a Maryland Hunter and Trapper*

By Meshach Browning

PANTIANOS
CLASSICS

Published by Pantianos Classics

ISBN-13: 978-1-78987-589-8

First published in 1859

Contents

Introduction

Having been in some degree instrumental in introducing the following pages to the public, it may not be improper to inform the reader of the circumstances which led to my connection with their publication.

For several years past, I have been in the habit of visiting the mountainous regions of the States of Maryland and Virginia, as well in search of the picturesque amid some of the wildest and grandest scenery in America, as with a view of recruiting my health, and enjoying a relaxation from engrossing business cares. Some years since, during these visits, I became acquainted with the history of the Author, as an old and very successful hunter in the Alleganies; and many of the incidents here described — as well those connected with social life, as others peculiar to the chase — were listened to with much interest, because narrated by persons familiar with the details, and frequently participants in them.

Supposing that others would enjoy these adventures with equal zest, several messages were sent to the Author, suggesting their compilation and publication; and offering, if necessary, to furnish any assistance required in furtherance of the measure.

This led to a personal acquaintance with the Author, which has ripened into strong feelings of regard and attachment for himself, and for many of his numerous descendants, now numbering over *one hundred and twenty*. More recent visits have resulted in the publication of the narrative — the manuscript having been submitted to me for such emendations and alterations as were deemed necessary; I promising, at the same time, to write an Introduction for the work.

In fulfilling this promise, it may be remarked, that although many of the incidents here given may, to the minds of some, savor of romance, yet no doubt whatever is entertained of their entire truthfulness and reliability. The character of the Author has passed unscathed through a long life; and, though he is now verging on fourscore years, it stands as high, to say the least, as that of any other individual, for integrity, strong intellect, generous feelings, and heroic courage, whether in combatting with savage beasts of prey, or in struggling against the stream of poverty and adversity with which he had to contend, not only in early life, but also for a long series of years.

He is not the man to indulge in fiction, in any manner, or on any occasion. Though uneducated — having had less than six months' tuition, and that when quite a boy — he has filled important and responsible positions in his own county, not only with credit to himself, but with advantage to the public.

There are a few incidents narrated, and expressions occasionally used, which I should omit if the work were intended exclusively for a particular class of readers; but as all classes will probably read it, and find portions suited to their tastes, the selection is left to the general reader, and these phrases and incidents are retained as furnished by the Author.

Few persons, it is believed, can fail to find something in the volume to interest them; as there are occasional touches of genuine humor, details of affecting incidents, and evidences of enduring energy and perseverance, conjoined with the most undaunted firmness, that seemed to know no fear in a hand-to-hand conflict with savage beasts of prey — in fact, even bearding the bear in his den.

Meshach Browning's life may be deemed an eventful one, considering the almost constant risks he ran of losing it in his many dangerous conflicts with bears, panthers, wolves, and wounded bucks; for the latter are scarcely less to be feared than the former, as their sharp horns, and keen, cutting hoofs, are wielded with as much strength and skill, both in attack and defence, as are the teeth and claws of the beasts of prey.

It is impossible to state with accuracy how many of the denizens of the forest have fallen victims to his unerring rifle and deadly hunting-knife; for he hunted regularly during forty-four years, and thus the greater portion of that time supplied his family, besides occasionally selling large quantities of venison and bear-meat. Comparatively but few of his many hunting scenes are here referred to; but he stated to me that, from the best estimate he could make, and from data considered reliable, he had killed from eighteen hundred to two thousand deer, from three to four hundred bears, about fifty panthers and catamounts (quite as ferocious, and not much less in size than the panther), with scores of wolves and wildcats. And although now incapable, owing to age and infirmities, of pursuing the game with his wonted vigor, the "ruling passion" is still strong; for within the past few weeks his skill and perseverance have been rewarded by the capture, in his traps, of an otter and a catamount, of the few now surviving his former achievements.

My task, though a "labor of love," is comparatively a very humble one, and has been mainly confined to the correction of grammatical errors; for I desired as much as possible to preserve the easy and rather peculiar style of the Author, as it came from his own sturdy and unpractised pen, because so plain and intelligible that he who runs may read: figuratively speaking, merely lopping out the weeds and bushes which tend to obstruct the view over a landscape, glowing and radiant with native beauties.

The incidents of social and domestic life are drawn so true to nature, and brought out so vividly to view, that the reader, though even a child, can readily trace out the full picture by the mere outline. From this cause his stories are not only never without interest, but often touch the feelings and enlist our sympathies before we are fully aware of it; and thus it is that "truth is sometimes stranger than fiction."

His is the best and most captivating narrative of hunting scenes that I ever read, because free from all attempts at display, and devoid of egotism. The abrupt, nay even rude style, as it may appear to some, seems to be exactly suited to the subject — as "an abrupt and plain style sometimes bears thoughts quickest to the seat of judgment" — and so readily comprehended by all, that the reader follows *his* game, feeling all the excitement of the chase and the energy of a Nimrod, without incurring either danger or fatigue.

After the revision of the manuscript, I placed it for perusal in the hands of a friend (himself, in early life, a successful hunter in Kentucky, and also personally known to the author), on whose judgment, in matters of taste or opinion, I strongly rely, requesting him to review the work. His opinion is appended:

Silver Springs, March 2d, 1859. Friend Stabler

The perusal of the manuscript memoir of the old Hunter who began his career more than half a century ago — and who now, on the verge of 80, is preparing for another bear campaign, gave me delight instead of labor. I advise its publication, just as given with his own sturdy pen, barely correcting the grammatical errors with which it abounds. Indeed, these mistakes give such proof of the difficulty with which, as an author, this man of the wilderness had to contend, and they are so thoroughly redeemed by the good sense, good feeling, the rustic humor of the narrator, and the interest of his story, that I would prefer to let these blemishes stand, but that this age of universal scholarship is so fastidious about correct spelling and making verbs and their nominatives agree. As a striking picture of the trying life which creates the character of an American backwoodsman, the face of the autograph and the peculiar phraseology (giving evidence throughout of a struggle with literature, yet making it subservient oy the power of intellect), has somewhat the effect of the harsh Scotch dialect in giving force to expression in our language. When our race of hardy pioneers is gone, I think this original work of the Bear Hunter's penmanship would have a value that should preserve it in some public museum. "The short and simple annals of the poor" were never better told, nor the difficulties and dangers which beset them in struggling into civilization in the midst of a wilderness, were never more graphically portrayed than in this black-letter manuscript.

If the public could make the acquaintance of Mr. Browning, as we did, in the midst of the mountain region in which he has lived from youth to age, it would add such a charm to his memoir, that I am sure it would be universally read. Found in the midst of a community which had risen around him in the course of three-quarters of a century, he was still the prominent figure among a host of strong-minded, stalwart mountaineers, among whom his own progeny, numbering more than an hundred intelligent, athletic men, and beautiful women, were conspicuous. In this region, so prolific of strong-minded and able-bodied men, old Mr. Browning, the son of the subaltern English soldier who escaped from Braddock's battle, and nestled in the neighborhood below the Alleganies, still holds pre-eminence, and yet he seems insensible of it.

He is the hero of every man's conversation in his mountain republic, but never of his own; and although he embodies in his own lifetime all its history, he makes a modest cital of himself in connection with it. Like old Nestor among the younger Greek chiefs, who all are willing to defer to his experience, wisdom, and eloquence, he chooses to defer to them in importance; and is, even in "narrative old age," the most striking instance of modest courtesy in waiving its privileges I have ever known. His own adventures as a hunter are often called out from him in social circles to renew the interest of early savage scenes which civilized life is now rendering tame; and no one has a happier vein in talk to give a living image to the eye.

It is the enjoyment derived by his neighbors from this faculty, and the knowledge of his probity and truth, that induced them to urge the attempt of perpetuating the story of his life in print. If it had been taken from his lips by a practised writer, his memoir might have had much greater attraction than as now given by his untaught laboring pen, which arrests the happy flow of recital; but even as it is, the public will find the impress of genius, of truth, of good feeling and happy humor, however veiled in the medium of conveyance, to recommend the work of this illiterate man.

Sincerely your friend,
F. P. Blair.

During a more recent visit to the mountains, I met with ray friend Judge Thomas Perry, of the Fourth Judicial District of this State — a gentleman not more widely known than he is universally esteemed and respected. Long personally acquainted with the author, and familiar with the recital of many of the startling scenes narrated by him, the judge promptly and most cheerfully offered to reply in writing to any queries I might propound to him — he being then engaged on the Bench. I am well aware that no letter or certificate will add to the fair fame of the author where he is known; but it is inserted as the freewill offering of the writer, and with the kindest motives for the benefit of an old and valued friend.

Cumberland, Md., March 7, 1859.

Dear Sir:

Your note of this day has been received, and I with pleasure reply to your inquiries. I have been acquainted with Meshach Browning from my infancy, and I have never known of anything to impair his character.

I have the greatest confidence in his veracity, and you can rely upon any statement he has made, or may make. In this community, where he is well known, no one doubts the truth of the many interesting incidents narrated by him.

Respectfully yours,
Thomas Perby.

To Edward Stabler, Esq.

This letter, comprehensive and complete within itself, is all that appears necessary to perfect the "Introduction."

To live far beyond the usual period allotted to man — "three score years and ten" — and receive the commendation, "I have never known of anything to impair his character," is a legacy which should be more highly prized by the descendants of an author, or indeed of any one. than silver and gold.

Edward Stabler.

Harewood, Md., 1859.

Note. — After the work was in press, the following unsolicited letter was received from a prominent citizen of Allegany county — viz.:

Accident, Allegany County, Md., March 30, 1869.

E. Stabler, Esq.

Dear Sir: — I have seen in the public prints, sketches of the life and adventures of Meshach Browning, for forty-four years a hunter in the Allegany Mountains; and understand that you are about to have his memoir printed, and published in book form. I beg leave to say to you, and to the public, that I have been personally acquainted with Mr. Browning for twenty-five years, and know him to be a man of sterling integrity; and that he is entitled to receive at the hands of the public full credit for every word that he has written.

This work is the narration of facts as they occurred; and having spent a great portion of his life in camps, erected in the wilderness for the purpose of hunting, many things may appear strange, and almost miraculous, to those who are not acquainted with a hunter's life; yet they are nevertheless true, and can be vouched for. Mr. Browning was among the first settlers here, and is one of Nature's noblest works.

Impatiently waiting the publication of this work,

I am, dear sir, yours very truly,
Blohard Faiball.

Chapter One

I WAS born in Frederick County, in the State of Maryland, in the year of our Lord 1781. My father's name was Joshua Browning, and my mother's name was Nancy. He was a farmer with limited means, and, with his wife, resided on a small farm; having little to recommend them in this world but an unsullied name, and known only as being strictly honest, industrious, and truthful.

They lived a happy life together until they had four children — one daughter named Dorcas, and three sons, Joshua, Jeremiah, and myself, called Meshach. My mother became a widow when I was an infant of two weeks old; and, after the business of the estate was settled, there was but a trifle left for the support of the little family; and she was obliged to maintain herself and children as best she could.

But it does seem to me, that when persons are left in such distress, that kind Providence has always something in store to supply their necessities, as was the case in this instance.

My mother's friends had all gone to the West, then so called, — I mean to the western part of Washington County, and had settled on the Flintstone and on Hurley's Branch, now in Alleghany County. But to follow them she had not the means. The next thing was, her neighbors advised her to put out her children to good places, and then she could see and attend to them. But this she refused to do, until she should try to keep them herself. But before she had rented a house and garden, she did consent to let a Mr. Aaron Lee have Jeremiah, to keep him until he was twenty-one years old.

Often and long did she rue that unthoughtful transaction. And it turned out that she never could, nor ever did get him home; he lived with that family until he was 16 or 17 years old, when he quit his place to shift for himself; but not before mother and the other three children left that country, and had gone to the West.

Mother managed by dint of industry and economy, with what my sister and Joshua could help, to keep us as well as other poor children; and sent sister to school one quarter, in which time she learned to spell and read a little in her primer. They worked together in the garden, and raised plenty of vegetables; and by spinning, sewing, and knitting, in which sister began to be helpful, they got along through three or four years. My mother was a woman of a medium height, strong and determined, but of very tender heart — rash when angry, out soon over, and kind again.

She continued in this situation until she found we were making nothing, and my sister was 16 or 17 years old, when a young man by the name of James Harvey then addressed her, and they were married, much against my mother's will. Then it was that she determined to leave Frederick county, and go out to the backwoods. Shortly after, she wrote to her friends in the West that she wished to move out to them; and a brother-in-law of hers arranged to get a Mr. Jacobs, who lived in Oldtown, as he was coming from Baltimore with goods, to take our things in his wagon and help us as far as Oldtown, within a few miles of his house; and in a few days Mr. Jacobs's wagoner, a large negro, called on us to go to the backwoods, then so called. We hurried and bustled into the wagon, while Joshua was sent to Mr. Lee's for Jeremiah to accompany us; but, to our great disappointment and grief, he was not to be found. Having our property all in the wagon, off went the horses, with whip cracking, mother crying, negro cursing and swearing, until we were in the main road to Frederick — then the insolent negro became quiet; and an old man met us with another horse, to help out with our too heavy load.

We went on in good order until we reached Sideling Hill, where the road was very rough and rocky: by and by we arrived at a very sideling place, with a considerable precipice on our left — the wheels struck a rock on the other side, and away went wagon, horses, and all down the hill, rolling and smashing barrels of rum, hogsheads of sugar, sacks of salt, boxes of dry-goods, all tumbling through one another, smashing the bed of the wagon, and spilling rum, molasses, sugar, and all.

My frightened mother called out, "Where is Meshach?" — knowing that I was riding in the wagon when it turned the dreadful somerset. All was bustle and alarm, until at length I was found under some straw and rubbish, stunned, breathless, mangled, and black with suffocation. Here was despair and weeping from a mother, in a dense wood, with no help but her little Joshua, the old man, and that hateful negro. The wagon was broken to pieces, the left hind-wheel smashed, and entirely useless. The man applied the spilling rum to use in handsful, until life began to return; and as mother saw hopes of my returning to her bosom again, she became quieted.

The loading was found to be greatly damaged, with the loss of two barrels of rum, and a great quantity of sugar mixed with dirt and trash. The next task was to prepare some shelter for the night, and in the meantime to mend the broken wheel: it was, however, soon found that the wheel was so badly broken that it could not be mended; and then it was that the old gentleman struck on the following plan: he told the negro to cut down a small tree, put the butt on the foremost axle-tree, leave the top end on the ground, and lash the axle-tree fast on the dragging tree. Thus we made a substitute for the broken wheel. By this time night had come on us; a large fire was made, and my mother took her place by the root of a tree, with Joshua by her side, who was about twelve years old, and myself in her arms: she has often told me that she never closed her eyes until day-light appeared next morning; when we made a breakfast of bread, cheese, and molasses gathered from the smashed barrels, and flat and hollowing stones, where it was in puddles.

This hasty breakfast done, and everything made ready, the whip cracked again, and off we started, Joshua walking and my mother carrying me on her back: we had twelve or fifteen miles to travel before we would be in Oldtown. We proceeded on our journey slowly, reached our destination, and found ourselves in Oldtown. Mother much fatigued, worn down, and in low spirits; the wagon, old gentleman, and negro all gone off, and we three left alone in a strange country. But in the morning a neighbouring gentleman to her brother-in-law, whose name was Joseph Robinett, came by chance into the village to trade; and mother by some means found that he lived near her sister, and prevailed on him to assist her in getting me along to her friends; which place we reached a little after noon. Here we are at Hurley's Branch, and among our friends.

We remained here two or three weeks, until my wounds and bruises were well, or nearly so, when we went to my grandfather's, on the head-waters of the Flintstone, and remained during that fall and winter. The spring following, mother's friends took her to a small piece of vacant land that was too small to attract the notice of others, and no person had any claim to it: it was very good soil, and something over twenty acres. Here her friends built her up a neat little cabin, and placed herself and her children in it; and we then had a snug home of our own.

In a few weeks our sister came to us, having lost her husband, Mr. Harvey, who died the same winter we left Frederick county. She joined us, and to work went all hands; Joshua and mother to chopping and grubbing, and sister to picking up and burning the grubs and trash that lay over the ground; and soon they had four acres cleared off, and ready for planting corn. This done, they went into it altogether; dug holes for the hills of corn to be planted in, and planted as they went; and when they were done making holes, they were done planting also; and had filled with pumpkins, cucumbers, and such things as they knew would be useful for the table. Their friends helped, and soon it was under a good fence: then when the corn came out of the ground, all hands went into it, and cleaned out all the weeds, and dug up the ground between the hills, and in that way they raised nearly one hundred bushels of corn.

At this time I had an aunt living near, who was always teasing mother to let me stay with her for company for her, as she had no children. And at last mother yielded and let me go with her; and I staid one summer with her and her husband, whose name was John Spurgin. He was a good-natured, kind man, but neglectful, lazy, and unlearned: they made it their aim to seduce me from my mother's love and from my home, and take up my home with them; but took good care not to let mother get the least knowledge of their interested design.

They had me so well into their scheme, that I was ready for any movement they might wish me to undertake. So, in September, they had all things in readiness, and a young man to assist in driving their cattle and horses: they then proposed to me to go with them into the prettiest country in the world; and that I should be their adopted son, and all the cattle and horses we could raise should be mine; and that I could stand in the door and see the pretty deer sporting and playing in the glades; and as soon as I was big enough to shoot, I should have a nice rifle to shoot those deer.

Fired with such prospects of sport, I was ready and willing to undertake the journey forthwith. I was put to bed, and told to go to sleep, and they would wake me before day, and take an early start, so that my mother should have no chance of stopping me. Sure enough, I was awakened a long time before day-light; all was ready for a move, with three horses loaded, and the young man Boon had the cattle ready to follow the horses. I was put on one horse, my aunt on another, and uncle drove the third; aunt in the lead. Off we went, as still as possible, that our movements should not be known to my mother until we would be sufficiently out of her power. On we went, without noise, over the mountains towards Cumberland; and, as the sun began to show its beautiful reflection on the high top of the Dan Mountain, westward of the town, we arrived in sight of the valley in which the town was situated. Here was a new scene to me entirely. The whole valley was covered with a dense fog — nothing was to be seen but the high tops of the western mountains, with here and there stripes of sun-light; whilst all around was in uproar, with cows bellowing, calves bleating, dogs barking, cocks crowing, and, in short, all sorts of noises. The fog was so heavy that I could not see any object until within a few paces of it. Here we halted for our breakfast. By that time the sun had driven away all the misty clouds, and the town was in plain view; and I think that there were not more than twenty or thirty houses, and they mostly cabins, surrounded by large corn-fields, containing heavy crops of corn.

Breakfast over, we resumed our march for the new country before us: on, on we went; and in the evening we found ourselves at the Little Crossings; here we halted for the night; the horses and cows were taken to pasture, for few houses of entertainment in those times kept oats or grain of any kind for feeding purposes, in summer, but depended altogether on grass. Supper being ready, we partook with others of a welcome meal, made up of buckwheat cakes, fresh fine butter, delicious honey-combs, venison steak, as also some fine jerk, [1] and sweet milk, of which we all took a good share.

We had our own bedding with us, which we laid down on the floor, and prepared for resting our tired limbs: soon we were down and sound asleep. The morning came, with a prospect of a good day; and, by the time I could see to walk, I was called up to fetch the cows, while my uncle saddled the horses, and got ready for breakfast. All this being done, and breakfast over, we bid good-bye to Little Crossings, and took the road again for the "Blooming Rose:" this place is a large tract of land, so called in consequence of the great variety of beautiful flowers that adorned the whole tract; and that part of Alleghany county is still known by that name. We travelled without halt-

12

ing, save to water our beasts, until late in the afternoon, when we arrived at the residence of my uncle's father.

Here we halted for a month or two, until uncle should seek a home away in the glades of the Buffalo Marsh, where I was to see so many beautiful sights. After a long time of anxious delay, as I thought, and after two or three different visits to the intended home, he at last determined to make a start for it, much to my joy and satisfaction. This day brought us to a home entirely up to my greatest expectations; for then, although late in October, there was great abundance of pasture for our stock, and uncle had cut plenty of wild grass, the summer before, for all our stock through the coming winter; and we had an excellent log-cabin to live in. This cabin had been the residence of an old hunter, whose name was Augustian Friend, or "Old Teen Friend," as he was called. He had squatted there, to hunt in those beautiful glades and the surrounding mountains; and he had left here to go on the Cheat River, to settle on a new place, where no other hunters would interfere with him. He left a fine potato patch and garden, which we took possession of as our own, and no person objected to our claiming the premises.

Here we were in the place I had so long been looking for, with so much anxiety; and I must say that what my uncle had told me as a truth was fully realized; for the country abounded with deer, bears, panthers, wolves, wild cats, catamounts, wild turkeys, foxes, rabbits, pheasants, partridges, wild bees, and in all the streams trout without number.

October being the beginning of the hunting season, my uncle commenced his task of laying in the winter's provisions: some days he would hunt for deer, other days for bees; and, as ho was most successful in bee-hunting, he spent more of his time in hunting bees than he did in pursuing the deer. Soon our table was abundantly supplied with venison and honey; and the high, fresh tame grass caused our cows to give large quantities of milk, from which aunt, who was a very industrious woman, made plenty of butter; and frequently a fat turkey being added to our table store, we began to think that there was not such a place to be found in all creation.

Things went on well enough until the news came to us that General St. Clair's whole army had been defeated and cut to pieces. This was such frightening news, that aunt was almost ready to leave all, and seek some better place of safety; and indeed I believe uncle too was a little frightened. Be that as it may, he continued but a short time until he took up his march again for the "Blooming Rose." In that neighbourhood there were some thirty or forty families, who were not so easily frightened. Here we continued until the next spring, being 1792; when uncle moved into Monongahela county, in Virginia, to a brother that he had living there. His name was James Spurgin: he was a business man, yet without any education, but managed his business well, and soon became a wealthy man. Those two married sisters, who were also sisters to my mother.

Here we all lived on the same farm. Uncle James's family consisted of five children, two sons and three daughters, of whom I became dotingly fond; and when our family left theirs, I was sorely afflicted. We did not move more than two miles apart, and I was allowed to visit often. It gave me great joy to meet them, more especially the second daughter, who was about my age. So things continued, until uncle became restless, and, wishing to have another new home, determined to go back to the Blooming Rose again. This was a hard trial for me. I had all my playmates, and, the worst of all, my sweet cousin to leave. I was, as I thought, in a bad way. I had the cows to drive, and I got them in front, and pushed them hard, so that I could give vent to my feelings, for I was ashamed to be seen crying in the road. But by and by we arrived at our journey's end. Here I was a stranger to everybody, and of course kept close at home for at least a month or two.

Our nearest neighbour was an Irish family by the name of McMullen. They had five children, viz., Mary, Hugh, Jane, John, and Thomas. The father's name was James McMullen, and his wife's name was Rachel. One day another boy and myself were in the woods near the old man's farm, and our dog gave chase to something, we knew not what, and ran it into a hole in the ground. I sent the boy to McMullen's for the loan of a mattock to dig out our game. We soon had the fellow out, and he was a very large ground hog. He gave our dog at least fifteen minutes' hard fighting, and when the battle ended we went to the house to return the mattock. I sent the boy with it, as I was a stranger, and too bashful to be seen in a strange place. When the boy told that the ground hog was out with me, the three oldest children came to see the animal. Mary was then in her twelfth year, and I was six months older. She was a beautiful girl, and I was struck with her beauty, and soon got a small acquaintance with the family. I was at all times ready and willing to do anything that would please the old people. But soon there was a school to be made up, and my uncle signed me for three months, and, to my great pleasure, Mr. McMullen signed Mary and Hugh. This was just as I wished it to be, for they had to pass by our house on their way to and from school. In a short time they came, and oil' we went together, all merry and playful. All was as it should be for weeks and weeks, while I done everything I could to get into her favor, until the school broke up, for which I was very sorry.

I had learned finely, and Mary had taken every opportunity to assist me in my lessons, for she had been three months at school before the time we commenced together; and when we left school, I could read and write as well aa she could. But never did a boy exert himself with more ambition than I did on that occasion, for I was determined to be as fast as herself at all events, and either Mary or I would be at the head of the class almost every night. This caused an intimacy between us that convinced me that my kind attention to her, as well as towards her brother Hugh, had made a very favorable impression on her young heart. I believe that her father had some idea of our friendship getting stronger than he wished to see it, and he took care to keep us at a distance as much as he could; but her mother and all the children were my friends. Mary and myself were at this time about fifteen years old, and had passed many pleasant hours in social pastime, unknown to her father. I would watch his movements closely, and, when I knew he would be from home at nights, I would go to see her and the family generally. But I am free to confess that if Mary had not been there, I should have saved myself the trouble of making those visits to the family. This was kept up until I was very nearly found out by her father.

He had gone from home, as I thought, for all night, and I concluded I would see Mary that night once more, and have a chat. Off I went, heart in hand, but being afraid her father would come home unexpectedly, and as I dreaded to be found in her company (my fears were more for her than myself), as I was apprehensive that he would treat her badly, and that would be worse than any punishment he could inflict on me. In order to be sure he was not at home, I went to the back window and peeped in, and saw the mother and family quietly sitting at work, but no old man. Taking it for granted he was not there, I was about to turn the corner to the door, when, to my utter confusion, "Bow wow! Wow!" barked a large dog, and "Catch him, Prince!" screamed the old man. "Heaven and earth! thunder and storm!" thought I to myself, "what now?" As quick as thought could come, I determined to keep the house between us, until I could make a safe retreat. Behind the house I flew, and seeing a flock of sheep lying at a short distance from me, and, having light clothes on, I fell on my hands and feet, and began to gallop as fast as I could into the flock of sheep, hoping the old man would take me to be one of the flock. Off went the sheep, the old man screaming at his dog to catch what he took to be a prowling wolf — the sheep and myself both galloping for good life, until I was completely out of the old man's sight. When I found I had succeeded so well, I said to myself, "Clear once more, by gracious, and nothing to brag of! This shall be the last time I will go behind any person's house to see what is in it. I had better have gone in boldly, when I could have made some excuse for being so late, and got off like a man. But if I had been discovered, Mary would never have heard the last of it," These reflections past, I wiped the sweat off ray face, and fixed up my shirt, which had been nearly all drawn up towards my head, by my shoulders being so much lower than my hips in the galloping scrape; and in heaving and bounding forward to keep up with the sheep, my linen was all round the middle of my body.

After getting my clothes straight again, I started (or home. I told the occurrence to no one, with the exception of Mary, it being so mixed with fun I could not keep it from her. This just suited her, for she was fond of having a joke of that kind, and often when I would be a little hard for her in joking, she would say: "You are fit for nothing but to chase sheep," (and this is to this day a byword), or, "You are more fitted to chase sheep." No person but she and I, however, knew how it came into use.

15

This familiarity continued without interruption until my my other Joshua and his wife, with a fine little son four or five months old, came in search of me, as they were travelling from the west back to Flintstone. They told me that mother had married her second husband; that the newly married couple, with Joshua and his wife, had moved to the West; that they were going to see her friends at Flintstone; that my mother wished me to come to her, for she had no hopes of ever seeing Jeremiah again; and that my sister had died, and left her with only Joshua and myself. I had not seen my mother then for six years, and I had a strong desire to visit her; but being persuaded by uncle and aunt to continue still with them, I gave up the journey to my mother's home in the West.

I forgot to mention that my aunt, while living in Monongahela, unexpectedly to everybody, had become the mother of a little daughter, after being married about twenty years. This knocked my nose clear out of joint; for I was soon denounced as lazy, and everything but a good boy. But when my brother called on me to go to my mother, my aunt, to keep me with her, promised to make me as good clothes as Mr. McMullen's children had. This was as good as I wanted, and I agreed to stay and try it a while longer. I was then coming close to my sixteenth year, and Mary the same; but in a short time after my brother left, I heard nothing more of the new clothes, and aunt got still more and more cross. She had long been in the habit of flogging me very severely, and finding no preparation for my clothes, I hunted coons and wild cats, and sold the fur, which was then in brisk demand. I took it into my head to try the deer, and I procured an old rifle that carried an ounce ball. I had been out with other hunters, but they would always do all the shooting.

This time I loaded up my old gun, and set out in great earnest. I travelled about two miles, and found the tracks of a lot of deer. After them I went, and in came another hunter before me, and took the tracks from me. I turned another way, and presently I heard him shoot. "There," said I to myself, "if that rascal had staid at home, that deer would have been mine." But on I went, looking for more deer. By and by, I saw two standing looking at me. I immediately placed my gun against a tree, took aim, and bang went my old gun with deafening sound, till my ears rang; the cause of which was, that having no charger to measure the powder, I had put in enough for at least two loads. As soon as I recovered from the shock, I looked for the deer; and there stood one, looking at the other down and kicking. With the best speed I could make, up I came, with the empty gun in my right hand, and on to the deer I sprang like a panther. But no sooner was I on than I was off again, and sprawled, heels and head, gun and all, in the snow. I drew my knife, left ray gun, and sprang at my game a second time, and succeeded in giving her a fatal cut across the neck, which severed the two large veins, and left her my meat; then looking for the other deer, there it stood, looking at me as if nothing had been going on. I ran for my gun, and found the heat of the barrel had melted the snow all over it; loading was out of the question, until it was well dried, and in the meantime the deer trotted off.

I was in high spirits, for all the hunters had often told me that I would miss the first deer I would shoot at. Then to skinning it I went. That done, and the meat secured, it was time to start for home. On my way I had to pass Mr. McMullen's house, but I did not see Mary, because I only passed by the barn, where the little boys and a young man were dressing flax, and, their day's work being done, the young man went home with me. When I arrived, my uncle was away from home, and my aunt, as usual, being in a very ill humor, would not speak to me. It was after dark, and I was tired and hungry. At last she said:

"Do you think of getting your supper here to-night?"

"I hope so," I replied.

"Well you will miss it if you do," she answered.

At this time her little daughter had a low stool, one of the legs of which was loose, and often dropped out. I went to sit down on it, when, the leg coming out, I fell back and struck my head against the jam, and hurt myself. Thinking to myself that I would burn that worthless leg and put in a better one, I threw it into the fire; but when the child saw the leg in the flames, she screamed with all her strength. I then pulled it out again without being burned, and gave it to her; but as the little creature had been petted and spoiled, she came slyly to me and struck me in the face with it, when the blood flew out of my nose in an instant. I immediately slapped her on the head, and the next minute was sorry that I had done it. As aunt had seen me strike the child, she took a heavy wooden shovel and made a blow at my head; but luckily it struck me flatway and broke to splinters. I recovered from the blow, and shut my fist to knock her down; but Providence sent the young man to save me from the disgrace of striking a woman — in act which I have ever since kept clear of. I then told old aunty that it would be the last blow she would give me; and it was so; for from that time, being determined to stay no longer with them, I began to think of going to the West. But the tug was to leave my little Mary, who was then growing into womanhood very fast.

After a struggle of two or three weeks, I came to the conclusion that Mary McMullen could not leave her home to go with one who had not a dollar, and that she and I were altogether too young to marry. Yet I determined to see her, and let her know my whole intention. Accordingly, the old man being from home, I spent one sweet evening in social chat, and told her all I intended to do. She tried to keep a firm countenance, but I saw clearly that she felt as much at heart as I did; for when I took her hand, perhaps for a last farewell, I saw her soft, rising bosom swell with emotion, as she said, "Good-bye, Meshach; I wish you good luck, and a safe and speedy return;" for I had told her that, could I make money to keep me along right well, I would come back, some time or other, to see all my friends again. So saying, we parted for that

17

night, with the promise to see each other again before I took my leave of her and all my other acquaintances in Allegany. I staid all night, as I was assured the old gentleman would not return during that time. I slept but little, thinking of my adventurous undertaking. The next morning, at breakfast, the day of my departure was spoken of, when I named the second day after; which was objected to by Mary, because it was Friday, and was said to be an unlucky day to commence any important business. She said she thought my leaving my native residence to go into a strange country was of the highest importance; and I imagined I could see in her countenance strong emotions of the heart — for she very soon left the table and went into the kitchen. I made a light breakfast, too; and when Mary returned it was agreed that the following Thursday should be the day when I would leave Allegany; which allowed me six days to bid farewell to all my friends.

GUNNER'S VICTORY.

I then left this much esteemed family, intending to visit some other playmates and acquaintances. A friend proposed a deer-hunt, there being a fine tracking snow on the ground, to which I readily agreed, and off we went with dog and gun. After traveling a long time, in the evening we found a large buck. Having but one gun, and that being mine, I took aim, let drive, and off went the buck. We went to where he had stood when I had shot at him, and, from the hair and blood he left in his tracks, we saw he was wounded, and pursued him with rapid steps; for night was coming on We soon found him, for the poor fellow had lain down from excessive pain and loss of blood. As he made off again, we set on our dog, who was trembling with eagerness for the chase. Off went Gunner, for that was the dog's name, and we soon heard him at full bay. Who should be up first was then the question to be decided. Jump and jump we went, side by side, till my strength and long wind prevailed, and I ran up first. But in running through the bushes, some snow having fallen on the lock of my gun, wet the powder, and it would not fire. Here

18

we were, with no means of helping poor Gunner, or of keeping him from being injured by the buck's sharp horns. At length, while the faithful dog was holding the buck by the nose, I drew my hunting-knife from my belt and made a desperate pitch at the heart of the infuriated beast, which laid him out dead in the creek, where he had expected to be able to defend himself in the water.

My friend and myself were both wet to the knees, and the evening being very cold, it became necessary for us, as soon as possible, to make for the nearest house. With all possible haste we skinned the buck and secured the meat, when we started for the place of safety, which was about four miles. On we strode, with long steps, made in as quick succession as possible, until my friend began to complain that his feet were freezing. He swore they would be frozen off to his ankles before we could reach any house. I found mine were freezing too, and I waded all the little streams we crossed; but he would not go into any water, for he said he had been in too much already; so on we went, until we came to the house we had aimed for. As soon as the man of the house saw our condition, he brought some fresh spring-water, and put our feet and legs in it for at least an hour, when the frost was drawn out.

We lodged there that night, and found next morning that our feet were swelled and very sore; but from my frequently wetting mine in the little streams, they were not so much injured as his were.

From this time, I visited all my friends, and got ready for my journey west. The night before the appointed Thursday I was bent on spending, at any rate, within sight of little Mary. I determined to commence talking with her in the presence of the whole family. Accordingly, I went to the house, and spoke to the old man as respectfully as I knew how; and in a little while he said to me, in a friendly tone "So, Meshach, you are going to leave us, I hear."

"Yes, sir," was my answer.

"How long do you intend staying?"

"Perhaps I shall not return for years, and it may be that I may not come at all."

"Ah! when you get among strangers, you will soon be homesick, and back you will come."

"Well, Mr. McMullen, this is not impossible; but, sir, I assure you I do not think Allegany county will see me soon again."

I said this in the presence of Mary, whom I had promised that I should return again some time or other. I did not mean exactly what I said; but I knew it was what he wished for, and, that in hopes of this being the last visit I would pay to his house, he would not object to my having a last talk with Mary.

While I talked to the old man, I saw that Mary listened with attention, and I knew what she had in her mind about what I had told her. I watched the old man closely, and presently he began to ask questions of the boys about the horses and the stable, when he took his hat and went out to the barn. This was my time: I whispered to Mary, and informed her I had told her father such a tale, and that I did it in hopes the old man would not be so bad as to prevent me from having an evening talk with her, which I had much desired since I saw her last. I asked her if she would venture to undertake it in the presence of her father? After a little hesitation, she said she could only try it, and if he cut any capers, I must stop short, and wait till another opportunity to see her. This being agreed on, I went to the barn, and helped to feed the stock. It was quite night, dark, and very cold. Well, thought I, let what may come, I will try my luck. So, when I thought the right time had come, with trembling limbs and beating heart, I drew up my chair by the side of Mary, as she sat knitting. I was half-choked with fear of the old man, and so much embarrassed, that it was some minutes before I could speak a single word; but to my great satisfaction, the old man went off to bed.

"Stand still, boy," Mary said, with a sweet smile; "what is the matter with you? I believe you are speechless."

"No, no, Mary," said I; "but I was afraid that your father would turn me out this cold night, and that I would have no chance to see you again before I started to the West. It seemed to me that if he had spoken crossly to me I should have fainted on the floor."

This caused her to laugh heartily at my expense, which seemed to make her still more dear to me than she was before. By this time I had got my nerves quieted; and an interesting discourse sprang up concerning our school pastimes, and the great probability of our never enjoying the like pleasures again. By this I fancied I could bring her to an acknowledgment of what I thought I had seen before in her countenance; but, firm to herself, she would not gratify me with any admission of her affection.

However, we spent a very pleasant evening together, and promised to see each other for a parting farewell the next morning. At, or rather before it was light, the old man left home without saying a word to Mary or I. This was pleasing to us both; and I believe the whole family were glad that he was gone, as it gave us time to finish any little thing we had left unsaid the evening before. After breakfast I began to get ready for a start, all the time watching every motion Mary made; but she kept firm till the old lady had made me a present of a fine pair of socks and a beautiful pair of woollen gloves. She told me that she had knit the socks herself, and that Mary had knit the gloves for me; but that she was too bashful to give them to me. Mary was not present when the old lady handed over the very welcome gifts; but she soon appeared again, and helped to stow away my small stock of clothing. This done, I bade good-bye to all but Mary, who said she would accompany me as far as the bars. Off we started for the bars, which were only a few steps from the door, and here we had another long talk, though we both kept off from the subject of marriage; for I really did not intend to return. In our discourse, I told her it would perhaps be a long time before I should be back to see her again; and then I expected to see her a married lady.

"No, no," said she; "when you come, if ever you do return, you will find me as you now leave me."

"Will you promise me that in good earnest?" said I.

"If you come in five or six years, you shall find me as I am now in every respect."

"Well, Mary," said I, "if something unexpected does not happen to me, I will see you again before the half of that time."

I looked at her, and saw a tear ready to roll from her clear blue eye, and I was compelled to take her hand aa quick as possible, to hide my own emotion from her. I grasped her hand, drew her to my bosom, and kissed her: then wheeled from her, and was soon out of sight.

[1] Jerk: this is the fleshy part of the venison, sliced thin, salted, and dried over hot coals till cured: it is excellent eating.

Chapter Two

Having left Mary in such a hurry in order to suppress my feelings, I feared that she would doubt my sincerity in what I had been saying to her at our last two meetings; and I stopped in the road to consider whether I should not go back to make all right. But, after some little reflection, I said to myself, "Would I not look like a fool to be seen going back, no one but Mary knowing what had brought me there? But let her think what she pleases; hang me if I will go back!" So saying, I traveled the road as fast as I could walk; but my toes were so sore from being frozen only the week before, that I made rather a slow walk of it; trying all the time to dispel the thoughts of Mary, and the msinner in which I had leit her. Almost before I knew where I was, I found myself in full sight of Uncle James Spurgin's farm; having traveled seven miles on my way westward.

Entering the house, I was received kindly; and, a very cold night coming on, I was asked which way I was going. This was a tough question for me, as I was leaving his brother; but I resolved to tell the truth, anyhow.

"I am going to Wheeling, uncle," was my reply.

"So you have left John, have you?"

"Yes, sir. Uncle John is a good, kind man, but he is doing nothing for himself; and I can never do anything while I stay with him."

"That is true, Meshach; but what do you intend to go at, as you have no learning?"

"I cannot tell you, uncle, till I get there; and then whoever gives me the best wages I will work for."

"And how long will it take you to get to Wheeling?"

"I do not know, sir; for my feet were frozen so badly last week that I can't walk fast. But I have allowed myself four days at the outside. That is twenty miles a day; and if my feet do not get worse I can do it in three."

"How much money have you?"

"One dollar, sir."

"And do you think to get to Wheeling with one dollar, boy? "

"I don't know, sir; but I have this buckskin," — showing him the skin, — "and intend to sell that in Union Town for what it will bring; and it ought to be worth seventy-five cents, at any rate. I think that will take me there; and if it does not, I will turn out in the country and work a day or two, and then go on again."

"Well, Meshach," said he, "I will give you my advice if you will promise me to take it, and attend to it."

"That I will promise you to do, sir; for I know I stand in need of good counsel."

"Then," said he, "be sure to avoid bad company; avoid all drunken crowds of rowdies and houses of ill-fame. Never suffer yourself to be drawn into them, for you will be tried often. And when these temptations appear before you, then remember what I now tell you, and avoid them. Furthermore," he continued, "when you find a man who wishes to hire you, ascertain, if you can, whether be is honest; and if so, go to him, and do for him a just and fair day's work. And if anything goes wrong, either owing to your neglect or accidentally, never tell a lie to screen yourself; but speak candidly, and acknowledge the truth of the whole matter. This will give your employer confidence in you. But, on the contrary, if you undertake to lie yourself out of it, you will be sure to be detected in so doing, and then you will be disgraced. Take it for granted, Meshach, that all good people despise a liar as much as they do a thief; and let me tell you, boy, a good name is the best thing that a young man can have. If you will take ray advice, and never tell a falsehood, under any circumstances whatever, you will in the end find that, in any and every place, truth is far better than a lie. And now, Meshach, I do not blame you for leaving your uncle John; and I wish you may have good luck in your undertaking, and that you may become a good and an honorable man." Here he ceased speaking, being called to supper, which ended the discourse.

Supper being over, the old people went into another room, and left me to talk with my cousins. I was taxed strongly by Lina, for that was the name of the daughter whom I had left with so much unwillingness, and had cried in the road about, when I was driving the cows. She said she had heard I was deeply in love with Polly McMullen. I replied, it did not seem much as if I was in love with any one when I was then on my way to the West, perhaps never to comeback again. "But," said I, "let me tell you, girls, that Mary McMullen is one of the sweetest girls in all this country; and if I was old enough, and was as well situated as your brother Jesse is, I would like very well to marry her. Marry her! yes, indeed. Lord! wouldn't I like to take such a pretty little bird as Mary is!"

This was said in a joke; but my feelings were such that I feared that Lina would see something in me that would betray ray real sentiments. But it all passed off as a joke, and our time was spent very agreeably till the old people called out bedtime.

We all parted, and I lay a long time before I could persuade my eyes to close. Uncle's good advice had made a deep impression on my mind; and, seeing the benefit it was intended to be to me, I concluded that from that time forward I would never tell a lie. And I now declare solemnly that I have never, to this day, told what I knew to be false, except, perhaps, when I have been sometimes called on to relate some mischievous tales that were going the rounds; when I have said I knew nothing of the matter; and in this way, and this only, have I ever departed from the known truth.

And here I say, thanks be to the name and to the memory of James Spurgin; to whom, I am free to acknowledge, together with another very kind friend of mine, of whom I shall speak hereafter, I owe all that I now am. However, nature overcame my feelings at last, and I knew nothing of myself till the old folks called for the boys to rise and make fires. Up we all bounded, and soon had them roaring and crackling. Then for feeding the stock. Snow had fallen during the night above knee-deep, and the morning was stormy and very cold. But out we ran, as if we would defy everything like snow and wind; and soon we had fifty or sixty cattle fed with hay from the stack; two pitching it off and one scattering it out.

"Now for the horses!" cried Jesse, as he started for the barn.

Off went Jonathan and myself; but Jesse had the start of us, and was throwing the hay on to the floor; and in a few minutes the feeding was done, and we all gathered around the fine fireside. By this time the girls had breakfast ready, and all were seated; the conversation being mostly between the girls and myself, as to where I expected to make my residence, and when they should look for my return. To all questions I made the same reply — that it would be very uncertain when I should return, if I ever returned at all; when Lina took the opportunity to tell me when I would come back. That would be, she said, as soon as I began to think about that pretty little bird that I had been telling them of last night, I replied that I would go out to the far West and look me up a pretty little squaw, and live among the Indians and hunt buffaloes and bears.

"Well," said Lina, "when you undertake that, the Indians will take off your scalp; and really, I think it would be of no consequence if they did." She spoke with seeming warmth, which raised a burst of laughter round the table, and ended the discourse.

Breakfast over, I began to talk of starting on ray way; but all hands thought the day was too cold and stormy. Having now commenced my journey, however, I wished to see the end of it, and I would not agree to lose a day. So, bidding all farewell, I set off for Union Town, which was twenty-two miles distant. I traveled at a tolerable gait till I fell into Braddock's old road, which I found well broken. I proceeded on till I reached the summit of the great Laurel Mountain, and looked as far west as I thought I could travel next day;

while nearer to me, and in full view, laid the little town where I intended to lodge that night, which I reached as daylight was about leaving me.

Here was a boy, not sixteen years old till the following March, thrown out into a strange country, without friends, without money, and, worse than all, without education; like a wild colt in the wilderness, to stray where he pleased.

The landlord, being a friend of both my uncles, would act charge me anything when I was about to leave the following morning; for which I thanked him kindly, bade him good morning, and took the road for Wheeling. I traveled till late in the evening, when I fell in with a young man on his way home from a raising. He invited me to stay with him over night, saying that he lived with his father and mother, who were very old, and that he would be glad of my company. As it was but a short distance from the road, I accepted the invitation, and was treated kindly by the good old people, who would not charge me anything, but sympathized with me in my present condition

Bidding them good-bye, I set off again on Sunday morning, and, after traveling some eight or ten miles, I came to a rather better-looking house than many I had passed in my journey, when, feeling tired, I concluded to stop and rest myself. The owner of the house, who seemed to be a good man, asked me many questions as to where I was going and where I came from. He then inquired my name, to which I answered, "Meshach Browning, sir."

"Meshach Browning I any relation to old William, and his son John Browning?"

Thunderstruck at these words, I made every inquiry I could, until, recollecting himself, he said there was to be preaching at his house that day, and if I would .stay, perhaps several of the family would be there; and he felt sure the old man would come, for he never failed to attend. So I remained some time, till I became restless. After many persons had arrived, it was said by some one that old Mr. Browning was coming; when Mr, Foot, the gentleman of the house, asked me if he should introduce me to the old man as his grandson. Being fully convinced that it could not be otherwise, I consented; and, as the old man was looking for a seat to rest himself, he being then over eighty years old, Mr. Foot said, "Mr. Browning, don't sit down till I make you acquainted with one of your grandsons." The old gentleman looked astonished as Mr. Foot took my left hand and presented me to him, saying, "This is Meshach Browning, your grandson, sir."

The old man at first seemed to be completely confused; but after recovering himself he said, "Is this Joshua's son?" I told him it was truly so. He then sat down; and, after wiping the tears from his eyes, and when his feelings had become a little more composed, he said, "Well, Mr. Foot, you will excuse me for this day; for this youth may have some trouble in finding the road to his mother's, and I cannot miss being present at their meeting."

"Certainly, sir; I should like to witness it myself. But young man, tell your mother that I wish her much joy on account of her young son, and hope to see her as soon as she is able to be out again."

The old gentleman took his hat and started off. I followed, answering many questions, and hearing of many things that had taken place after I left Flintstone, till we approached a farm; when the old man, laying his hand on the fence, said, "Meshach, this is the farm where your mother lives; we shall soon see her. Yonder she is now."

The old lady had gone out to get a bucket of water, and was then near her own door, but did not notice us till we stepped into the house. She took the old man's hand, and, after asking how he was, said, "Who is this young man with you, father?"

"Look at him, Nancy, and tell me if you think you have ever seen him, or if you know any one he favors." She seemed confused, and after some time replied that she did not recollect ever having seen him before, nor did she know any person whom he looked like. "Well," said the old man, "does he not look like yourself?"

"For Heaven's sake, father, what do you mean? is it one of our relations?"

The old man replied, in a calm tone, "Be composed, Nancy; it's your son, Meshach."

"Lord be praised!" said the poor old lady; and she Bunk back in her chair, breathless.

Her husband, who had been looking on, immediately threw cold water on her hands and in her face, and in a short time she began to recover; when the old man told me to go out of the room until he called me. I walked out, and in a short time she entirely recovered. I did not return until she became fairly composed. She seemed almost afraid to speak to me, lest her nerves would give way again. By little and little, however, she became composed, and began to converse freely. The day being now spent, the old man bade us good night; first making my mother and my step-father promise to bring me to see him as soon as I was rested.

The evening was passed in relating what had occurred after we had been separated by that selfish couple, John Spurgin and his wife. I told my mother that her sister was a great deal worse than uncle Spurgin was; and as a proof I recited the following story:

"Before they took me from Flintstone, they promised me that I should be their adopted son, and that all they and I could earn should be mine. But after they had an heir of their own (when I was about twelve years old), she became as cross as a wounded bear. She was an even-tempered woman, for she was always mad. One morning uncle sent me out very early to feed the cows; and a light snow having just fallen, sufficient for tracking rabbits, I called my dog Gunner. After the cows were fed, off I went to the woods in search of rabbits, and succeeded in taking two very fine ones; which detained me one hour, perhaps rather more. I went home proud enough of my two rabbits, for I knew that my uncle was very fond of their meat; but unluckily for me, uncle was away from home. I entered the house, thinking that my game would amply pay for the time spent in catching it.

"As soon as I was seated at the fire, I saw aunt shut the door and bolt it, when I looked around to see what was coming; and observing a bunch of switches at each side of the room, I knew there was an approaching storm.

"'Where have you been all this time, sir?' said my aunt.

"'Catching these rabbits,' I replied, pointing to them, in hopes that when she had seen them she would let me off.

"'Well, you have caught two rabbits, and you mu.st have grease to fry them in; and I'll give you that now.'

"So saying, she took me by the arm, led me into the middle of the room, and began to pour the grease on without mercy. Round and round we went, as fast as she could turn me. I soon found out what she was at by waltzing me round the room so fast: it was to have a new switch at hand as fast as she broke one over my back and shoulders.

"Round, and round, and round we went, till I found the switches were still plenty, and that I must either fight or die. I thought I might as well die fighting as to tamely submit to be beaten to death; and at it I went, with all my strength; pulling her hair, scratching her face, and biting her arms and hands, till she at length got my head between her knees, and holding me by one arm, began to beat me most unmercifully. I could not help myself in any other way than by twisting my head round until I brought my mouth directly in contact with one of the *stocks* that held my neck fast. Nothing being between my keen teet and her leg, I took hold of her flesh and skin a little higher up than she ever tied her garter, and there I hung, like a bulldog, trying my best to bite out the whole of what was in my mouth. She stopped whipping me, and said that if I did not let go my hold she would beat me to death.

"'Will you let me go?'" she said.

CATCHING RABBITS.

"Ah, old fellow, thought I, if I let go to tell you I won't do it (which I am determined not to do), then, when my hold is broken, I may not again get so good a chance; and when she repeated, ' Won't you let go, you devil? ' I shook my head in token that I would not, clenched my teeth, and threw my head from side to side to get the mouthful out. But her skin was so tough that I could not tear it. Finding me deaf to all she said, she had no remedy but to fight; and at it she went again. She tried to kick me off with the other foot; but I was in such close quarters that she could do me but little harm. Finally, I began to suffer for want of air, on account of my mouth being pressed down so close to her flesh, and my head being covered up under her clothes; and from long fighting, the old woman had become so hot that what little air I did breathe was as stifling as if it had been heated in a stove. Completely exhausted, I was compelled to open my mouth to catch my breath, and trust to chances for the balance of the fight. I rose to my feet; and, though by this time she was quite out of breath, she picked up another switch and laid over me with all her strength, saying, 'Won't you cry for me, you --- you?'

"I told her that if she beat me to death I would not cry for her; 'For,' said I, 'that would please you too well; and I tell you that you are not able, nor you never shall make me cry again.'

"'Yes, you --- scoundrel, I have been suckling till I am so weak that I can't master you any more.'

"'Thank God for it!' said I 'You have not made much by this job; and the next time you try it you will make less.'

"So saying, I walked off, and she went to the bed and laid down; and from that time she never undertook to beat me in that way again."

My mother heard this story with excited feelings. But when I told her that the fight had cost my aunt a considerable spell of sickness, her anger was somewhat appeased. We retired to rest at midnight, and slept soundly till sunrise the next morning. We breakfasted on a fine dish of fried chickens, with fresh butter, light rolls, and different kinds of preserves.

Well, thought I to myself, this is a fine place, surely, to make a living; and if Mary only lived out here I never would wish to see Alleghany again. But Mary will have to take care of herself, and I must do the same. I will try to forget her as fast as I can, and seek some business at which I can make something for myself.

My mother and friends prevailed on me to spend a week with them; and in the mean time I helped one of the young men with a job he had to finish for a certain General Biggs, who held an appointment from the Government to survey the State of Ohio, and lay it off into sections. While I was working for him with my friend, the General asked me how I would like to go with him on that expedition; and as it was certainly just such a place as I would like to be in, I told him it would suit me first-rate if I would be allowed to take a good rifle with me, and hunt every evening and morning. He asked me if I understood handling a rifle. I told him I did; and that if I had one I could prove to him that I was no slouch with it, either.

"Well, my boy," said he, "there is my rifle in the passage; let me see you try yourself."

All being ready — a paper about the size of a half-dollar being put up as a mark, and thirty steps measured off, bang went the rifle.

"Excellent!" cried the General; "half-ball in the paper. Try it again; maybe that was an accident."

I loaded as quick as I could, to let him see I knew how to handle the rifle as well, if not better, than he did, and fired again.

"Well done!" said he; "whole ball in the paper. One more shot, and I am satisfied. "

I loaded and shot again, when the General exclaimed, "By gracious! almost in the centre. The three balls may be covered with a dollar. That's hard to beat. I thought myself a good shot, but that is more than I ever did in my life. Three times in succession I why you could shoot a buck's eye out every shot, couldn't you?"

"I think I could at that distance, sir."

"Well," said he, "if you will go out with me I will give you ten dollars a month, and find you in clothes and boarding."

I told him I thought I would go.

"You may hunt," said he, "as much as you please; for I want a hunter with us, if not two of them."

After finishing our job, I went home, fully satisfied that I had struck the right nail on the head. But when I told mother what I intended to do, she grew sad, and said that but three years since the Indians were killing and scalping every man they caught on the other side of the Ohio; and that they would be sure to murder the whole party, for she supposed there would not be more than twenty or thirty men with us; and what would that be against their numbers!

"They will murder you," said she, "and leave you to be eaten by the wolves; for I am told that these animals are so plenty that the" are very dangerous of themselves. I will lever consent to your undertaking such a perilous journey. And so, my sun, if you don't want to send your old mother's gray hairs to the grave, let that trip alone, and let General Biggs get hands where he can. Every poor fellow that goes with him will wish himself at home long before he gets there again. It would have been much better if you had not come to see me at all, than to stay with me only two weeks, and then go out into the wilderness, where your flesh will feed the wolves, and your bones soon lie bleaching on the ground."

At that time a young man named Francis Dodd and his wife were boarding with my father and mother. Francis was working for an old gentleman in Wheeling, by the name of John Caldwell, who paid him ten dollars a month. He joined with my mother and her friends, and succeeded in getting me to abandon ray surveying trip.

The next Saturday there was a parade in West Liberty, a small village within two miles of our residence, and Caldwell was going there to seek hands. Francis and I went there together to see Mr. Caldwell, when we met him in the town, and I made a bargain with him for ten dollars a month and my board. On returning home, my mother was much rejoiced to hear that I had given up my trip with the surveyors; and it was decided that I should go down to Wheeling with Francis Dodd.

The afternoon of the next day, which was Sunday, we set out for that town, distant fifteen miles, and reached it after dark, having traveled through mud up to our ankles. I had but little opportunity to see where I was going; but at length we found Mr. Caldwell's house, in which were several travelers, together with the family, consisting of Mr. Caldwell, his wife, and seven children.

We had no share in the night's chatting, which was carried on between the lady, Mr. Caldwell, and the travellers. Being tired, Mr. Dodd and myself retired early, and were soon fast asleep.

When morning came, the rain was pouring in torrents. The old man called me to him, and told me first to make good fires in the kitchen, and then in the house. Dodd assisted me, and we soon had blazing fires in both places; and then we fed the cows, six mules, and four or five horses; which the children and old Dinah, the black woman, usually attended to. This task was soon done, and all the family, together with the travelers, seated themselves by the blazing fire. By this time, the rain having ceased, and the clouds scattered, I began to view the strong walls that surrounded the house and kitchen. They were made of trees, split into two pieces, and planted in a ditch five or six feet deep; one-half of a tree being placed over each joint, to keep the balls of the enemy from coming through. The clay was beat so hard round the ends sunk in the ditch, that they could not be moved; and these walls were so arranged that the enemy could not approach them on any side without being exposed to a fire from within. Inside the walls a strong log house, called a block-house, was built, in the form of a double square; leaving room upon all sides to shoot, and also making it impossible to set fire to any part of the fort or houses.

This was all new to me, and I thought I would like to have been with the braves who had defended themselves so nobly in similar places. Mr. Caldwell told me that I should be his house-hand, to attend to the hauling of firewood, go to mill, make fires, etc. "Now," said he, "don't you see those mules at the stacks yonder?"

"I do, sir."

"Well, go yoke up the oxen, and haul rails, and make a fence that will keep them out; after which, if you have time this evening, haul a load or two of firewood."

I gathered up my team and hauled the rails, with which I built a good fence by one o'clock, and then set off for a load of wood. As soon as I came back Mr. Caldwell called for me, and I went in.

"You have made a poor thing of that fence, and these mules are at the stacks again. Go now and make the fence so that they cannot get in."

"I will, sir, if I can; but they are very hard to turn, sir."

I went at it, and made it eight rails high, and locked it at each corner. I then went to the house and said, "Mr. Caldwell, will you come with me, and see if you think I have it now sufficiently strong to keep them out."

He went with me, it being but a little distance; and, after walking all round the lot, he said, "Yes; if they break that they ought to be killed before they get out," So saying, he went off to the house, and I started for another load of wood.

On my return to the house, all six of the mules were in at the stacks again. I let them stay there, and went to the old man and told him the mules were at the stacks again.

"Well," said he, "go and kill every of them, or drive them off the place; and if they come back, set both the dogs on them, and drive them over the river, if you can."

Off I went; and selecting two or three round creekstones, I approached close to them, and threw one at the leader, which was the worst beast on a fence I had ever seen. I threw the stone with such force that it missed the leader, but struck another on the shoulder, and crushed the bone. Out they went, and ran off; and they continued running as long as I could see them. I was much disturbed in my mind as to what I should do; but, thought I, if it comes to the worst, I will try uncle Spurgin's plan, and tell the truth, if I have to work a whole year to pay for it.

Having come to this conclusion, I waited the return of the mules; but they did not come till the third day, when it was evident they had been in mischief; for one had been struck on his ham with an axe, and another was very lame in one leg. However, the thing passed off without any inquiry as to who had done the mischief, and I kept my own secret.

Everything went on very well, and I saw that I was rather a favorite in the family; for singing songs was then a common amusement, and I knew a great many of the most current at the time. I was often called on to sing "Sinclair's Defeat," or some other song for which the family had a fancy; and I could change my voice to sing with the girls or with men, as it best suited the company I was in.

The oldest child of Mr. Caldwell was a daughter. She was very handsome, with eyes as black as jet, long, fine black hair, hanging in beautiful curls round her temples, well-formed face, and clear white skin — in a word, I thought her a full match for Mary McMullen. Her father doted on her, and he was a rich man. Well, thought I, I have often heard it said a faint heart never gains a fair lady; and if I can keep the old people in a good humor I think I can manage the girl; for I had heard nothing of any sweetheart of hers, nor do I believe she had one.

All seemed well, till one day the old lady sent me to the woods, to hunt for a young cow, that had a calf. I went after dinner, and searched three or four hours, but could not find her. This displeased the old lady, who told me I was good for nothing. "Nancy," said she, "you must go and hunt that heifer, or she will be ruined. Go, you booby," said she to me, "and put the saddle on one of the horses, and I'll be bound she gets her."

O Lord! thought I; what would I give if I had found that --- cow! But off I went, and very soon I led the best riding-horse up to the block, and helped Nancy into the saddle; and as she turned she said, "Browning, mother has frightened you out of one year's growth; you are as pale as a cloth yet;" and off she dashed at a gallop, and was soon out of sight.

Well, thought I to myself, if she should find the cow won't I be in a fix! But I hope she may fail, and save me this evening. I'll be up to-morrow by daylight, and hunt till I do find her, if it takes me till night.

But by and by Nancy returned with the cow and calf, though she had been gone less time than I had.

"Browning," said the old lady, "take off the saddle, put the mare away, and then turn the cow into the meadow."

"Very well, madam," said I; and I soon had all done.

Neither the old lady nor Nancy said a word to me about my not finding the cow, till I went into the kitchen to make up the fire; when Nancy said to me, with a playful smile, "You are surely a great soldier, to be scared at an old woman!" and then she enjoyed a good laugh at my expense till her mother came in and relieved me.

Next morning, being Sunday, I rose betimes and made the fires; which I had scarcely done when in came Nancy. Now, thought I, we shall hear of the cow again. But I was pleased to find that she sympathized with me, by her saying she had told her mother it was not to be expected that a stranger should find them, who knew nothing of the woods, nor of the range of the cows. "And," said she, "you were going the right way till you took the left branch; the cow having strayed along the other."

We passed some little time in agreeable conversation, till the old lady made her appearance, when I left the kitchen.

After breakfast, which was later than usual, the old lady told Nancy to take Dinah, the black woman, and go to the meadow and milk the heifer. In a little while the negro came back and said that Nancy could not do anything with the cow, she was so cross.

"Go down, Browning, and help them," said the old woman.

I was far more willing to go than I wished her to understand. However, off I went, and we tried to get the cow into a fence-corner; but she would always break by us. At length, as she was passing, I seized her by one horn and by the nose, by which I held her until she was milked. Nancy then laughed at me again, and said, "You are no coward, Browning, though mother did scare you so last night. That heifer was dangerous: did you see how she ran at me with those sharp horns?"

"Oh, to be sure I saw her run at you, and was afraid she would catch you; but I was determined to stop her." By this time we were on our way to the house; and hearing a great noise there, I said to Nancy, "What does all that mean?"

"Why," said she, "they called out 'a bear, a bear!' Run, Browning, and see what is the matter among them."

I went off at the top of ray speed; and on arriving at the house, I found that four or five gentlemen, who, with their ladies, had come to visit Mrs. Caldwell, and had brought with them their bird-guns and little dogs, had seen a very large bear passing through the field in front of the house, and had started in pursuit with those little animals, two of which would make but a mouthful for the bear. Mr. Caldwell was a successful bear-hunter, and had two fine dogs, which were well trained to fight bears. I called the dogs, took the old man's gun, and ran in the direction of the noise till I overtook the party; they having halted as soon as the bear had reached the woods. The little dogs would not leave their masters; as if they were afraid the bear would tear them to pieces. As soon, however, as Mr. Caldwell's animals scented the bear, off they went, heads down and tails up. I scarcely stopped to say anything to the back-track gentry, but followed after the dogs, so that if they overtook the bear I would be near to help them in the fight, if need be. As I passed the party, they gave me many curses for being such a fool as to follow the bear after he had got out of sight.

But on went the noble dogs, and I after them. At length, hearing them in full fight, I made all the haste I could, till I saw them all turning somersets down a very steep hill. Over and over, and down, down, towards me they came, until what I made up the hill and they made down brought me within shooting distance. By this time the fight became so desperate that the bear, finding his hind-quarters were suffering severely, thought it better to try and save his breeches from being torn any worse than they were. He concluded to climb a large tree; but seeing me coming up the hill, puffing like a locomotive, he was frightened, and attempted to come down. As he descended I fired at him, and sent a small rifle-ball through the middle of his body Down he came, making two or three somersets; but finding no quarter, he immediately ascended another very large oak.

This tree being forked, and very high, he went up to the first fork, and, being sick, laid himself down in it and refused to move. By this time the back-track gentlemen had ascended the hill, pulling themselves up by the bushes. Many of them had never seen a bear before, and they began to consult as to what was to be done.

I had no more balls for my little rifle, and they had nothing but small shot, while there lay the bear. It was agreed, against my advice, to try what a load of shot would do with him; though I argued that it was an impossibility to kill him with that. I told them to let him alone until they could go for more balls, or get some one to come and shoot him. But my advice was not listened to; and I was directed to stand back and keep my mouth shut, or I should have it shut for me. I am free to acknowledge that I felt like resenting the insult, but

32

was deterred from it by being among strangers; and I submitted to it without making a reply. They then took aim and fired at the bear's head; which only made him give a snort or two, scratch his face, and climb up the tree as far as he could go, where he seated himself in another fork, and all the shooting they could do, he would not budge.

After a long parley, they concluded to send for John Martin, who could shoot a squirrel off the highest tree in the woods. When the sun was about two hours high, the messenger returned with Mr. Martin, who brought his gun, which carried nearly an ounce ball. He had also plenty of ammunition. Great anxiety was manifested for the moment to come when Mr. Bear was to get the fatal shot; and after Martin had had full time to recover his breath, which climbing the high hill had rendered rather short, he placed himself in a good position, and let drive. The bear, however, kept his place. Several more shots were fired with the same success, when it was agreed to let Captain Morris, an old Revolutionary officer, who had killed many an Englishman, have a shot. The brave captain gave notice that he would not shoot him in the body; but blow his brains out, or not kill him at all.

The gun being cleaned and loaded, the captain took aim, and off went the rifle. But, though the bear snorted, and groaned, and made a great fuss, yet he remained in his place. Another load was made ready, and the captain tried his luck again; when the bear, provoked with such treatment, rose from his resting-place, and made a bold offer to come to the ground. But on arriving at the lowest fork, and seeing a many enemies together, and the dogs standing at the root of the tree, ready for the fight, his courage failed him, and he quietly lay down again. Then Mr. Martin again took the gun, and tried two or three more shots. It may be remembered that I often asked them to let me have one more shot at him; but in return I only got curses, was asked what I knew about a gun, and told to stand out of their way, or they would knock me out.

It was by this time getting dark, and I had been at that tree from ten or eleven o'clock, and many of the others had been there quite as long. It now became so dark that Martin could not see the powder in the pan. The gun missing fire, the powder was thrown out; and in his great confusion, he did not think of the situation of his lock, but snapped and cursed, cursed and snapped, till I saw he was discouraged.

I then went up to him in the dark, and told him I could set the gun off. He gave me some curses, and told me to take it and be ---; at the same time handing it to me. I felt for the powder in the pan, and found it empty; but having some in a horn, I placed it carefully in the pan, and was ready to try my luck. By this time there were fourteen men round that tree. I could only see the bear by getting him between myself and the sky. I took the best aim I could, and fired; when down he came, and at him went the dogs. Then a shout of horror arose from the back-track party for every man to climb a tree, or the bear would tear them to pieces; and at it they went, climbing as best they could. Among the number was an Irishman, called Burk, who, in the hurry of the moment, dashed himself against a young honey-locust, which was full of long sharp thorns, and many of the points were sticking deep in his flesh, he roaring, "O Jasus! I'm ruint, I'm ruint! O Jasus! it is ruint that I am!"

Over and over, down the steep hill, tumbled the bear and the dogs, till they foil into a sink; where they stopped, and I came up with them.

The last shot had disabled the bear so much that he lay on his back defending himself by striking the dogs off as they attacked him. As I had nothing to shoot with, I went in search of a club, to help the dogs; and, pulling a dry pole out by the root, I broke it as short as I wished and went up to the fight.

Creeping behind the bear as he was reaching after the dogs in front, and leaning from me, I struck him on the head, between the ears, and down he went, while the dogs attacked his hind-quarters, and held on until I had finished him. I stood and watched the dogs worrying him till I felt safe in approaching; when, on examining him, I found his head was crushed, and that he was certainly dead.

All being now quiet, the back-track gentry began to call:

"Halloo, Captain Morris! where are you? "

"I am here."

All hands called answered. Then one asked, "Where is Browning? "

"Oh, the knows," was the reply; "for I expect the fool has run on the bear, and is killed."

"Halloo, Browning! " was called.

I wouldn't answer.

"It's no use to call," said one: "he's as dead as ---"

"Halloo, Browning!" was repeated.

Still I did not answer, for I wanted to hear what they would say.

"Halloo, Browning!" resounded a third time.

"What is wanting? said I.

"Where is the boar?"

"Here he is."

"What is he about?"

"He is dead."

"That's a lie, I expect." "How could you kill him without a gun or a tomahawk?"

"I beat him to death with a club."

"You be ---; though you are fool enough to do anything. "

So saying, they began to come nearer and nearer, till they were at the edge of the sink; but they would not come any closer till I took the bear by the foot and shook him; when they were certain he was indeed dead. Then I showed them the club I had killed him with; when each one took it and struck the dead beast on the head, to have it to say they had helped to kill the bear.

34

The question then arose, how was he to be carried home? Some were for getting the oxen and cart; but I told them they could carry him on a pole, by tying his feet together, putting the pole through between his legs, and one person taking each end. This matter decided, they inquired what they were to tie him with. I told them that freshly-peeled bark would be as good as ropes; and at it they went, to hunt a pole, while I was to get the bark. We all soon returned, with bark and pole. I tied the bear's legs, and put the pole through, when two persons took hold, one at each end. But the head of the beast hung so low that the pole wabbled from side to side, and they stag-gered like drunken men. Such cursing, staggering, and tum-bling as then occurred, is not often seen. I stopped them, and tied the head close up to the pole,

MY FIRST BEAR FIGHT.

when they got on pretty well, and soon arrived home with their prize — for they claimed the whole credit of what had been done, without naming me in any way other than as a --- fool.

The bear was laid in the kitchen, and old Mr. Caldwell came to see it, and to taunt those fellows for their cowardice. When the bear was closely exam-ined by Mr. Caldwell, all present saw that Captain Morris's two shots had struck him — one passing through his ear, the other breaking two of his tusks — without doing any serious injury; and that not a ball from Martin's numerous shots had touched him at all. This was a bad decision for Martin, and, as the result proved, for me too; for the old man decided that my two shots had killed the bear; and he spoke of their climbing trees during such a fight as being cowardly in the extreme, and said that if the bear's back-bone had not been greatly weakened by my last shot, his dogs would in all proba-bility have been killed; "For," said he, "it is clear that his was the shot that brought him out of the tree; and as soon as he was on the ground, you not only ran off, but hid yourselves, and let the dogs shift for themselves. And the same thing would have occurred had you been engaged in a fight with the Indians."

This was very galling to them; but they had no redress, except to wreak their vengeance on me; which they certainly did; for I believe they told tales about me to the old lady, and caused her to suspect that I was fond of her daughter. But be that as it may, they envied and abused me subsequently whenever they had a chance.

It being necessary to skin the bear, at it they went; but they made a poor hand of it, though they got through at last. When the meat was to be divided among the hunters. Captain Morris required his share, and all were included but myself.

"Well," said Mr. Caldwell, what share does Browning get?"

They said that they did not know that I wanted any.

"Browning" said he, "do you want any of this meat?"

"I have no use for the meat, sir," said I, "unless you desire to have a piece. If you do, I will give you what should be mine. But I would like to have the skin."

Mr. Caldwell immediately took up the skin and handed it to me, saying, "It is justly yours; for my dogs treed him, and you killed him; and you have a right to the skin; for it has always been a rule among hunters that the first blood drawn takes the skin, be it bear or deer."

This last decision completely fixed their malice against me. The meat was then shared out, when Mr. Caldwell secured his piece.

This was the first bear-fight I was ever engaged in. The adventure raised my reputation as a fearless boy, and the old man often told it to persons who happened to spend a night with him, much to my gratification. And frequently, when Nancy and the other children happened to be in the kitchen during the evenings, they would induce me to relate the whole tale, when they would ridicule the back-track party for their cowardly conduct. I saw, or thought I saw, that it had raised me in the opinion of the old man and the children; for on one oc-casion Nancy said, in a pleasant way, "Browning, when mother frightened you so I thought you were a great coward; but I don't think so now. And I heard Pappy tell a strange man the other day that if he had you in an Indian fight lie knew you would attack them as fearlessly as you did that bear. Browning," she added, "I have often wished that I had been born a boy; then I would be a man some day, and help either to kill or drive off the yellow rascals so far, that they would never come back again to murder the whites. If you had seen as much of their murdering as I have I know you would fight." She then related the following story:

"Some years ago, before General St. Clair lost so many men in a great fight with the Indians, father and mother were compelled to leave This place, and we all went up to the town fort. The neighbors were obliged to leave their farms and go into the fort also. My father and three or four of his friends used to go out, and some stood guard while the others worked, and either dressed their corn or chopped their wood, all the time expecting to be shot by those yellow savages.

"At length news came that the Indians were in the neighborhood. The fort was put in the best condition for defence, and we awaited their approach. But no attack was made. Several days passed by. when it was supposed they had given up the assault. At length two Indians made their appearance on the high hill above the town. This hill runs from north to south, while Wheeling Creek runs from east to west, passes this elevation about a mile north of the town, and then turns south, coursing along the foot of the hill, until it arrives at a point a little south of the fort where it empties into the river; thus leaving the hill a mile north of the mouth of the creek, with that stream on one side of the hill and the river on the other — with a space of not more than three-quarters of a mile between them. Whenever the river is a little high, the water is backed up the creek to the depth of ten or twelve feet. On this hill, opposite the fort, those two Indians showed themselves, fired a shot or two at the fort, and then went off slowly, slapping their hands behind them in token of derision and contempt of those within the fortification.

"Fired with such an insult, our men commenced running out, and would have all gone, had not the commanding officer stood in the gate and stopped them; though not till twenty-four men were running up the steep hill after the Indians, who were to be seen still retreating, as if they did not intend to make battle. When the whites had reached the top of the hill, to their great dismay, they found themselves between two galling fires. They could not cross the creek, if they ran that way. Seeing themselves pent up by the creek on the east and south, and by the river on the west, with three hundred Indians to contend against, the only hope left them was to break through the north line of the enemy, and escape down the river to the fort.

"As they approached the enemy, they made a desperate push through the line, and many fell; but some escaped unhurt, though they were pursued, and shot as they ran. My father was one of the last three of this brave party. As he was running for his life, with a friend of his a little before him, he saw his friend fall. As he passed him the wounded man called to him, 'John, don't leave me.' But on he ran, and after that he saw him no more. My father, however, perceived a white man, who had left the settlement some years before, and whom he recognised at first sight. This fellow carried a spear, mounted on a handle like that of a pitchfork, and ran before all the Indians. He was close at my father's heels when he arrived at the break of the hill next the fort. There was a large tree lying on the ground, and another small one standing very near it. Something tripped up my father's feet, and in he fell between the two trees; and as he went down the white Indian made a furious lunge at him. The spear, however, glanced off the log, turned its point upward, and stuck .so fast in the standing tree that the white savage could not withdraw it before my father slipped out of his position, escaped unhurt, and reached the fort safely.

"The man who culled to him for help had had his thigh broken; but he crawled on his hands until he found a hollow log, in which he hid himself till dark, when he crawled to the fort. A short time after, in came another, with one arm broken; but the balance of the party fell a sacrifice to the savages.

"Thus fell twenty-one of the best and bravest men of Western Virginia, without even having had a chance to defend themselves. Their death was a great loss to the frontier settlements, as also to the strength of the fort; which in a few days was besieged by the same band. Their previous success emboldening them, the fort was in danger of being captured. Having intercepted a boat loaded with cannon-balls, destined for the use of the garrison, the savages procured a hollow tree, bound it round with ae many chains as they could, drove wedges under the chains, to tighten them as much as possible, loaded it like a cannon, and at a favorable time let go a most tremendous charge of ordnance — such as was never heard of before. The gun burst, killing several, wounding others, and frightening the rest.

"But in a little time they renewed their attack on the fort. The ammunition had been divided between tie garrison and Colonel Zane's house. The attack was directed mainly against the latter place; but the assailants were driven back. The powder becoming scarce in the house, it was proposed that some men should run to the fort for supply; and among the volunteers for that dangerous journey was a sister of Colonel Zane's, who said she would go. This, however, was objected to, and the young men insisted on going themselves. But she was firm in her purpose, and replied that the loss of a woman would be less felt than that of a man. And pinning up her dress, to let her feet have fair play in the race, off she went. But the Indians, astonished at the sight, did not tire a single shot at her, and she reached the fort in safety. Soon she had secured plenty of powder in a slim belt round her waist, and off she bounded again for the house. But the enemy, seeing her returning, suspected some mischief, and fired a volley of balls after her; all of which missed her, and she reached her destination in safety, with plenty of powder to carry through the siege.

"The Indians, somewhat discouraged, hung round a while and hunted up a fat cow; and while some were engaged at the fort, others killed the animal and roasted it by quarters. They then took turns to go and fill themselves, while those who were not eating kept up a hot fire on the fort. But when the feast was over, they all marched off in profound silence. In the last onset, a chance ball passed through one of the port-holes just as a man was in the act of firing at the enemy, and, striking him in the forehead, killed him instantly."

Thus ended Nancy's story of Indian murders upon the whites. She continued, "I think, Browning, that if the Indians were to commence hostilities again, while you were living with us, you would fight for our family, wouldn't you?"

"Indeed, Nancy," said I, "no infernal Indian should ever take off that pretty black scalp of yours while life and strength were left in my body sufficient to save you from their cursed hands."

"I do really believe you would," she replied; "and father thinks so too: I heard him say so "

After this, our leisure time was spent in much pleasantry; and almost every evening: I would sing a song, or two, or three, for some of the family, to which the old lady would listen with seeming; pleasure. The old gentleman never failed to listen when he was home, and everything was going on as well as I could wish it, till the last month of my time was approaching; when I thought that I could see a change in the old lady — nay, I was sure that her behavior was entirely different. If we youngsters got by ourselves, singing and telling riddles, she would come and take the girls into the house, and spoil our pastime as often as we would undertake it; and the longer I remained the more crabbed she became.

All the hands were obliged to sleep in the same room, and in addition, those who were at the bear-fight — fourteen in all. Having become jealous of me, on account of the old man's decision in regard to the light, they took every opportunity they could to annoy me, and make my situation as unpleasant as possible. The days and nights being disagreeably warm, we were obliged to sleep on the floor; and, in order to harass me, my enemies would begin a scuffle with each other, in which they would soon include me, and thus I could not get to sleep till late at night. To get rid of that annoyance, I asked Nancy to give me a blanket, with which I would go out to a shed which the joiners used to work in when it rained, take my bear-skin, and pass the night on the shavings.

In that way I slept finely for a week or two, when one day I was told to saddle a horse for Nancy; and as she was about to start I said, "Nancy, where are you going to ride to?"

"I am going to my aunt's, in the country."

"How long will you be gone?"

"Lord knows," said she; "mother says I must stay till she sends for me. But," she added, "I would much rather stay at home. She will not better herself much by it; for she will have all to attend to, and no one to help her except that old sleepy negro; as Pappy swears he won't hire a girl. But farewell, Browning; you will not belong here." And off she went, at a rapid pace.

I watched her receding form as long as I could see her, for I was very sorry that she had left. From what she had said to me during a minute or two, I concluded that the old lady was suspicious that our friendship was becoming too warm; and I thought then, and have always since thought, that something

39

of that kind was the reason why her daughter left home. That was the last I ever saw of Nancy; who, in my opinion, was as fine a girl as Western Virginia contained.

After Nancy had gone, I went to the stone-quarry, in which I, with others, was engaged in preparing stone for building a very large house. Hands of all trades were also gathered there to finish the building.

Several days passed by before I understood why Nancy said to me, "You will not belong here." The very morning on which my four months were up, I was lying on my bear-skin in the shavings, with my blanket thrown over ray head to keep off the mosquitoes, when I felt it drawn off ray face, and presently down came a large bucket of cold water all over me. I bounded to my feet, and inquired of the old lady what that was done for. She replied, because I should not be lying there till that time in the morning, and receiving high wages; and she said that she would do the same thing every time she caught me so late in bed; though at that time there was no one up but herself.

I said to her, "I have been at all times ready to do all in my power to keep you in a good humor; but you will never again have an opportunity of treating me thus; for I will never strike another stroke on your farm while I live and keep my senses. For," I continued, "you must not think, because you have wealth, that I am your servant. I am as free and as white as you are, madam; and I have done with you, and you with me, for life."

"That's just what I want," said she.

"And that you shall have," I replied; "though really hate to please you so well. But it shall be done; and as soon as Mr. Caldwell returns I'll be off."

About twelve o'clock the old man came home, and I immediately called on him for a settlement; telling him that I could not stand Mrs. Caldwell's rough treatment. She complained to him that I had told her that I was as white and as free as she was.

"Well," said the old man, "that's all true, as he is free, and white too; and if you had let him alone he would not have meddled with you. He is the only one that I can send to do any business and depend on. You have sent Nancy away, and there are two of the best hands gone by your fault."

She left the room, and dinner was soon on the table. I had not eaten any breakfast, and being told to sit down I did so.

As soon as dinner was over, the old man got his money, and paid me all my wages in silver dollars. This was very pleasing to me, for it was ten times more than I had ever previously been the owner of.

After the money was transferred to my pocket, the old man said, "Browning, I wish you would remain with me, and I will pay you ten dollars a month as long as you please to stay. The land on the other side of the river will soon be in market, when I will show you all the choicest pieces; and if you should get a wife, you can have the best of the land, and live on venison and bear meat, like I have done many times when I first settled in this bottom."

To all this I replied, "Mr. Caldwell, your offer is very good; but, sir, I know your wife has been angry with me for the last month, and I do not wish to be in her way; for neither she nor I can have any enjoyment of our lives under such circumstances."

We then shook hands in the most friendly manner, and I left Wheeling. That was my last interview with any of the family, of every member of which I was very fond, with the exception of the old lady. And, indeed, when I now think of the whole matter, if she thought what I believe she did, I don't blame her at all; for I am sure there was nothing in the world to recommend such a shabby looking boy as a match for her fine-looking daughter; backed, too, as she was, by a wealthy father. But I have been informed that the old gentleman, by some means or other, subsequently became involved, and failed in business, and that Nancy married a man who managed badly, and became poor. Whether my information was correct or not, I cannot say; but on account of the respect I always entertained for the family, I hope that it was not true. Her father was very wealthy when I knew him; and I am sure that I saw more silver in his possession than I have ever, either before or since, seen at one time.

Chapter Three

Having said good-bye to Wheeling, I traveled to ray mother's the same night; and meeting with my uncle, he told me that Mr. Poot, the gentleman who had introduced me to my grandfather, had offered a dollar a day to any good gunner who would shoot the squirrels that were destroying his corn. So we agreed that we should both go together, and have fine sport, besides being paid for our services.

The next day we started off to the corn-field before daylight, and as soon as we could see, found ourselves surrounded by the greatest number of squirrels I ever saw. which were running by hundreds in all direction. At them we went, shooting sometimes half a dozen on one tree. My partner would place himself on one side while I would take the other; and between us, we killed and took home so many squirrels that Mr. Foot would have no more brought to the house. We went home every night, the distance not being more than a mile. We carried away as many as we wished; but after two or three days we left them lay where we shot them; and I think it was on the fifth day that uncle left me to manage the balance. I continued shooting for nine and a half days, till I could see but one more squirrel, and that was a black one.

When I had completely exterminated the squirrels, Mr. Poot paid me nine silver dollars, which I added to my stock, and thought I was quite well off. Still further to help me, my step-father and my mother had bought me a complete new suit of clothes; but I had to work for the tailor who made them.

I went to work at my new job heart and hand; and when I was through I began to think of the "Blooming Rose" again, and Mary McMullen. I labored on, however, till at length I proposed to mother that I should go and see my old friends; to which she agreed, on condition that I would promise to return to her again; which I did in the most positive terms.

In a week or two I was ready, and set off for Allegany County again. Two days subsequently I was at my uncle James Spurgin's, in Monongahela County, in a very different situation from what I was in when I left there the previous January, though I had only been gone about seven months. I showed them my clothes, besides from twenty to thirty dollars in silver, which I had in my pocket, and described all that I had seen. I told uncle how near I had been to getting in a scrape by breaking the mule's shoulder, and also how I remembered his advice, and had made up my mind, if the question had been asked, to tell the whole truth, and see what it would do for me.

"Well, Meshach," said he, "if Mr. Caldwell is the man you represent him to be, he would not have made you pay one penny for it; and on the other hand, if he had discovered that you did break the mule's leg, and that you had tried to clear yourself from blame by telling a lie, he would probably have made you pay for all the damage done to the mule."

After supper, the girls, Jesse, and myself, went into another room, where we spent almost the whole evening in relating past occurrences; as well those which had happened to myself in the far West, as it was then called, as what had happened during my absence in the two neighborhoods in which I had formerly resided. I carefully avoided all inquiry about the McMullens, and expected an allusion to Mary every minute.

At length Lina remarked, "Well, cousin, you have asked after all your associates, and have not mentioned your little bird. You need not think to slip off that way, for we all know what you mean."

"Well, Lina," said I, "I was waiting for Jesse to say something about her; for, don't you know, I left him in charge of that pretty little girl, telling him to take care of her, and if I ever could, I would do the same kindness for him."

Jesse replied that he had not seen her, but that lie had heard that she was improving in her looks every day.

"Well," said Lina, "if you say much more about her he will leave us, and start off to-night, in order to be there soon in the morning; for you can see how uneasy he is getting."

"Indeed, girls," said I, "it would be a cold-hearted boy who, at my age, would not love to see such a girl as she is."

Having run me as far on that score as they wished, the conversation was turned to other subjects, and time passed very pleasantly till a late hour, when it was proposed that we should go to bed. Jesse and I occupied the same room; and, after we lay down, we continued talking till nearly daylight. The first thing we heard in the morning was the old gentleman calling the guys to get up; "For," said he, "boys, we have a great deal of hay down, and we must have it secured while it is in good order."

After breakfast was over, I staid to help with the hay till it was all safe in the mows. This was a fine frolic; girls, boys, and old people all being at it, each one trying to surpass the other in skill and activity, till all was done. The evening was our own, and we enjoyed it with the greatest glee, singing songs, of which I had learned perhaps half a dozen new ones while I was away.

The next day I left for the "Blooming Rose;" and as my cousins had informed me of the death of uncle John's little daughter, I thought I ought to visit his family before calling on any of my acquaintances, for I knew their affliction was very great. Accordingly, I spent a week or two with them. They were very anxious that I should live with them again; but this offer I declined, by telling them that I had promised to live with my mother, at least till I should marry a wife — if ever I did take one; for that was an uncertain business, as the one that I wanted I could not get; and I never would have any girl upon whom my affections were not fixed.

In the mean time, I visited many of my friends; but I did not go to Mr. McMullen's, as I had not been apprised of his being from home, and as I well knew my presence would be unwelcome to him. I wished to see Mary before I attempted to pay another visit to the family.

Some days passed thus, till at length there was a funeral, to which I went with uncle and aunt, and there I met Mrs. McMullen and Mary. After the funeral service was over, uncle, aunt, Mrs. McMullen, and Mary, together with several others, walked about a mile in company over the same road. I took Mary's hand, and walked by her side until the others had all turned off at different roads; when she her mother, and myself were the only persons left. The old lady stopped a little while with my aunt, but Mary and I kept on till we drew near her home; when we seated ourselves on a fallen tree by the roadside, and spent what we both thought and acknowledged was far too short a time in which to say all we wished.

When the old lady came up to us, I told her that I would have been better pleased if she had made her stay with my aunt a little longer — Mary having informed me that her mother was truly my friend, but that her father was much displeased at ray return. Mrs. McMullen smiled, and asked why so. I told her that Mary and I had sufficient to say to each other to occupy another hour.

"Well," said the old woman, "you can both go back to the house instead of sitting in the road, and there spend an hour or two; but be sure not to stay till sundown."

I pledged myself that I would see her daughter home before sunset.

We were both pleased — at any rate, I knew that I was, and I had good reason to believe that Mary was; for, as her mother walked away, I said to her, " What a blessed old lady she is, to let me have such a splendid chance to court her daughter, at the very moment when I expected her to take you off home with her!"

"That seems to be the case with all the men, I believe; every one is for his own interest. But I can tell you that my mother has all confidence in you; and I don't believe she would have given any other young man living but yourself the same privilege with me; but if father knew I was here in your company, I don't know what he would do, or what I should say; for he is determined to keep us as far from each other as he can. Mother and he disagree about you; and she tells him that if he drives you away he will not better himself in this neighborhood. Is it not strange, Meshach. that he is afraid of what we never spoke to each other about, and, indeed, what we are both too young to think of doing?"

"Well, Mary," said I, "if I went back to live with my mother, and was then to hear that some other young man had come to court you, and your cruel father (for he is cruel to me) compelled you to marry him, I should be mad enough to commit murder."

"You will never have occasion to do anything wrong on my account," said she; "for neither father, mother, nor any one else, shall ever persuade or force me to marry a man I do not love."

"Well, Mary, have you ever yet seen a young man whom you loved well enough to marry?"

"That is a hard question; but I will tell you that I love your company better than that of any other whom I have yet seen; but marrying I have never taken into consideration; and it will be time enough to think of that five or six years hence."

"But, Mary, if I should make my home with my mother, and stay there five or six years, you will be married before half that time passes."

"Well, that will not be my fault; for, if you go and leave me, you cannot expect me to come after you, or send for you to come to me. No, sir, if I did, you would despise me; and well you might, if I was to do anything so much out of place. If you are so fearful of my marrying, you had better stay and keep the advantage you have gained, and make as much more of it as you can. I have informed you that I love your company better than that of any other young man, and that is all I intend to tell you; and, if I had not foolishly divulged my secret to you, I would not do so now, for you seem to have lost your confidence in me. I have given you no reason for such a change of opinion. I promised you, when you left last winter, what if you came back in five or six years, you would find me as you left me; and have you not found me as good as my word? You know, also, that everything you ever told me, I believed as firmly as if I had seen it myself; and yet you seem doubtful of me. I have always had confidence in you, and all my family, except ray father, have a good word for you at all times; and you know that if my mother was not particularly friendly to you, we would not be here together. Really, the sun is getting low, and I must be going. Don't you know what you promised?"

44

She put on her bonnet, and I took her hand, and on we went. As we walked, I said: "Mary, you never told me you loved me, nor have I ever told you that I loved you, but we are both left to our own conjectures; yet, if you were to tell me you thought I loved you, I should say you had made a very shrewd and good guess; and that is all I will tell you."

This raised a laugh; and she said we were nearly even, and she supposed there would be no more said about loving each other, but that all would be left to conjecture. That being agreed on, we turned our discourse to other subjects, and too soon arrived at her home. We waited for the sun to go down, being bent on having the last minute of our time together; and in the meantime I apologized for having given her reason to think that I doubted her sincerity. She readily accepted my acknowledgment, and it seemed as if it had redoubled our affections to each other; indeed. I thought she was the sweetest creature in all creation.

Notwithstanding all our precaution not to betray our love to each other, out came the acknowledgment from both, accompanied by a promise not to make any different engagement without each other's consent, until we should be old enough to marry. We then parted; I going to my uncle's, and she to her home, fearful of being suspected by her father. But she afterwards told me that he never mentioned it to her.

My uncle then proposed a hunt and a fishing excursion to the Buffalo Marsh Glades. This place took its name from the fact that the carcass of a large buffalo had been found in the deep mud of the marsh by the first white men who, perhaps, ever set a foot in that beautiful glade. I agreed to accompany him; and we set out for the same house from which we fled when St. Clair met with his defeat, mentioned in my first chapter. When we arrived at the place, we found that the house had been destroyed by some mischievous hands; so we built a fire under a large oak, and there slept comfortably at night.

In the morning we set off for our sport, taking a small path that led to Deep Creek; and as we walked along I saw a very large buck standing within gunshot of us. Having but one gun (for my sport was designed to be in fishing), the old man (who, by-the-bye, was a poor shot) fired at and wounded the buck in the foot. A fine swift dog we had with us, soon ran the buck down, and he became our venison. The old man told me he he would attend to the meat, and I should try my luck with the trout. I waded into the water, hip and thigh, with a piece of the venison for bait, believing that anything I liked so well would surely please a trout; and I was not mistaken; for just as fast as I could bait my hook, and let it into the water, I pulled out the largest kind of trout, till at length they refused suddenly, as is their habit, to give me another bite.

I gathered up what I had caught, and counted forty-seven, making as much of a load as I wished to carry in one hand. I then struck for our fire again, as the morning was cold: there was a heavy dew on the grass, which was as high as a man's belt, and I was cold, wet, and hungry. The old man was in with his buck, and had some venison before the hot coals, which was nearly ready for eating. I handed over my long string of trout to the cook, who soon had as many as were necessary for our late breakfast, nicely fried in his little pan, and butter gravy swimming round them, until they were beautifully browned all over. Then we sat down to the finest kind of venison steaks, fried in the same way, and good light rolls, well buttered, all placed on pieces of chestnut bark just peeled from the tree. All this, together with a sharp appetite, made the meal, I thought, quite good enough for a Governor, or even the President himself, if he were there, and as hungry as I then was. After helping ourselves to as much as we needed, we were satisfied with what we had done.

Our next business being to get home with our venison and fish, before they could get spoiled, our horses were saddled in haste. We loaded up, and off we went for home. We had about ten miles to travel, which we completed by the middle of the afternoon. When we arrived at the house, who should be there with my aunt, for company, but my little Mary! Well, said I, is not this good luck? I'll bet this has been done for me. I shall go part of the way home with her again, at all hazards; and we will keep it from the old man's knowledge the best way we can.

After taking a long and earnest look at her, and admiring her well-shaped form, which was about medium size — she then weighing one hundred and twenty pounds, and having well-proportioned shoulders and breast; full, clear blue eyes, expressive of the wildness of a fawn in its most playful moments; and cheeks like roses, Lord! said I to myself, won't she be a prize for me some day, if I can only keep things as they now are, till the time comes? But I think I can manage that, unless some enemy interferes between us, as I think they did at Wheeling. Yes, yes, I must let nothing of that Wheeling business come to Mary's ears, or she will be off at once, I reckon; and that would be the --- indeed.

I told my aunt to send Mrs. McMullen one dozen of the best trout, as a present; and I requested Mary to hand them to her mother, and tell her that I caught every one of them myself, and that I sent them to her. My old uncle also sent a present of some of his venison; and the old people said, that if I was not too tired with walking, I ought to help Mary to carry her venison and fish home. I looked at her, and replied, that I had been walking so much lately, that it tired me but little to walk a whole day, and I did not feel the least tired now. Mary made no reply, but she gave me a mischievous look, and smiled, which almost fevered the blood in my veins.

In a few moments we set off for her home, and we related to one another how everything had worked for our advantage. She said: "After yourself and your uncle had gone, mother said, in the hearing of father, that Aunt Polly would be very lonesome there by herself; and that the late loss of her child made it still worse. 'Well,' said the old man, 'some of the children may go

over and stay overnight with her.' The old lady, however, said that it would
be of little use to send the small children; and it was agreed that I should go.
Whether mother thought of you or not, I can't say; but I expected every moment that father would think of you, and break up the whole plan."

"Very well, Mary," said I, "you think it fun to go where you will see me, do
you? "

"Well," she replied, "I know very well that if I don't think it fun, you do;
and I don't think you will offer to deny it. Now let me see if you will deny it,"
said she. joking playfully in my face. "If you do, I will have to tell you, for the
first time, that I don't believe what you say."

We were then at her father's fence, and had stopped to take leave of each
other; but we delayed parting till the last hour of her allotted time, which
was sunset; but when the time came, we parted with great reluctance, promising to take advantage of every opportunity to see each other.

It is of little use for parents to try to keep young people apart, after their
affections are firmly settled on each other. They will seek each other's socie-
ty, as it was in this case with Mary and myself. We were determined to see
each other; and after all the old man could do, we did meet, somehow or other, every week.

I would advise parents to give good advice to their children; then let them
take their own way, and let the responsibility be on their own heads. That
has been my course through a long life, and under many trials; and I have
never repented of it. So it was: we saw each other frequently, when no one
suspected us; and so it continued till I went to the West again, which was in
September. We then parted, with a hope of meeting again in a short time; for
I had determined to endeavor to persuade my step-father and mother to
move to Allegany; and I told Mary that, whether they came or not, I would
return and stay at some place within reach of her, until we should attain a
sufficient age, when she should be mine.

I again travelled to Short Creek, in the West, and joined my mother; but
did not find it a hard task to persuade the old folks to move to Allegany,
which they did in October; and in a month's time my mother, step-father, and
myself, were neighbors to the McMullen family, and were pleased with their
new home.

Not long after we had settled in our new home, there fell a light snow,
when I took my rifle, and calling a dog which I had brought with me from
Wheeling, which was of the stock of old Mr. Caldwell's hunting-dogs, I went
into the woods after deer. I had not travelled far before I found the tracks of
four deer, which had run off; for they had got wind of me, and dashed into a
great thicket to hide themselves. I took the trail, and into the thicket I went,
where I soon saw the deer running in different directions. I got between
them, in hopes that I should see them trying to come together again. I kept
my stand perhaps five or six minutes, when I saw something slipping
through the bushes, which I took to be one of the deer; bat I soon found that

it was coming toward me. I kept a close look out for it; and directly, within ten steps of me, up rose the head and shoulders of the largest panther that I ever saw, either before or since. He kept behind a large log that was near me, and looked over. But though I had never seen a wild one before, I knew the gentleman, and was rather afraid of him. I aimed my rifle at him as well as I could, he looking me full in the face; and when I fired he made a tremendous spring from me, and ran off through the brush and briers, with the dog after him.

As soon as I recovered a little from my fright, I loaded again, and started after them. I followed them as fast as I could, and soon found them at the foot of a large and very high rock; the panther, in his hurry, having sprung down the cleft of rock fifteen or twenty feet; but the dog, being afraid to venture so great a leap, ran round, and the two had met in a thick laurel swamp, where they were fighting the best way they could, each trying to get the advantage of the other. I stood on the top of the rock over them, and fired at the base of the panther's ear, when down he went; and I ran round the rock, with my tomahawk in hand, believing him to be dead. But when I got near him, I found he was up and fighting again, and consequently I had to hurry back for my gun, load it again, creep slyly up, take aim at his ear, as before, and give him another shot, which laid him dead on the ground. My first shot had broken his shoulder; the second pierced his ear, passing downward through his tongue; the last entered one ear, and came out at the other, scattering hit brains all around. He measured eleven feet three inches from the end of his nose to the tip of his tail. This was the largest panther I ever killed, and I suppose I have killed at least fifty in my time.

I took from this fellow sixteen and a half pounds of rendered tallow. It is something softer than mutton tallow, but by mixing it with one-fourth of its weight of beeswax, it makes good candles. I continued hunting the balance of the season, with little success — not killing any bears, although there were great numbers of them in the woods. However, I knew but little of the art of hunting.

I continued with great glee to partake of all the pastimes, attending the dances, shooting matches, etc.; and courting Mary occasionally, till our love was so confirmed, that we were never so well pleased in any other company but that of ourselves. In the year 1799, we being each then in our eighteenth year, by the advice of both our mothers, we agreed to put an end, by marriage, to a courtship of five or six years' continuance; and, accordingly, the last day of April was fixed on for our wedding.

As the day began to draw near, the old folks had to be consulted; but when I called on Mary's father, I told him that I had but few words to say to him, having only to tell him that I had been a long time in love with his daughter Mary, and that I knew she loved me also; that we had determined that nothing but death should part us; and that, if he would please to give me his consent, I should be very glad; but that, as for me to live without her, was out of the question. I also said: "Some man will marry her, one day or other; and I have determined that, at the risk of my life, no man shall ever have her but myself."

The old man kept quiet till I had done, when he said: "You have had this matter all arranged among yourselves, and I shall not meddle with it now. You may take her as soon as you please." But he was very angry.

I thanked him, and was going to apologise to him for not being more open and above-board in courting his daughter; but he refused to hear any excuses, and left the house. Though much mortified at such treatment, I felt that I would be satisfied if he only kept his word, and did not forbid her to comply with her promise; for she had always told me she would not marry against the will of her parents, and I had but little hope of getting the old man's consent.

However, there was no time to be lost, as I wished to see my brother Joshua, who had once been in company with myself and Mary at a party; where, having seen that I was fond of her, he said to me, "Brother, you may love that girl as much as you please; but don't think of matrimony."

I told him that thoughts flew into people's heads very quickly, and sometimes continued uncontrollable.

"Yes, yes," said he; "and if that is your case now, you are a gone coon. She is a beauty, it is true; but you are both only children yet, and should not think of marrying till you are twenty-one at least."

"And in that time," said I, "something may turn up to prevent me from getting her at all. No, no; I shall take care that she shall never be the wife of any other man while I am alive."

"Then do as you please, boy; for she is a sweet girl, and good enough for any man; but I hate to see children so fast. However, go on, boy, and see where you will stop."

This conversation had occurred a year before, and I intended he should have an invitation to my wedding. I had young horse, which was old enough to ride; and as we both wanted some things from Cumberland, I went thither for them. I set out from that town to my brother's, twelve miles below, and made him acquainted with my intentions. He made no objections to the match, but said he could not attend. I staid two nights and one day with him, and then returned home.

The next week we made our preparations, and Thursday, the 30th day of April, 1799, was appointed for our marriage.

Our friends assembled to ride with us into Pennsylvania, to get a magistrate to perform the marriage ceremony; which in those days was the only way open to all the young people to become joined in wedlock. The morning being a fine clear one, with the prospect of a good day, I thought it certainly was the beginning of some great jubilee, when all creation would be restored to the highest summit of its glory.

Everything being ready, we all set off in great spirits, and at a rattling pace; for all the girls in the company could ride like show-masters. In a few hours we found ourselves at the magistrate's office, and were soon called on to stand up before that sagacious officer, who was a Presbyterian, and professed great piety. He gave us such a lengthy exhortation that I became tired of his noise; but at length he got into the right way by saying, "What God hath joined together let no man put asunder." Then, after putting the necessary questions, and obtaining the proper answers, he pronounced us man and wife.

"Thank you, Mr. Squire," said I; "that is what I have wanted to be a long time."

After receiving the old man's blessing, he dismissed us, and we were soon on our way home, which we reached about four o'clock.

Mr, McMullen, having become somewhat softened, through the advice of his friends, had prepared a dinner for our little but light-hearted party, and the night was spent with music and dancing. The next morning, after our friends had taken their leave, with many good wishes for our happiness, we were left in my father-in-law's house; when I thought I could see in the old man's countenance that I was not welcome there.

This being Friday, I proposed to Mary to go to my mother's, and spend the next evening with her; which she had requested us to do. This was agreed on, and the rest of her family promised to come over in the evening. As we had but a mile to walk, Mary and I set off by ourselves, and were soon at my mother's door. The two old people greeted us with great kindness, calling Mary their child, and were greatly pleased with her; in fact, not only my friends, but every one who knew Mary, loved her. In the course of the evening, a little company of our friends again collected, to have a second evening's diversion; but Mr. McMullen did not come. I asked Mary what it meant that her father did not accompany his family, and she went to her mother to learn what was the reason, but received none.

After supper, the music struck up, and many a light-footed reel and jig was danced that evening. Time passed away very fast; and, much to the dissatisfaction of our little company, they soon found it to be after midnight. They bade us a pleasant good-night, and left Mary and myself alone with my step-father and mother. Our own company, however, was amply sufficient for our own pleasure, and we passed that night and the next day with the old people.

On Sunday we returned to her father's again; and then it was that I began to consider what I should do to make Mary happy; for I had previously thought that if I only had Mary I should want nothing else in the world; but I now saw that I wanted everything else but her. I had been preparing a home for her, having traded my horse for a small squatter's farm, with fifteen or twenty acres of cleared land, three acres of wheat standing in the ground, and a good little cabin; but not a cow had I, to give us any milk, nor a bushel of grain, nor a pound of meat of any kind; it being very scarce, and not to be obtained without money; but I had not a dollar.

Seeing that something must be done, I had determined to leave Mary, and set to work to earn sufficient to buy bread and meat to start upon, and manage some way or other to get along. This was the conclusion we came to on Sunday evening, after she and I had gone to our room.

In the morning, at peep of day, in came her father, saying, as he opened the door, "Rise up, sir, and go to work at something to maintain your wife, whom you would have, at the risk of your life. And you, too, madam, get up and go to your own home; for you shan't roost here any longer."

Indignant at the insult, I attempted to jump out of bed; but Mary caught me by the arm, saying, "Bear it a moment or two, Meshach, for my sake. He will be off directly." And so he was, in a very short time.

I turned out of bed, and dressed as fast as I could; but Mary, only half dressed, came to me, and threw her beautiful white arms round my neck, saying, "For God's sake, and for my sake, don't quarrel with him. Will you promise me you won't quarrel with him, Meshach? Only promise me. Remember, it is your Mary asks you for that promise."

"Yes, Mary," said I; "I will not speak to him this day, on your account. But this very morning I intend to leave this place. Now, Mary, I shall go to mother's for my breakfast, and do you get yourself ready to follow me, I will come and wait at the fence for you, and we will stay at mother's till I can make some other arrangement."

I left her in tears, and went home, got my breakfast, and walked out to the fence to wait for her. She saw me, and, with her mother, hurried to meet me. The old lady had bundled up her clothes, together with two plates, two knives and forks, two cups and saucers, two tin-cups, and two spoons; which were all rolled up in Mary's clothes and placed in a woven basket. The old lady looked serious, but remained firm. Poor little Mary's heart, however, was so overcharged that she could not keep back her tears, which flowed abundantly until we came in sight of my mother's; when we sat down, and she gave utterance to her feelings in these words:

"Oh, my hard-hearted father, I have never given you any reason to treat me so cruelly! But my heart loved, and you did not feel it; nor yet do you consider my situation. Oh hard and cruel father!"

This was too much for me: our tears mingled plentifully together. And at this moment the thought of that hour brings them into my eyes, so that I have frequently to drop my pen and wipe them away; for the narration of this event, although it occurred sixty years ago, so plainly recalls all the attendant circumstances to my mind, that it seems to me I can see her, and hear every word she then uttered.

But after she had got a little the better of her feelings, I took her hand, and said to her, "My dearest wife, you know I love you as well as you ever could love me; and although your father has no sympathy with our feelings, the world is wide, and kind Providence will not let us suffer if we put ourselves under his protection. Mary, I am strong and active, and we can make our living without his help. You don't know but that he may yet be compelled to come to you for sympathy."

"Well, Meshach, if such a thing ever should happen, I will never mention his cruel treatment to me this day; would you?"

"No, no, Mary; and I thank God for placing so good I heart in my dearest wife." [1]

With her handkerchief we dried our tears; and, the day being well advanced, we walked forward to the house.

"What is the matter with you, Mary," said my mother; "have you rued your bargain already?"

"Oh no, mother. But you know Joshua told Meshach that we were but children. Children will cry when their mother leaves them; and I think it just as bad to leave my mother as if she was compelled to leave me. I have been crying a little about it; and indeed, mother, Meshach cried too. You know that if you have two babies together, and one cries, the other will cry also. And that is just the way with him; for as soon as I began to cry he did the same. I am ashamed of it; and I am sure he ought to be also, as he pretends to be a man. But Joshua calls him a boy; and if he is only a boy, it will not look quite so bad if he does cry a little sometimes."

She said all this in such a playful way, that it raised a hearty laugh; and the conversation was changed to a discussion as to what should be done to supply us with provisions. It was agreed that Mary should stay with my mother, while I went out and worked for flour and meat. So off I went, on Tuesday morning, and worked till Friday evening; when I had earned two bushels of wheat; but I could get no meat without money.

On Saturday morning, as I had some arrangements to make at my little cabin, it was agreed that my step-father should go to the mill for me, while Mary and I fixed up our cabin, so that it should be ready for us to go into on Monday. We finished our job before dinner-time, and we had been all day thinking how we should get provisions with which to commence keeping house.

I had a wooden trap, which I had made the previous fall, for the purpose of catching coons and wildcats in; and I had made it very strong. In the afternoon, I said to Mary and my mother that I would go and see my trap, and perhaps shoot a wild turkey. I started off for the trap; and as I came near the place I saw a flock of wild turkeys flying up into the trees to roost. I left them till it began to grow a little dusk, when I crawled up and shot one, which proved to be a fine fat bird. "Well," said I to myself, "this will be a beginning for us on Monday, anyhow; and I will see how my trap comes on."

I had set it in a pine grove, which was very dark; but when I went to examine it I found it down; and as it was too dark to see what was in it, I took a small pole and poked it in, when I soon found that I had to contend with a large bear. Jobbing him set him mad for fighting, and he raised the trap up;

but as he attempted to come out it fell again. I saw that it was too light, so I jumped out and my weight made it too heavy for him. After several trials, finding he could do nothing, he became still; when I crept off slily, and carried large logs, which I piled on it till it was impossible for him to raise with it any more. I then shot at him through a crack, and wounded him in the head. I tried a second and third fire, but did not succeed in killing him, though I exhausted all my balls. I was compelled to leave him as he was, and go home; where I told them that I had a large bear in the trap, which was so badly wounded that he had no chance of escape.

Next morning, which was Sunday, Mary, mother, father, and myself, accompanied by the dog, set off as soon as we could to the bear-fight. We found him yet alive, and ready for the combat. I raised the trap a little, in order to let him and the dog have a tussel through a small opening. They fought a long time; but the bear was so badly wounded in the head that he could not bite, though he tore the dog badly with his claws. I then called the dog off; and after the old lady and Mary had obtained a full view of him, I shot him dead at the first fire, when I could see how I was shooting. We then took him out, and found him to be not only a large, but very fat animal, weighing three hundred and nineteen pounds. We took a pole, and after tying his feet together, put the pole through, and the old man and myself carried him home in about three hours, where we dressed him. On Monday Mary went home, and got her brother to come over and carry one quarter to her father, who was very fond of bear-meat.

Mary soon returned; for her father received her so coolly, that she made her visit very short. After giving my step-father one quarter of our supply of meat, it became necessary for us to see our remaining two quarters taken care of; so we hurried and got our little goods (and little indeed they were, the whole not being worth more than twenty dollars) on a sled, when my mother and stepfather accompanied us to our new home. The two old people returned the same evening, and left us to shift for ourselves. I had procured a barrel to pack my meat in, and to work we went. We soon took all the bones out, and laid the meat carefully in the barrel, which we placed in a cool house, on a dirt floor, where it kept good till the last of August, being all the time under pure brine.

While we were cutting our meat and securing it, Mary said to me: "Meshach, how truly your words have come to pass, 'That if we trust in God, He will not forsake us.' Little did I think, when you came home without any meat, that we should have this day as much as we need; and I think we shall do well enough, after all. But what we shall do for milk and butter, I do not know. I ought to have a cow from home, but I shall not get one, I am pretty sure. But," she continued, "we have got together, and I am content; for I know you will do the best you can, and I will help you all I am able. I will let nothing be wanting on my part; for mother says no man can make a living, unless bis wife takes care of what is earned."

[1] How little do parents and others know, when indulging in unkind and harsh feelings, what changes may take place in after life! To illustrate more fully the lovely character of Mary, it may be stated that the father who so unfeelingly turned his child out of doors, was for many years indebted to these children for a roof under which to shelter his gray hairs, and for the means of averting actual want and suffering. After becoming old, and incapable, by reason of age and infirmity, of providing sufficiently for his own and his wife's comfort, they were removed into the family of his daughter. Here they lived about twelve years, when the old gentleman was stricken down with paralysis, and for many months lay as helpless as an infant, requiring equal care and attention. All that the most devoted kindness and affection could do was done by Mary to alleviate his sufferings, and minister to his every want, both bodily and mental, until death came to his relief. It may truly be said of this estimable lady, that, though reared in the wilderness, every trait that adorns the female character shone brightly in her: she was a dutiful child, a most exemplary mother, a devoted wife, and a true friend.— E.S.

Chapter Four

After several days had passed, without our being able to obtain any milk or butter, except what our two old mothers would send us occasionally, I remembered that there was m the neighborhood a man who had long wanted my rifle; and although I disliked to part with it, yet as necessity compelled me to do so, I sent him word that I would let him have it, if we could agree on the terms. In a day or two he came to see me; and we had no trouble in making a bargain, by which Mary became the mistress of an excellent cow, which yielded us as much milk and butter as we wished to use. This made all right, as we then had, in abundance, meat and bread, milk and butter of our own. It is probable that a happier man and wife were nowhere to be found.

And so we continued, models of happiness and contentment. I planted corn and potatoes, had a garden, and our three acres of wheat were very fine indeed. About the first of October, as I thought it was high time to take ray dogs and gun a little, I asked Mary if she would stay at home by herself, or would go to my mother's and stay, while I went hunting? She said she had plenty of work to do, and did not wish to leave her home, when she had anything to do there. I promised to return home before dark; and was about to start, when Mary said to me: "I feel afraid on your account, for I know you have neither fear nor care of yourself when among the wild beasts; and some day you will be crippled, if not killed. What would you do if you got in the claws of such a bear or panther as you killed last fall, or in the trap this spring? Meshach, they could tear you as easily as a cat would a mouse; and I beg you to take care and not get into their clutches."

I assured her that I had plenty of powder and balls; and that, if they attempted to run on me, they must take care of themselves; or, as they raised up to take hold of me, I would be sure to let out a part, at any rate, of what they had inside of their black wallets. She said: "Ma; God protect you!" and I started.

I knew where there was a swamp of black haws, which bears are very fond of; and off I started for the swamp. When in sight of the place, I went round to let my dogs have the wind of the thicket, and sent the oldest dog into the swamp to raise the game. In he went; but he was scarcely out of my sight, when I heard the fight begin. Then off went the young dog and the best one also. I found the old dog had not stopped the bear, but as soon as the young fellow closed in, I found there was hard fighting going on, and therefore I ran as fast as I could ii the direction of the battle. When I came up, I saw the fellow on a small tree, just out of reach of the dogs. The noise I made in rushing through the bushes attracted his attention; and, as he saw me coming, he let go his hold, and dropped down, when the dogs immediately attacked him. I ran the muzzle of my gun against him, and sent a ball whizzing through the middle of his body, but too far back to save a hard fight. As the gun fired, the dogs closed on him, and the fight became desperate, first one dog crying out and then the other.

I had lost my gun in the weeds, and I had no means of defending my dogs, except with a large knife in my belt, which I drew, but not till I vainly tried to find a club. My dogs were getting the worst of the battle; and while he had one of them on the ground, and was biting him badly, I ran up and made a lunge at him, but, like my shot, it struck him too far back, and only entered his liver. Still, he fought on, though my stroke released the dog, who rose and went at him again; but as the bear attempted to go under a log that was raised a little off the ground, the sound dog caught him by the nose, while the other seized him by the ham. Both held fast; and he being tightly wedged between the log and the ground, I ran upon him with my knife, and dealt him two or three severe blows, which finished him. I expect he would have given myself and my dogs a harder tussel, if, somehow or other, during the fight, he had not broken one of his hind legs, which gave us the advantage.

In a week or two afterwards, Mary and I went out to get us some chestnuts; and as we were going only a short distance, I did not take my gun. But soon after getting into the woods, off went both dogs at full cry. I could not tell whether they were chasing a deer or a bear. By and by we heard them fighting; when I ran for my gun, and left Mary to get home as best she could — though she told me not to wait for her. After running a mile or more, I found they had a she-bear up a tree, and that she was so completely whipped by the dogs that she would not come down to fight any more. As she was entirely in my power, it afforded me but little pleasure to kill her; for even in a bear-fight I like to have something to do: the harder the fight the better I like the fun.

In February of the year 1800, myself and another young man went out to the woods to catch a young deer, which I intended to raise as a pet. They will become tame in two or three days; and even the oldest bucks will yield in a week, and become quite docile. I have so tamed two during one week, that they would come to me, put their noses in my pocket, take apples or moss out, and eat it, and search all my pockets for more.

Louis Vansickle and myself went into the laurel swamps, where all the deer had taken shelter from a snow, which had fallen to the depth of four feet generally on the highlands. As we drew near the edge of the swamp, we discovered the roads made by the deer, which had been out of the thicket, browsing on the small bushes and eating the moss that had fallen from the timber. We had pursued these paths but a short distance when we observed even large deer running, or rather jumping up and down; the snow being so deep that they could advance no more than three or four feet at a jump. We pursued at our best speed, which was about as fast as I could walk on dry laud; for we had snow-shoes tied fast under our moccasins, which were nearly as large as the seat of a chair. On, and on we went; but finally I proved too long-winded for Vansickle, and left him far behind.

When I drew near the hindmost deer, the foremost ones, being tired out, had stopped to take breath. The last one, attempting to pass by those in front, leaped into the deep snow, where he stuck fast, when I caught hold of him, with the intention of tying him; but he was too fat and strong for me, as the snow had not been long on the ground. lie was also ill-natured, and fought viciously until Louis came up, who had a hawk-bill knife in his pocket. I took this knife, and with it cut the throat of the buck, and left him with my companion. With the knife in my pocket, I ran after and soon overtook the others, as they were crossing a small branch with steep banks on each side. A large tree, which had fallen over the stream, lay a short distance from the ground, and many leaves had drifted under it. One of the bucks, being hard pushed, and greatly frightened, threw himself under this log among the leaves, and thus escaped my notice, as I was watching the deer in front of him. I passed by, and, after pursuing the others some distance, caught a very large buck, which I undertook to tie; but he fought me desperately, and was so strong that I could not handle him.

While I was engaged with that buck, hearing Louis hallooing behind me, I seized the animal, cut his throat, and ran to the relief of my friend; thinking, as I ran, that he had fallen among the rocks and broken his leg, as the ground over which I had passed was very rocky, and full of holes. I said to myself, as I was running to him, "If he has broken a leg, I will first take my rope and tie him to a tree, when I will pull his leg straight, and set the bone; after which I will tear up some clothes and wrap them round the limb, scrape a place clear of snow down to the ground, build a good fire, and leave him there while I go for a horse and sled on which to carry him home."

I was soon agreeably disappointed, however; for as I name in sight of him, I observed him lying on his back, with his knees drawn up toward his face, and his great snow-shoes turned up to the sun; the snow having drifted so deep in the hollow that he could not touch bottom with his hands. Before him

56

stood one of the largest bucks, with his tail spread, and all his hair bristled up, watching poor Louis; and every time he moved the buck would spring on him, and beat him over the head and face with his feet until Louis became quiet again; when the buck would take his stand again until my friend made another move; and then he would repeat the same performance.

It seems that, after I had passed the buck which had hid under the log, and the animal had recovered his breath, Louis came on him suddenly, not knowing the deer was there. He ran so near that the buck sprang at him, throwing him backwards into the deep snow; and every time he would attempt to rise he would again sink down, when the buck would attack and beat him until he lay still.

How often the buck had repeated this chastisement before I came in sight, I do not know; but when I first saw them Louis was lying motionless, but hallooing vociferously for help. Standing, as I was, on the rocks above them, the fun appeared so fine that I could not help him for laughing. He made several attempts to rise, but in vain; the buck giving him a beating at every move, until Vansickle was furious with rage. He swore that I intended to let him freeze to death in the snow; that it was but death any way; and that he would get out of that place or lose his life in the trial.

He made another move, and, as the buck sprang on him, and commenced beating him again, he reached up, and first passed one arm around the animal's neck, and then the other, with which he drew the deer close to him; and the scuffle was so close that I could scarcely decide which would be victorious. At length the buck seemed to be getting exhausted, and lay quiet, when Louis began to bite his ears, which caused him to struggle; but my friend had lapped both snow-shoes crosswise over his kidneys, and drawn him so close down that he was almost powerless. Louis then withdrew his right hand from around the buck's neck, and, as he lay under him, commenced striking him in the ribs, giving a great grunt at every stroke, and saying, "It is my time now, you rascal; you have had your turn, and now mine is come." He would then give the buck another blow, and ask how he liked that; and then another stroke and a heavy grunt.

After my fit of laughing had subsided a little, I went to him and told him to let go his hold of the buck; but he refused, saying that he had got a good hold, and he did not intend to let go until one or the other should lose his life. He still continued to strike heavy blows on the buck's side. I took the animal by the ear, and told Louis to let him go, and I would cut his throat. But he refused, saying that he was determined never to loose his hold until one or the other should be dead. I told him that if I then cut his throat the blood would spurt in his face and over his clothes; but he would not let go, though he insisted on my cutting the buck's throat. I did so, when all the blood flowed over him; and a bloodier man I never have seen during my life. But he retained his hold until the buck was dead. He was so frightened, however, by the beating given him by that animal, that he would not hunt any more unless I went in advance; and if a bush rattled, he would jump back for fear another buck was coming at him. He was badly hurt, having many black-and-blue lumps on his head, and one very black eye. Two or three days subsequently, he showed me a long war-club, which lie had made to defend himself with, as well as to attack those wicked fighting bucks. It was eight feet long, with a large knot on the upper end, but shaved down at the lower end so as to form a small handle. But he would not again venture himself in the woods unless I went with him; which as I did not do, he never had an opportunity of trying his club.

Everything went on first-rate until the leaves began to fall. I had a two-year old colt, which I got when I traded my horse for the farm, and it ranged in the woods where the bears were plenty. I went out one day to look for my colt, but did not find him; and as I was returning home in the afternoon, I saw that some animal had been rolling over the leaves. "Well," said I, "this must have been ray colt, which has been here rolling." But upon further examination, I found it had been a bear, which had got so heavy and fat that he lay on the ground and drew himself along, and ate the chestnuts that were to be found in great numbers among the fallen leaves.

As soon as I found what it was, I left; making as few tracks as possible, lest the bear should return, scent my presence, and make off.

I told Mary, the following morning, that I was going after the biggest kind of a bear, and felt almost sure of him.

"Well, Meshach," she replied, "you know that all the time you are out I am so unhappy, that if we could get along without your risking yourself as you do, I should be glad if you would keep out of the woods."

"Don't be afraid of me, Mary," said I; "for I am good for the biggest of a bear there is in these woods. "

In the morning I was up before it was light enough to see, and off I started for the bear's feeding-place. As he was not there, I began to consider where he was; for I knew he would feed somewhere that fine morning. Having settled upon a place, I went in search of him, both dogs following close at my heels; and when I reached the outskirts of the ground, where I expected to find him, they began to whine, and show every sign of game being near. There being many large rocks scattered over the ground, I stood still, fearing that if I moved I should scare the game; but in a minute a tremendous bear came trotting out from behind one of those rocks, within fifteen or twenty yards of me. Not being conscious of my presence, he was busily engaged hunting chestnuts, standing with his head towards me, I could not wait to get a shot at his side, lest my dogs should spring at him before he turned around; therefore I let fly at him, when down he went, and dogs and bear were at once in close quarters. I ran up quickly, and made two or three blows at him with my knife, and killed him in two minutes from the time I first fired my gun.

58

I then returned, in order to devise some plan for carrying him home. He was so old that his teeth were as black as the top of a cow's horn, and worn quite blunt at the end; but he was exceedingly fat and large. Having no other way of conveying him to my cabin, I concluded to try my colt, which I had brought home the evening before. I bridled and saddled him, telling Mary that she must go with me and hold the colt while I fastened the bear on his back.

She did not refuse, but only remarked, "Is it not enough for you to hunt and kill bears, without making a squaw of me?"

However, she quickly put on her bonnet, and off we went for the bear. We first skinned him, and then cut him in two; but even after that I could not raise one-half of it high enough to put it on the colt; so I quartered him, and laid one quarter on the other, on the top of a high rock, which was square on one side, and rose up perpendicularly to the height of about five feet. I took off my hunting-shirt , which I tied over the colt's head and eyes, so that he could not see what I was about, and then brought him close to the rock, where Mary held him, while I rolled one quarter on his back, and then another, until I got them all on, when off we went, the colt bending under his burden at every step. But he stuck to it like a fine fellow till he got home with his load, which weighed not less than two hundred and fifty pounds.

A few days after this was all taken care of, a fine snow fell, when off I started again to hunt bears. I saw several tracks, but took the largest one, which I followed rapidly, as the snow was still falling fast; and I had every advantage of the bear, for he could neither hear nor see me. I pushed on after him, until I arrived at a small branch, which the bear was compelled to cross, and in which he had stopped to take a drink. The bank being very high, I did not see him till he bounded up the opposite side into the thick bushes. I could not get a good sight of him till he was at some distance; but knowing that would be my last chance, as he reached the top of the hill, I fired at him, hit or miss. I reloaded my gun, and went to where I last saw him, when I discovered he was badly wounded, there being a great quantity of blood along his trail.

Encouraged at the prospect of coming to a closer engagement with the old larky, I followed the trail with all speed, well knowing that he was making his way toward a large laurel swamp, and that, if he got into it, he would be beyond my reach, until I went home for my dogs. The bear was obliged to retreat about a mile through cleared ground, where I could not only run as fast, if not faster than him, but where also I had a fair chance for a hand-to-hand fight. I followed the trail, running with all my might. Observing him making all the head-way he could, I increased my speed till within close gun-shot, when I fired at him a second time; but seeing no change in his speed, I loaded as I ran, in order to lose no ground, and, coming still closer to him, I gave him a third shot. Still, on he went; but as I saw he was failing, I loaded again as I ran, and poured in a fourth fire, which I found made him stagger considerably in his gait. I then saw that one of his thighs was broken. By this time he had entered a small ravine, having steep banks on each side, where I could run round and head him off; in doing which, I saw a large tree laying across the branch he was travelling up. I went out on this log till I got about the middle of the branch, where I stood, unseen by the bear, till he was almost under me, when I notified him that I was there, by saying, "Old fellow, you are mine at last." He stopped to see what was the matter, when I took the fifth shot at his head, and down he went into the water. In the twinkling of an eye I sprang from the log, knowing that I could cut his throat before he recovered from the effects of the shot. I seized him by the ear, and, holding his head up, I slashed his neck through to the bone, and from ear to car, in a couple of cuts.

The next morning, it not being a good hunting day, I got Hugh McMullen to go with me, as his sister Mary could not, and help me to put the bear on the colt's back. So he and I went out, loaded the colt without blinding his eyes, and brought home the bear in fine style.

In a day or two, finding the snow soft, and fine for hunting purposes, I took my dogs into the woods, and over the same ground; but discovering no bear tracks, I took them to the laurel swamp, and sent them in to find a bear. Almost immediately, they started a very large buck, which, being frightened, came dashing toward me, but as he passed me I shot him, and broke his shoulder. The dog followed after him, and into the Big Yough river they went, where I found them fighting desperately, and the dog almost drowned.

I shot the buck in the head, and he floated down the river; but after going several rods, he lodged on a rock, when I waded into the water nearly to my belt, against a very strong current, and succeeded in bringing him to the shore. He was very large; but he had fought so much with other bucks, that his meat was not fit for use; so I took only what I could conveniently carry, as food for my dogs, and went home.

Everything seemed to progress to the satisfaction and happiness of myself and my beloved Mary. There having come on another snow, I started out before day, and was on the hunting-ground by the time there was sufficient light to take aim. Discovering the trail of many bucks, I took a stand, and watched for others to come the same way. In two or three minutes I saw a buck, with a fine pair of horns, coming directly toward me: he was so beautiful to look at, that I became excited, and trembled so much that I thought I would let him come so near that I could not miss him. On he came till he was within twenty steps of me, when I fired; and he started off, with the dog after him. But the buck had one leg broken, the ball not striking within two feet of the place where I wished it to lodge. After I shot the buck the second time, when he and the dog were in close contest, and saw what a wild shot I had made the first time, I was really ashamed of it, although I was away out in the woods. The same day, while on my way home, I saw a fine buck rise up, he having got some hint that he was in danger. As he popped up to look where the danger lay, I was within short gunshot, and let him have a full charge, which brought him down, with his back broken.

By this time our cabin was supplied with as much meat as would last us all the winter; where, although there was plenty of all kinds of game within three or four miles of home, having heard of a fine hunting-ground out on the Negro Mountain, I left my little Mary, and spent a week out in that dense wilderness; at the end of which time I returned with only one small buck and a she-bear, which was a very fine animal. I had just killed the buck as a heavy thunder-storm was coming up, and I was pushing on as rapidly as I could for my camp, when I spied a bear running as fast as it could. The ground being clear of underbrush, I ran after it, thinking it was only running to get out of the storm. It kept its hind parts all the time toward me; but as I found I was gaining ground, I reserved my shot until I saw it could not run any faster. I increased my speed, and began to draw quite near, when she turned to make battle, with her mouth wide open from fatigue and want of breath, and her belly hanging almost on the ground with fat. She then stood looking at me, and I at her, till I shot a ball through her brains. She was the best, though the smallest, bear I had killed. When I got all this meat home, I suspended my labors in the chase for that fall.

I do not pretend to say that I hunted no more, for I dare say I hunted some days after that, though nothing occurred to make any lasting impression on my mind But whether I hunted or not, I know I killed no more bears or deer.

Some time in February, I took out my dogs early in the morning, to chase a fox, when I found the tracks of a wolf, and blood in them. I discovered, also, that he traveled on three legs. I followed his trail over the roughest hills, along the Yough river, and at last traced him into the river. As I could not think of stopping in a chase like this, I went down the river until I found a canoe, in which I crossed to the other shore, followed up the river until I again struck his trail, and traced it to Bear creek, where I found he had crossed. Down the creek I went to a saw-mill, then crossed over, and went up the creek until I found his tracks again, which I followed for about a mile, when the dogs winded him on the steep side of a hill. Off they broke down the hill, till they came to a large rock, with a shelter under the south side, where the sun shone warmly. The wolf was here found, so fast asleep that the dogs were on him before he knew anything about them. Being prime animals, they dragged him from his lurking-place, and held him, while I beat him to death with a club. A premium of eight dollars was paid for his head by the county, and this sum was set apart for Mary to buy ware for her dresser.

Everything seemed to be going on to our entire satisfaction, until toward the close of the winter, when there came a false claimant for my farm, who demanded immediate possession of my premises, and threatened that, if I did not comply, I would be ejected according to law. By this time I had, by trading, managed to obtain three cows and eleven sheep, which, with my colt, constituted all my property; and, being afraid of a prosecution which would strip me of all I was worth, I concluded to surrender possession, turn out, and endeavor to get me some other residence. I could secure no farm in the neighborhood; and knowing that I had no means of buying farming utensils, I consulted with my wife, and proposed removing to the Glades, where we would be sure of plenty of grass for our stock. I told her that I could supply our table with meat at any and all times; and that, if she would go with me, I would risk it anyhow. She made no objection, but very cheerfully agreed to go to any place where I thought I could make a living. This being agreed on, we gathered up our little stock; and her father (who was, as I thought, glad that I was leaving his neighborhood) helped us with two of his horses, and Uncle Spurgin with one of his.

In those days, there being but few roads suitable for wagons, and only narrow paths leading from one settlement to another, and this being especially the case where we had to travel, pack-horses were the only mode of conveying goods from one place to another.

Our goods being all packed up, Mary and our little daughter were placed on uncle's horse, and we took the path for Bear Creek Glades. As we were late in starting, we did not reach our destined home that day, but stopped at Mr. William Hoy's farm, within three miles of our destination. He and his lady were not only exceedingly kind to us, but rejoiced at having a neighbor so near to them. In the morning, after eating a late breakfast, Mr. and Mrs. Hoy saddled their horses, and accompanied us to our new home, which I will here describe.

It consisted of the remains of an old cabin, which had been torn down to the joists by hunters, and burnt for firewood. I had it again raised to its former height, and covered with clapboards; but it had neither floor, chimney, nor door — a hole cut through the wall being the only way of getting in and out. After we arrived at our house, the first thing which greeted us was a very large rattlesnake, which lay coiled up in the house, but which we soon despatched. We commenced stowing our bed and clothing on the ground in one corner of the house, while the horses were nipping the grass outside. Another rattlesnake was discovered outside of the house, but was soon killed. The loading being all laid in the house, the two pretty women (for Mrs. Hoy was also a very pretty lady) seated themselves on the clothes, to rest a little.

In a short time, it being proposed to take a cold dinner of meat, bread, and butter, Mary took her bucket, and asked me where the spring was. This was situated on the edge of a large swamp, matted with high weeds, twisted with wild hops in all directions, making the worst kind of a thicket. I pointed her to the little path I had made while I was working at the house, and told her to look out for snakes.

"Oh!" said she, "I will keep the dogs before me, and they will smell them. I am not afraid if I have Watch with me."

Off she ran for water; but no sooner had the dogs reached the swamp, than out rushed five wolves, some passing on one side of Mary, and some on the other; she hissing on the dogs, and calling to me to look out for wolves. But they all escaped my rifle, owing to the high and thick weeds. Our dinner being finished, Mr. and Mrs. Hoy, together with Uncle Spurgin and Mrs. McMullen, got ready to go home. "Now," thought I, "I shall see my poor little wife have another cry."

When her father bid her farewell, he said: "You have got yourself into a hard-looking place."

"It is so, father," she replied; "but outside this dreadful thicket, it is the most beautiful country I ever saw."

They all departed, leaving Mary and her brother Hugh, whom I had forgotten to mention, till now, as being one of our party. He had agreed to remain with his sister a week or two, till she became a little acquainted with the place. Mary and myself proposed to walk a little through the beautiful glade, which was covered with grass knee-high, and intermixed with wild flowers of all the kinds and colors that nature had ever produced. All that fancy could desire was here to be seen at a single glance. This pleasant walk finished, we returned to the house, where Hugh and our little daughter were playing on the bed, she being much pleased with the appearance of the place When the sun began to sink behind the tops of the tall pine-trees, the deer and bears might be seen stalking over the open glades, feeding leisurely in the cool evening air.

I asked Mary if she would stay in the house by herself while I went out to shoot a deer, for she had beer, a long time wishing for some fresh venison; and I told her that her brother wanted to go with me. She said yes, if I would leave Watch (her favorite dog), which would not suffer man or beast to touch her in a rough way; for, if I was playing with her, and she called Watch, he would jump at me, and would bite, too, if I persisted. Then she took two forks, and putting one through each corner of her bed-quilt, she hung it up as a substitute for a door. I made her a good fire, to keep the gnats and musquitoes from eating up herself and her child; for these pests were there by millions. Hugh and myself then started off to a deer-lick, which was near our path, toward Mr. Hoy's.

When we got there, we climbed a high tree, to keep the deer from seeing or smelling us; and took our seats on the limbs, thirty or forty feet up the tree. After sitting a short time, I looked toward the far side of the glade, when I saw some animal coming out of a thicket into the glade. I said to Hugh: "Yonder comes one of Hoy's cows;" and, without examining it closely, I turned my eyes in another direction, to look for deer.

Presently Hugh exclaimed, "Be — if that cow ain't turned into a bear," Directing my eyes toward the animal, to see what it was, I told Hugh to go down the tree with as little noise as possible; and that, if I got on the ground without scaring the bear, he was surely ray meat. "For," said I, "he is in that large glade, and before he can get out of it I will be on him, as sure as you live, and he must die."

We got off the tree safely, without alarming the bear. "Now," said I, "Hugh, do you stand quietly here, and keep Gunner still, until I shoot. You see the bear is coming nearer to us, and I will meet him at the bridge over the branch. There you shall see the grandest fight you ever witnessed, unless I should kill him at the first shot. Have him I will; for there was never a better place to fight in, and out of this he shall not go alive."

By this time the bear had traveled at least a quarter of a mile, all the time approaching nearer to us. I then left Hugh and Gunner, to be ready to reinforce me, in case I should be unsuccessful at the first shot; for the bear was a large one, and would fight like the d — I if he got the chance to do it. I walked carefully down towards the bridge and seeing him coming toward it, I placed myself in his way; and, with ramrod drawn, two balls in my mouth, and the big knife hanging by my side, I was never in my life better prepared for a fight than at that time; for I had full opportunity to make my arrangements before he came within reach.

GLADE CABIN.

He moved forward so slowly that it was beginning to grow dark before he was where I wanted to make the attack. When he was within eight or ten paces, I spoke to him in a low tone, saying, "You are in the right place, old fellow." This I did to stop him while I took a good aim for his heart. He did stop, and looked at me until I fired; when off he started, with Hugh and Gunner after him, who had been watching for the battle to commence till their patience was almost worn out. No sounds of fighting being heard, I loaded again, and ran into a little thicket, where the bear lay dead enough; my ball having passed through the middle of his heart, and thus prevented the fight which had been so well arranged.

After taking out his entrails, and cleaning out the blood, I sent Hugh to Mr. Hoy's, with directions for him to meet me at that place in the morning with a horse, when he should have three-quarters of the bear. Hugh started one way, while I went the other; making all possible haste to my dear little wife, not knowing how she might like to be alone so long; for it was at least two hours after sundown.

I found her quietly waiting for me, and she said she was not the least afraid. After listening to the description of my hunt, she said that if I had staid at the house I could have killed a deer close by; for she saw one passing along while she was milking her cows.

Next morning I went after my bear, and reached the place before Hugh and Mr. Hoy arrived. We soon had him quartered; Mr. Hoy taking three parts, and Hugh and I the rest; which, with the skin, made us a good load home. Mr. Hoy brought a negro man with him, who carried the head of the bear home, and he told me afterwards that it weighed eighteen pounds.

As Mary wished to see a little more of the beauty of the glades, we all three walked out after the grass was dry, and traveled a distance of between one and two miles. The scene was delightful to view — our cattle and horses pasturing in grass reaching to their knees, the birds of different kinds, singing as if each was striving to outdo the other, and numerous turkeys roaming about, followed by large flocks of young ones. I told Mary that as soon as they were large enough to eat she should have as many of them as she desired to use. And if woman's eyes were ever pleased by beholding beautiful flowers, then was Mary gratified; for she gathered many bunches, and still saw new ones which she coveted; but we could carry no more. The whole face of the country was like a beautiful sheet of wall-paper, variegated with all shades of color.

We took this walk at a time of the day when all the animals were hidden, and we saw none of any kind; but in every soft piece of ground were to be seen foot-prints of all kinds, from those of the bear down to those of the rabbit. After Mary was satisfied with looking at and pulling the flowers, we returned home, highly delighted and having a fine appetite for our dinner of fresh bear-meat, good, pure, sweet milk, and butter which she had brought from our old home.

All three were soon seated round our primitive table, made of a large sheet of maple-bark, tied down on two laths, to keep it from curling up at the sides; this was laid on a scaffold made by driving four small forks into our clay floor, on which little cross-poles were placed, to hold up the bark. This table was made in a very short time, and without expense. We had a smooth, clean table, large enough to accommodate at least half a dozen persons. Our meal was made cheerful by the liveliest chat, and by pleasant expectations; for we had everything in common, and, like the sheet which was let down to St. Peter, we had nothing to do but "Rise, Meshach, slay and eat,"

My next care was to put a floor in the house, so that my wife's health should not be injured; for at that time there was no fairer or healthier woman in all our country; and I was very proud of her, for she was thought to be the best-looking female in those parts. I commenced splitting puncheons to make the floor, and had to carry them on my shoulders to the house. In laying them down, some laid badly; and I would say, "Mary, I will put that one under the bed, where it will neither be seen nor be in the way." But not long after that we would have another bad one, and she would assign that a place under the bed, too; until at last she declared that all the puncheons would have to go under the bed, and that she would be compelled to sit on the ground after all our labor She teased me about it till I was really ashamed of my job.

I mention this little matter to show how far she was from being low-spirited; and I have often thought what some of our young ladies of these days would do if placed in a like situation — particularly our city girls — if, at twenty years of age, — for that was the age of Mary, — they were located amongst bears, panthers, wolves, and rattlesnakes. And what would they do? I would like to see a few of them tried, just to learn how they would come through what she so bravely stood up to for four or five years.

After finishing my floor, I found I must have a lot to keep my calves in, separate from the mothers; and to work I went alone; Hugh having gone home for his clothes, intending to stay a month or two with us. I had ray rails to make and carry on my shoulder; but in three or four days my pasture-lot was enclosed, and then I felt at liberty to take a hunt every morning or evening, as the wants of our table required.

When Hugh returned, his sister Jane came with him, to spend a week or two with us. She was then a young woman, and quite good-looking; and as women always wish for something new on their table, Mary asked me to catch a mess of trout for our breakfast next morning. To gratify her, I went to Deep Creek, where success was certain. But just before I reached the fishing-ground, I met a bear standing in the path, within close gunshot. He saw me first, and ran into the bushes, followed by Watch. At it they went, up and down, over and over, until, by the time I came in sight, the bear had become so afraid of Watch's sharp teeth, that he was in the act of climbing a tree in order to save his hams from being scarified any worse; for Watch had torn him in many places, and some of the wounds were very deep. Yet when he saw me coming at full speed, he came down again; but as he did so, I sent a ball through his liver; which, however, for a few moments, did not seem to weaken him any. Watch and he then had another tussle; for the bushes were so thick that I dare not venture my knife, as I could not get out of the bear's reach speedily enough to save myself. However, I loaded the second time, came up as closely as I wished, and shot him through the head. I hid him away carefully, and went home considerably after night. When the two sisters found that I was going to the fishing-ground with my horse, for the bear, they determined to ride on the animal to the creek, and fish for trout, while I would bring the bear.

In the morning we set out, — Jane, Mary, and our little daughter, Dorcas, who had been named after my only sister, — and in due time we arrived at the creek.

There was a little shelter, made of pine bushes, that were very dry, and I had to make a fire to keep the gnats from the child while the girls fished for trout. I made the fire, then stood my rifle against the tree which formed the mainstay of the camp, hung my bullet-pouch, containing half a pound of powder and twenty or thirty balls, on the muzzle of the gun, and, after showing the girls how and where to fish, I went for the bear. I loaded him on the horse, and had returned almost within sight of the fire, when I heard an explosion like that from a heavy blast in a stone-quarry.

I hurried to the place, where stood the two girls, greatly frightened, and my ammunition was blown to the four winds. While the girls were busily fishing, the fire had crept along in the dry grass, and got into the bush-camp, which was burned up, and thence the fire had communicated to my powder-horn. My gun was considerably injured, but not so much as to hinder me from using it. The child having become tired, Mary had taken her away not more than two minutes before the blow-up.

The girls having caught as many trout as they wished, and the burning having so marred their pleasure that they would not fish any longer, we all went home. The girls were rather out of heart with fishing; their faces, hands, and arms being so badly stung with gnats and mosquitoes, that they would not try the sport again.

We were not intimate with any of our neighbors, though, indeed, we had but three. Colonel John Lynn, who lived within two miles, I had seen several times, bin I had formed no acquaintance with him. He was very prominent, and, perhaps, one of the most influential men in the county. He could do more in an electioneering campaign than any other two men in the county. Nor was this to be wondered at; for in his every action toward his neighbors, and all persons who had any business with him, honor, honesty, kindness, and charity were clearly manifested.

Mr. William W. Hoy, who lived within three miles, was a very generous and kind neighbor, but not popular; and Mr. James Drane, who lived within five miles, was a very kind, gentlemanly, and truthful man. These were my only neighbors. Neither Mary nor myself had ever been in any one of their houses except that of Mr. Hoy; so we were compelled to wait till circumstances gave us an opportunity for forming an acquaintance.

This state of affairs did not last long; for all except myself being engaged in clearing farms, wanted help; and as I was a good hand at log-rollings and house-raisings, we all soon became acquainted, and really fond of each other.

Mary was contented in her new home; and while I furnished meat and bread, she made as sweet butter as ever was eaten, and laid away enough for winter use. There were thousands of wild bees, and from each hive I discovered I got from two to ten gallons of honey. I could sell deer-skins at any time in the old settlement; for in those days many men, and almost all the boys, wore buckskin pants and hunting-shirts; which made skins bring a good price. I used to take my skins to the mill, and leave them there, and the farmers would leave me their value in grain and for bear-meat I received four dollars a hundred. In that way I bought flax and wool, and Marj carded it by hand, spun, wove, and made it into clothing. She done washing, knitting, house-work, milking, and churning, besides keeping herself, her children, and myself always cleanly and nicely dressed.

This was the manner in which people lived in those times; and I have often thought that if time could be suddenly set back sixty years, and everything restored to the same condition it was in then, our young people would not know what to do. At the present time, if the plainest farmer's daughter gets married, she must have a girl hired to help her with her work; and at the same time she has not more than she could do with all ease, if she would go into it with resolution.

In this way, Mary and I lived in quiet and peace with the world, and ourselves, till fall came on. One rainy morning I rose early, and told Mary that I would make a short hunt. I took my gun, called Watch, and went about half-a-mile from the house, when, as the rain poured down in torrents, I ran under a large tree for shelter from the storm. I kept a look out (for I had got accustomed to be always on the look out), and presently I saw a very large buck coming straight toward me. I was afraid the lock of my gun would get wet when I uncovered it to shoot; so I took a patch, which, being used for a cover to my balls, was well greased with tallow, and slipped it over the pan of my lock. The buck moved on till within eight steps of me, when I made a slight noise, which caused him to stop suddenly. Having my gun ready before he stopped, I immediately sent a ball into the middle of his breast. He did not run out of sight before he fell dead. I took out his entrails, and started for home, being as wet as I could be; and had got in sight of the house, when up bounced one of the largest-sized bucks, which, after making a few jumps, stopped to look back at me. He was such a tempting mark, that I shot him, and he fell dead within sight of the house. I dragged this one home whole, and was in season for a late breakfast; having secured two large, fat bucks, equal to a small beef in value.

A few days after this, a fine morning succeeded a showery night, and as there was a sufficiently strong wind blowing to keep the game from hearing my footsteps, I told Mary I would take a hunt. She rose early, and had breakfast ready before day-light. I told her the day would be a good one for hunting, and that she need not look for me before night. She offered me some bread and meat for my dinner; but as I did not want to be encumbered, I did not take it, and off I started, light footed and light hearted.

On I went, from place to place, seeing thousands of signs of bears and deer, but not one living animal. Tired with looking for and not finding any game, I got out of humor, and determined to cross the large valley between the Negro Mountain and the Meadow Mountain, which was four or five miles wide. Through the valley I went, though I had some long laurel swamps to cross; but I finally reached the Meadow Mountain, without starting any game. I was then eight or ten miles fi-om home, when it began to rain; and, provoked with my bad luck, I turned my course for home. I had traveled but a short time before the rain was mixed with snow, and presently there was nothing but snow falling. Having, as usual, left my hat at home, in order that I should have a fair chance to see everything that came in my way, I soon found my face and hair full of the drifting snow. Not content with walking, I ran some distance, and had, as I thought, nearly got to one of the large beds of laurel, when I suddenly came to a steep hill, and heard the roar of a waterfall below. "What can this be?" said I to myself. "I never knew of this place in these woods before. If this is Cherry-tree Meadow Creek, it will run to my left; but I will go and see." I went down; and finding it running to my right, I knew it to be the Little Crossings, instead of Cherry-tree Meadow Creek. I turned my course for home again, for I had travelled two or three miles further away, and I began to fear those laurels I had to cross. The snow had now covered them all over; and if night came on me before I got into them, it would be impossible for me to cross them in the night. I therefore ran at full speed, and by-and-bye I came to another steep hill, and another roaring waterfall.

"Well," said I, "this looks very like the same place I was at a few minutes ago, and I think it is the same." I ran down the steep hill, and at its foot saw the tracks in the snow, which I had made just previously. Feeling irritated, and as crabbed as a wounded bear, I again walked up to the top of the hill, "Now," said I, "I will take three trees in range, and keep on that course till I come out of this desolate place."

Having ranged my trees, I started off at full speed, thinking that, if I could yet succeed in passing the laurels before dark, and get a glimpse of the high Negro Mountain, I could go home in the dark. Encouraged at the thought of home, I ran on till I came to another steep hill and another roaring waterfall. "Merciful Father!" said I, "have I got back to that again?"

As I was carrying my gun in my right hand, I laid it on my shoulder, and walked coolly along till I came to my tracks the third time; and then I made up my mind I would have to stay in the woods all night. It was then getting dark, the snow was ankle-deep, and both hail and snow were falling very fast. I searched for a hollow tree to creep into, but could find none, nor a shelter of any kind. At length, finding two trees laying across each other, I gathered the bark from them, and, by laying it over the cross-logs, thus made a poor kind of resting-place for that night. My next job was to make a fire, which I was afraid I would be puzzled to do, everything being wet and covered with snow. However, I succeeded in kindling a large fire before my camp, when I crawled under the shed, which was not more than two feet high, and lay there half the night; first turning one side of my body to the fire, and then the other, in order to dry my clothes While I lay with one side up, the fine hail would fall into my ear; and when I turned over, it fell into the other. Finally, I took the tow I used for cleaning my gun, and with it corked up both ears; and after laying down again, I found I had hit on an excellent way of keeping the hail out.

I worried out the night, troubled with many anxious thoughts about Mary; for I knew she would think I had fallen in with some beast, and been killed. As soon as it was light enough to see to walk, I set off for home, being determined to get there as fast as my feet could take me. I steered my course as well as I knew how, taking good care not to go back to the Little Crossings again. After travelling a long time, at length I heard my dog barking in a thick swamp of laurel. I went in slowly, to avoid making a noise; and seeing a small bear up a tree I shot it in the head. It was a fine little bear, as fat as butter; but what to do with it I did not know. If I left it in the woods, and the snow should melt off, I never could find it again; and besides, I knew not how to get there with my horse. So I determined to carry it as far as I could, and then leave it where I could find it another time. I thought of making a fire, and roasting a part of it for my breakfast; but considering that it would take too much time, and how uneasy Mary must be, I concluded to try and get home without delay.

I stripped the skin from the legs of the bear, which I cut off close to the body; and, tying the loose ends of the skin together, I put my head and one arm through the loop thus made, by which the bear was securely fastened on my back. In this manner I could travel pretty well, and continued on till I struck the road leading from Col. Lynn's to Cumberland. It being then about twelve o'clock, I proceeded up the road as fast as I could walk, though I was frequently obliged to stop and rest, for my load did not weigh less than from eighty to a hundred pounds. The Colonel seeing me coming toward his house with my load, met me at the stile, and called to a black man to have his horse saddled by the time I had eaten my dinner.

I went in the house with my host, to whom I related the details of my hunt, and of the disagreeable night I had passed. He seemed to appreciate my sufferings, for he had himself once been lost seven days in a dense wilderness. There was part of a roasted turkey on the table, and Mrs. Lynn had the first joint of the leg cooked in some way that I knew nothing of. She called it the turkey's devil, and asked me if I would have a piece of her deviled turkey. Not knowing what it was, and thinking that if I took it, I might not be able to eat it. I refused it, saying, "Mrs. Lynn, I had devil enough yesterday and last night, and I don't want any more to-day." The two old people enjoyed a hearty laugh at my expense, and I got out of the scrape.

By the time I had finished my meal, the horse was at the stile; when the old gentleman put my load on the animal's back, and we soon arrived at my own home. The good old man, after hearing Mary relate her many fears and conjectures, and enjoying our happy meeting, mounted his light footed horse and rode off like the wind; leaving Mary and myself as happy in each other's company as if we had a dozen of our best friends with us.

As I had no other way of procuring our winter's provisions, I went hunting; and it was not long before we had plenty of meat salted away for that season. When the hunting season was over, which lasts till the first day of January, I took ray skins and traded them for a sufficient quantity of grain to last until spring. All this being done, the balance of the winter was devoted to the care of our little stock of cattle; which then numbered seven or eight head, beside one horse and ten sheep. The sheep gave me more trouble than all the rest; for if they happened to be out of their pen only one night, it was ten chances to one that the wolves killed at least one of them. But they seldom made much at this business; for if they killed a sheep or a calf for me, in two or three nights after I would catch one of them in a steel-trap; and his scalp, being worth eight dollars, was equal to the price of four sheep.

I thus always kept a little in advance in my account with the wolves and the bears; and as for the rattlesnakes, I have slain my thousands without ever having been bitten by one. I was at all times prepared to receive their attacks; for before leaving home I always took hay, or long grass, and twisted it into a large rope, with which I wrapped my legs up to the knee; and this they never could bite through. When thus provided, I would go where I pleased in daytime; but being afraid they would creep to me in the night, if I was where I thought they were numerous, I would stuff leaves round my legs, inside of my pants, and sleep with my moccasins on; and making ray dog lay down, I would lay my head on him; knowing that then no snake or animal could take me by surprise. Both ends being thus fortified, I could sleep as comfortably as if I had been in the most secure house and on the best bed in a city.

Mary and I passed the winter as contentedly as heart could wish, as we were well provided with milk and butter, honey and venison; but still we were anxious for the return of spring, when the flowers and sweet-singing birds would add to the enjoyment of our leisure hours.

At length spring came, and all the beauties of nature lent a new charm to every hour in the day. This was the time also to commence bear-hunting again; and accordingly I told Mary one evening that I would try to kill a bear the next day.

"Well, Meshach," said she, "you have always heretofore came home safe; but I am afraid you will some day or other be found unprepared for the bears, and be torn to pieces."

I answered her that there was no danger; for, being well acquainted with all kinds of animals I would not engage with them unless I had the advantage; and that, as in no case would I come to close quarters with them, but would remain at a sufficient distance to keep out of their clutches, she must not be uneasy about me; for I would surely take care of myself.

The following day, I saddled my horse and started for my camp — distant about ten miles in the wilderness. I reached there about four o'clock, and hobbled my horse, to keep him safe till I had finished my hunt. This done, I took my two dogs, entered the woods, and hunted till late in the evening, but could find nothing. However, on my return to the camp, as I skirted the edge of a largo laurel swamp, I started a very large bear, which, with two or three jumps, got into the laurel and out of sight. The dogs followed him in full cry, and I ran through the laurel after them, till I found myself out of breath, and could no longer hear their yelping. I continued following them till I got on the top of Meadow Mountain; when I sat down to rest and listen, I soon heard the dogs barking at a great distance, when I descended the wild, steep hills, till I came in sight of the bear. I saw that he was standing upon a large limb of a tree, and crept slily along until I got within a good distance for shooting; when I took a deliberate aim at his heart, and fired. Down he came, so badly wounded that he could not fight. It was then late in the evening, the sun being down, and I was at least four miles from my horse. I commenced skinning him, and by dark I had the hide off and the carcass cat in two; which I laid on a large fallen tree to cool. It was dark, and a heavy cloud was coming up, with thunder and lightning, and every appearance of a dreadful storm. I groped about in the dark for some shelter, but could find none. Seeing a large fallen tree, I took poles, and, laying one end of each on the ground, I placed the others on the log, and spread my bear's skin over them, with the greasy side upwards. The skin was sufficiently large to shelter me from the rain, and the tree protected the west side of my lodge. By the time I had seated myself under my shelter, the rain was pouring down in torrents, accompanied by vivid lightning, and such appalling peals of thunder that the earth seemed to tremble under me. Two trees were torn into splinters within a few rods of my lodge.

It continued raining till about midnight; and having made no fire, I concluded to remain where I was for the balance of the night. So, taking the bear-skin and wrapping it round me, I lay down and slept soundly till daylight.

When I awoke I felt hungry; but having left my provisions at the camp with my horse, I immediately set off thither. I had at least half a mile to travel through a dense laurel-swamp, which was so drenched with the heavy rain that it was like swimming through a river. But into It I went, half angry at myself for going so far from home to hunt. On I went, however, breaking and tearing through the thick laurel like a frightened ox would have done if he had had a hornet's-nest tied to his tail. I was as wet as I could be, and was obliged sometimes to crawl on my hands and feet under the laurel; at other times, to walk on the tops of thick beds of it, until I was so heated that I stopped to take a drink; when the reflection of my face in the water looked like the full moon, setting behind a cloud on a murky evening in Indian summer.

On I went, till I got to my camp; when, finding that my horse had gone, I ate my breakfast, and then followed his trail till I found him safe at home. As the day was very warm, I knew that the flies had by this time been so long on my meat that it would not be worth anything; so I did not go for it: and all I got for that job was the hide.

Being much dissatisfied with that hunt, I took with me Hugh McMullen, and went on Deep Creek to seek another bear. On account of the high water, we had to travel about four miles down the stream, in order to cross on a large drift, to get to the ground on which we wished to hunt.

We found the drift, and got over; and as soon as the dogs entered the hunting-ground, away they went, at full cry, Hugh and I followed at our best speed, until we were near the creek; when we heard a bear and the dogs plunging through the water. Not knowing what sort of a bear it was, and fearing that the dogs might be killed, we hastened to the creek, which was from fifteen to twenty feet wide. Thinking that I could clear it with a running jump, I started at full speed, and sprang for the other bank, which I reached; but, not being able to recover my balance, down I went, to my arm-pits, and my gun went entirely under water. After a smart struggle, I mounted the bank, and ran after the dogs; whom I found under a large pine-tree, and the bear sticking on the side of it, about fifteen feet from the ground. The bear wanted to come down, but seemed afraid.

Hugh came soon after; but as we were without any means of shooting, I told him that if I could get the bear down I could kill it with my knife, as it was only a common-sized fellow. I directed him to take a good strong club and go behind a tree, in order that the bear should not see him, while I would coax him down and try to kill him.

All being ready, and Hugh concealed, I called the dogs to me, and stepped behind the tree the bear was on; thus giving him a chance to run.

As soon as he saw such a good opportunity to escape, he began to come down; but the dogs, hearing him scratching the bark of the tree as he was descending, both darted round the tree. The bear was not yet within their reach; and to escape them, he scrambled round to my side of the tree. I jumped up as he was peeping at the dogs, caught him by the hind-foot, and brought him to the ground; and in a moment the dogs were into him for death or victory. The bear seized one of the dogs by the shoulder; but the instant I saw that I sent my knife into his side, through the lights, and stretched him lifeless at my feet.

When the fight was over, my brother-in-law accused me of being crazy; and said he would not run such risks for all the bears and dogs in the woods. We then skinned the animal; which we found to be a very large female, though we thought we had been fighting a common-sized he-bear. She had wounded my dog so severely that he was unable to hunt any more during that season.

I then turned my attention to bee-hunting, and killed no more bears or deer than would keep my table supplied with meat; which was an easy matter to do; for there was no time when I could not kill a deer, as I always saw from ten to twenty in a day. I thus kept my house well supplied with provisions at all times.

About this time, Mary's eldest sister paid us a visit; and as she arrived at one o'clock in the day, Mary asked me to bring home some young turkeys for supper. Telling her I could soon do that, I called Watch, who had been lame for more than a month, from the bite of the bear, and was still stiff; but I thought motion would be good for him. Into the glades I went, where I soon saw three or four old turkeys, with perhaps thirty or forty young ones. I sent Watch after them, but they flew into the low white-oak trees; and when I would walk fast, as if I was going past them, they would sit as still as they could, for me to pass on; but after walking twelve or fifteen steps, I would stop and shoot off their heads. I thus kept on till I had shot off the heads of nine young turkeys, and I don't believe I was more than an hour away from home.

I continued till fall hunting bees and shooting turkeys, and as many deer as I wanted. In September old Mrs. McMullen visited us, arriving in the afternoon; and Mary said to me that she wanted some fresh venison, as she knew her mother was very fond of it; whereupon I took my dog and gun, and set out for an evening hunt.

As the movements of my dog showed me, beyond a doubt, that there was game very near, I ordered him to go on, when he bounded off to a large mass of rocks. I then knew it was not deer he was after, but that there must be a bear hid in those rocks. Gunner presently came to a great crack in the rocks, and, after scenting around awhile, I told him to go in and fetch the animal out, believing that I should see a poor bear crawl out; for at that time all bears were poor. Down went Gunner, while I ran to the other side of the rock; but to my astonishment a panther bounded out, and, jumping from rock to rock, soon got out of sight. The dog followed among the rocks as best he could, and soon I could neither see nor hear anything more of them; but, after some minutes, the dog opened again, as if he was coming back on the other side of the rocks and laurel.

I turned to follow the dog; but all again becoming quiet, I listened with anxiety, when I heard something moving behind me. I looked around, and beheld the panther coming toward me, but not near enough for me to shoot. He made a short turn, which brought him opposite me, and within ten steps; but he went on the off side of a rock, that covered him from my shot. As I saw he would have to come from behind the rock, and be exposed to my view, I held my fire till he came out; and as soon as he made his appearance, I let him have a shot, which I directed as near as I could for his heart. As the gun cracked he sprang into the air, snapping at the place where the ball had struck him; and then turning towards me, he came on till within about five steps of me, put his paws on a small fallen tree, and looked me full in the face. While he stood looking at me, I saw the blood streaming from both sides of his body. He stood but a short time, and then sprang up a leaning tree, where he sat only a minute or two, when he again came down to the ground, and disappeared. I was really glad of it, for I found myself so nervous that I could scarcely load my rifle; and when he was looking at me, I was determined that, if he made an attempt to come nearer to me, I would seek safety in flight; for he would have been obliged to ascend a steep hill, and as I had at least five steps start of him, I don't think he could have caught me. If any man would run at all, I think that would have been as good a cause as he could wish for; and I know I should not have been distanced in that race. In the meantime my dog returned, and I sent him to see what had become of our enemy. He left me in great glee, and descended under a large mass of rocks, where I heard him worrying the panther. I then ventured to the den, and found the beast dead. He was a very large animal, and I felt sure that he had ranged these woods a long time; for many dead deer had been found there, which had evidently been killed by a panther, and after that fellow was dis-posed of, no more deer were found dead in those woods.

This fight postponed my deer hunt, and Mary had to wait the luck of an-other day. In the morning I rose at break of day, and hunted the grounds I had been over the night before; but found nothing. I then crossed over to the Meadow Mountain. The morning being cool, and the sun shining warmly on the east side of the mountain, I hunted that side, and presently saw an un-common big buck, but he was too far off for me to shoot him. I crept a little nearer to him, but was still too far, as I thought, to shoot; but finding that I could not get any nearer, I prepared myself, and took a fair aim at him. As soon as the gun went off, he came running towards me at a gallop; but by the time he got near me, I had again loaded my gun, and as he was going at a moderate gallop, I shot as ae ran, and killed him. I then skinned him; and tak-ing the saddle, skin, head, and horns, I carried them up a high mountain, and was never more fatigued in my life, than when I got home with my load — the saddle weighing eighty-seven pounds, the head and horns nineteen pounds, and the skin eleven pounds. I believe that was as good a deer as I ever killed in my life, although I have killed larger animals; but he was so fat, and the venison was so tender, that I thought it was fully equal to, if not bet-ter, than any I had ever eaten; and Mary and her mother had as much of the best venison as they could wish for.

The fall was advancing, the weather was becoming cold, and the leaves had nearly all fallen, when one evening I said to Hugh that we would take the dogs into the cornfield, and catch some coons which had been eating the corn. We went to the field; and as soon as we arrived there, the dogs set off in fine style, and we, being full of fun, screamed after them, expecting every minute to hear the coons squealing. But the dogs ran on until they almost got out of our hearing, before they came to bay. We followed by the light of the moon till we came up to them, when we found they were barking up a stout oak Presently down came a good-sized bear, and the dogs went at him; but it was so dark under the tree (it being a red oak, with very thick top, and the leaves still green on it), that we could not see the fight. But the dogs being more than a match for the bear, he again ascended the same tree; and as he did so, observing him between myself and the sky, I fired at him; but he still went on, until he got among the thick limbs of the tree, where we could not see him at all.

I was about to reload my gun, when I found I had not a single ball left. Here was a predicament, and what to do we could not tell. At last I told Hugh that I would climb the tree and with my knife cut a long pole, on which I would tie my knife, and stab the bear with it. He objected to the plan; and said that if we got into a fight in the tree, I would be sure to fall, and that would make it doubly dangerous. I told him that if I got that big knife into the bear's lights, or into his heart, he could not fight long, and I would not strike at him till I could take a sure aim. So up the tree I went, till I got on the limbs, and within ten or twelve feet of the bear, when I stopped to rest, and tie my knife to a pole. I then heard something like water falling on the leaves, and I thought it was caused by fear of my coming after him. I called him a cowardly negro, and told him that he must do something before long; but as I was cutting my pole from the limbs of the tree, and making it ready to tie my knife on with my moccasin string, I heard a crashing among the limbs of the tree, when, looking up, I saw the bear pitching headlong down through the tree-top, and heard him fall on the ground. I screamed to Hugh to pelt him with the axe, for he had one with him; but as I heard no noise, I called out to know what was the matter; — when I was told that the bear was dead. I then came down, and found that the shot had done its work, and that he had hung on to the tree as long as life remained. We tied his feet together, put a strong pole through, and carried him home. It appeared that, while I was ridiculing the poor bear for his cowardice, the water I thought I heard falling was his heart's blood; and as he had no strength to move, he was fairly excusable for not fighting.

This fight encouraging us to seek another, in a few days we took our dogs and guns, and started for the Little Crossings. After hunting there a long time, the dogs started off in full cry after what we were pretty certain was a bear, and in a short time we heard the fighting begin. The dogs would run awhile, and fight awhile; and after a chase of at least three miles, all the time coming nearer home, the bear at last ran into a large glade, in full view of Colonel Lynn's house. It so happened that General Lee, an old Revolutionary officer, who fought with General Washington, was on his road to the West, and had stopped with Colonel Lynn a few days. When the dogs and the bear came in sight, the whole family, together with General Lee, came out to see the sport. Hugh and I came into the glade, and commenced hostilities at once; and after three rounds fired at him, the bear yielded to superior numbers, there being four to one; and he died like a hero, fighting till the last breath left him.

As the time was approaching when it would become necessary for me to prepare my winter stock of meat, Hugh and I took our dogs and guns, and set off for the Little Crossings, which, in those days, was the best hunting-ground I knew of. We were late in reaching our camp; but I started out, and soon encountered a herd of deer, of which I shot two. We brought these to the camp that evening; and agreed to meet at the camp the following morning, if either one saw any bear tracks, there being a light snow on the ground. We met at noon, as Hugh had found the tracks of a bear; and, having eaten our dinner, we started to follow the track, which, after tracing it three or four miles, seemed to terminate in a small thicket of laurel. As neither of us had ever been there before, we did not know how to take advantage of the ground; there being two thick swamps, one on each side of a hill, and this little thicket situated on the top of the latter, with clear ground on both sides.

As we found that our dogs winded the bear in the little thicket, we slipped them into it; and in a few minutes they were in the midst of I know not how many bears, but it is certain that seven of the largest kind ran out on the south side of the hill; and Hugh told me that he saw at least a dozen run out on the north side. Our reason for separating was, that as soon as the dogs got among the hears, each selected a bear for himself. When I saw this arrangement, I sent Hugh after one dog, while I looked to the other. I pursued mine into a dense laurel thicket, and was many times within ten steps of him; but as, with all my activity and strength, I could not get within sight of him, I continued the chase till it was so dark that I could not have seen him if he had been on clear ground. With tired limbs, and shirt saturated with moisture, I was compelled to retreat without obtaining a sight of my stray dog. I went to the place where Hugh and I had parted, and hooted, [1] but received no answer. I then waited, and after an hour or two Hugh returned, with precisely the same bad luck I had met with. I mention this circumstance to show the great number of bears ranging those wilds during the olden time, and I have many times seen ten and twelve during one day's quiet hunting.

During this hunt, Hugh killed a deer, and hung it upon a tree. He then told me that he would go home, for he did not like to live so long in the woods — a bed and a good warm dinner being more to his fancy than staying out in the snow, and getting nothing to eat but frozen bread and meat half raw; that he was going home that night; and that, if I would stay, I might take his deer and keep it, for he would not go for it. He started for home, and I for his deer, which I soon discovered had been destroyed by a bear. The dogs scented him, and being keen for a chase, I told them to try him, and off they went. I waited till I found it was useless to stay any longer, when I travelled about half a mile, and again waited for the dogs. As I was about to leave the last place, I saw deer feeding, thou another and another, till I counted four.

One, a very large buck, was lying down, and all the rest walked off, leaving him fast asleep. After his companions were out of reach, I crept from my resting-place to take a shot at him; and having marked the place he lay in, I lost sight of him, but still approached nearer and nearer, till I was within eight or ten steps. While I was out of sight of him, I thought he had got up and followed his company, and so continued to think until I had walked within eight steps, when there he lay, fast asleep, with his head flat on the ground. I took deliberate aim at his head, and when the gun went off he did not kick, as he was killed instantly. I then skinned him, and took his saddle to the camp; where, having lost my dogs, and Hugh being gone, I felt lonesome, and determined to go and see Mary and my two little daughters.

I took my dinner, though late in the evening; and, it being ten miles to my home, I tied up about fifty or sixty pounds of skins, and started, travelling as fast as I could, determined to be at home as soon as my strength could take me there.

I traveled on, resting occasionally, until I was about half-way home. I was lying on the ground, with my shoulders and back resting on my load, when I heard one of my dogs barking at a great distance. I left my load and ran at my best speed, not feeling the least tired. I suppose I ran a mile, when I halted to listen, and heard him still barking. I started again, and ran, as near as I could guess, for the place where he was barking, and then stood still, for fear I should scare the bear.

Being anxious, as the sun was then down, and I in strange woods, far from home, I gave a shout to the dogs. They were both lying under the tree, resting themselves; but they immediately sprang up, as I was near enough to see them rise. Looking up, I saw the bear coming down the tree; when I ran up, and as he struck the ground I shot him — but too far back. He seized my best dog across the back, and laid him out flat; but while he was at it I sent my knife into his heart. This I did with a very good will; for I was sure my dog was done for. He lay there till I disposed of the bear and started for home; when the poor fellow howled piteously.

I traveled on till I got home, late at night, and found my old uncle Spurgin, together with Mary and the children, who were all very glad to see me; for I had been nine days out, and had killed several fine deer and a large bear.

Here I found my true pleasure — my wife, dressed clean, her beauty, in my estimation, unsurpassed, the children, as clean as water and soap could make them, a plenty to live on, and not an enemy on earth. I say, who could be happier than I was at that time? It would be difficult to find any man who had less trouble, and enjoyed more real pleasure than I did, until the last year of my residence in that place — of which I shall speak hereafter. Having passed the evening in conversation, mostly about the hunt I had been engaged in, it was agreed that the old gentleman should assist me next day to bring in the bear.

After a good night's rest, I felt as if I was ready to encounter any kind of a beast that ranged those woods; and I said so at breakfast.

My uncle reprimanded me, saying, "A pitcher which goes as often to the well will some day or other come back broken," meaning that I would some time or other be killed by the bears or the panthers.

Mary joined in with him, remarking that she had said and done all in her power, and that she really expected that some day or other I would either be killed or left in the woods, like her poor Watch was left the previous night. She said that she thought it was a sin to have such a faithful creature as Watch was torn to pieces and loft ill the woods to starve or die, as the case might be. She lamented her faithful dog, that had always been by her side, to keep anything from harming her.

I told her that, having given him as much of the bear's liver as he would eat. he made a tolerable meal of it; and that I would attend to him, and bring him home as soon as I could do so.

I soon got ready; but as the old man and I were about to start I called Gunner; when, as he came running, I heard Watch howling to go with us also; which he could not, because he was too sore. Mary, recognising his howl, ran to him with a pan-full of sweet milk, which he immediately drank; and she was delighted to see her favorite dog in a fair way of recovery. He must have made his way home during the night; for I called him before I went to bed, but he was not there.

The old man and I then started to bring home the bear. Having learned how the Indians carry their bears, I tried their plan, and found it the best I could adopt: first, I skinned the head of the bear; and then, having split the skin of the head from the ears to the nose, I put the snout through the hole in the skin; thus forming a kind of rope. I then split the bear's back-bone without touching the skin, laid him on the horse's naked back, with his head toward the horse's tail, which I passed through the hole in the skin of the head, and thus the rope made a fine soft crupper; and by pulling the bear forward, the crupper became tight, and prevented him from sliding forward; I then passed his two hind-feet around under the horse's breast, and there tied them firmly; then, making a rope fast at the lower edge of the bear's ribs, opposite where the girth would go round the horse, I cut another hole in the near side of his ribs, and pulled the strap or rope as tight as the horse could endure it; and thus the bear was turned inside out, the soft skin being next the horse's back. The carcass, thus fixed, cannot turn one way or the other; and it was decidedly the best way I ever found to carry a bear through the woods.

Old uncle and I brought my bear home without difficulty in that way. Watch was laid up for a long time; but in a month or so he was again ready for service, and as good as ever he was. My uncle advised me to change my ground, and hunt in the glades; which I did, and killed twenty-two deer in two weeks, and then ended the fall hunt.

In January my old uncle again came up to see us, and to hunt a bear in his den.

The following morning, we went to Meadow Mountain, and into the rock and laurel; where, by some means, we got separated. Hearing him halloo for the dogs, I sent them to him as quick as possible, and they were soon in full cry. I ran off, leaving the old man to follow the best he could, and pursued the dogs and the bear. I ran on till near night, — for it was late before we started him, — when, finding that only one dog was after the bear, I went home, much out of humor, and very tired.

The dogs had each pursued a bear, and had got home before me. Watch was very bloody, but Gunner had not been in a fight. Neither of them was hurt, and we could not imagine how Watch had got so bloody without being injured.

The following morning, Colonel Lynn came over and asked where Watch was. I told him he was somewhere out of doors.

"Well," said he, "that is the best dog I ever saw; for, as my black Moses was threshing in the barn, he heard barking and fighting, and went out; when he found a bear in the shade-tree at the spring. The negro ran to the house with the news, and I took a musket, and my large bull-dog, and went to the spring, which was nearly a hundred yards from the house. As I drew near, the bear came down off the tree, and the bull-dog ran in and laid hold of him. The bear gave him one slap on the jaw. when he bawled out and ran home. Watch seized the bear by the ham, and ran round and round with him, till he was glad to run up the same tree again. As I was then quite close to the bear, I took aim, and killed him at the first fire."

The Colonel said he had come lo tell me to send for my bear. But as it was the first he had ever killed, I told him to keep the skin and half the meat, and I would send for the other half another day.

The winter continued to be very severe till March; when there came on a thaw, which melted off the old snow.

I had heard of a great den of bears on Meadow Mountain, called the Big Gap; and on the 4th day of April, 1803, Hugh and I started to hunt bears on our old hunting-ground; and during a chase, we found ourselves on the ground of which we had heard so much about bears denning in, or, as the hunters call it, "holing." I proposed to Hugh to look for their dens; to which he agreed, and so we went in search of the place.

In half an hour we were in the greatest place for bear's holes I ever saw in my life. I really believe that at least twenty had lain in one acre of rocks. However, they had all left their holes, to go out and eat acorns, except an old female and her younglings, which were located in a deep place in the rocks. Our dogs found them before we got near the place, and the old one fought with great fury, while her cubs ran for life. As they passed me, I shot one, and killed it, though Hugh missed the one at which he fired. We then went to the assistance of the dog.

The old bear had left her hole, and tried to follow her young; but the dogs kept her so busy, that she did not get out of sight of the hole before we shot her dead at the first fire. Two of the young ones escaped.

We continued the hunt, and in the evening of the same day fell in with another old female and two young bears. The dogs ran them all up the same tree; but the laurel was so thick, that as soon as I shot the old one, the young ones ran off while the dogs were worrying her. However, we sent the dogs after them; and after a chase of a mile or so, they put one up a tree, which we secured. We then commenced carrying our booty to camp, and got all secured in time to enable us to reach home the next evening, in high spirits.

The worst of the job was yet to be done; for we had to go with two horses ten miles, to carry the bears home. However, we succeeded in getting them all in safe, and they furnished us as much meat as we required for that season.

Having raised a little money, I laid it out in young cattle; and, there being scores of wolves about, on the same night that I got my cattle home I missed one yearling, which I found had been killed by a wolf. I told Mary he should pay me for my calf; but she said she thought it was a bad debt.

I took a shoulder of the calf, laid it in a running branch of water, and there set my steel-trap; and on the third morning following, I went to the place, and the trap was gone.

Rain having fallen all night, every trace of the wolf's trail was destroyed. I returned home, after hunting till I was tired, and got both dogs; but they could not scent him, on account of the great rain. I knew that he would go to the nearest laurel-swamp; to do which, he had a creek to cross. I went into the middle of the creek, and waded ap it, till at last I discovered where the trap had struck in the bank as the wolf was crossing the stream. I then followed the trail, with great difficulty, till it became fresher; when off went the dogs, and immediately they were on the old fellow in a hollow tree; and such fighting, and cutting with teeth, I never saw before or since. He was the largest and strongest wolf I ever met in ray life. He remained in the tree, with his mouth wide open; and every time a dog came within reach, he would sink every tooth into him. I encouraged the dogs to make another set at him; when the strongest took a deep hold on one of the wolf's ears, while the other seized the remaining one. He then bounded from the tree, and the two dogs threw him on the ground. He tried again and again to recover his feet, but they tumbled him down, until they were all tired; when I took a club and beat him on the head until he was dead. I took off his scalp and hide, which were worth nine dollars — the price of two calves. That was the way I served every bear and wolf: I always, to a certainty, took my own out of them for every trespass they made on me.

I still continued to shoot what deer and young turkeys I had need for, and caught trout when we wanted them. When hay-cutting time came, I usually got some young man to help me; for by this time I had ten or twelve head of cattle, and two horses.

On one occasion, I had one young man helping me, and we had come to the house for our dinner; but as Mary had gone to see her mother, we had to prepare our own meal. After we had eaten, we sat ourselves down in the door to rest a while, when a hog began to squeal. I knew what was going on.

I took down my rifle, and told the young man to keep the dog quiet, and I would catch a bear stealing somebody's hogs. Off I ran, and soon found an old bear, with a hog, which he had nearly killed.

Colonel Lynn bad desired that, if ever I found a bear on a hog, not to mind the hog; but to kill the bear, even if I killed the hog too. "For," said he, "if the bear escapes, he will kill half a dozen other hogs."

So, thinking I would make sure work with him, I took the leeward side of him, to keep him from smelling me, and approached within ten steps of him. The hog was very badly bitten, and very weak; while the bear was lying flat on the ground by his side, but not touching him. I wanted to shoot the bear in the heart; but the short bushes hid his body from me. I waited, and presently he reached out his paw and scratched the hog on his hind-parts. The hog grunted, and tried to crawl down the steep hill; but whenever he would drag himself out of reach, the bear would rise suddenly, jump on him, and give him a severe bite. He would then lay low again, but hold his head up, and look and listen, to see if anything was coming. He did this three times.

I saw it was Mary's pet hog, and I determined the next time he held up his head to try a shot at it. He soon gave the hog another bite, and listened again. "Now, my fellow," thought I, "you shall get your turn." I took a clear sight for his ear as he lay with his side to me, and bang went my rifle.

Down went the bear; when on to him I sprang, like u panther would on a fawn, and sent my knife into his lungs; so that, if the ball had not done the work of death effectually, the knife would have made up all deficiencies. But the ball had done all that was necessary, not leaving a particle of his brain that was not mixed with clotted blood. However, he was worth little except for the hide.

After my hay-making was over, I continued to shoot deer and turkeys till the hunting season came on, which was the first of October. During this summer, Dr. Brooke came into our neighborhood; and, being a Methodist, as well as a wealthy man, he brought with him a Methodist preacher, whose name was John Wirsing. The preacher had a new house to raise, three miles out of the settlement, and in the midst of the wild animals. He notified the people that, on the next Thursday, he wished to raise his house, which was to be a large-sized log-cabin.

The neighbors turned out in force, as it was for a preacher. There was plenty to eat, and plenty of whiskey to drink, and all the hunters were there. One of them, called Henry Dewitt, said he would bet a buckskin that he and David Clark could kill more game than any other two men in the company.

He did this because Clark, when out a day or two before, had found a place where the bears had gathered in great numbers to eat beech-nuts.

"Well, brother Henry," said a middle-aged man, called John Friend, whose sister Dewitt had married, "I will take that bet; and how long shall the hunt continue?"

"This evening, to-morrow morning, and to-morrow evening," was the answer; "and then we will meet at Dr. Brooke's, and count out our game."

This being agreed to, the next question was: "Who will you take with you, brother John? "

"I will take Andrew House," was the reply.

Mr. House was his brother-in-law; but he refused to be one of the party.

"Well," said Friend, "here is young Browning. I hear he is not afraid of any bear. I will risk him."

This nettled Clark; for, when he found the beech ground he now purposed going to, he shot a cub, when the old bear ran at him, and he fled, leaving cub and all, and never went back. However, Clark said he did not believe that he, or Browning, or any other sane man, would stand and let a bear come on him. He said that when the cub began to squall, he saw two other old bears coming at him, each of which had cubs. They were all united against him, he said; and any hunter might think as he pleased, but he never would stand the like of that.

We all enjoyed a laugh at his story; and having finished the house, and eaten a hearty supper, we regaled ourselves with a stout horn of good old rye whiskey, and all parted in great glee. Friend being acquainted with those woods, which I was not, he walked before. At length we came to a fine beech ground, just as it was getting dark; and, as we entered the outskirts of the beech, we found bears had been feeding there that evening. We expected to see one every moment; and, sure enough, a bear which we had both overlooked, started up and ran off within a few steps of us. It made a few jumps, and then stopped to look back, when I pulled trigger on it. It ran a few steps afterward, and fell dead, being shot through the heart.

We took out the entrails, and then left the beech ground, so as not to frighten the others which fed in that place. It had rained during the day, and everything was wet; and as we were obliged to enter a low laurel swamp, to hide from the bears, we could get no wood to keep us warm. But daylight came at last, and I was glad to get out of that place. After eating some of the liver of the bear, which was badly cooked, for want of enough fire to roast it properly, we started into the beech ground again. Friend desired me to lead, as I could shoot quicker than himself; and if a second shot was necessary, he would be in readiness. As the leaves on the ground were frozen hard, and cracked under our feet, we kept on old logs and rocks, and at length I heard what I thought was a bear, pawing among the frozen leaves, in search of beech-nuts. I remarked to Friend that I thought the noise was made by a bear, and as he was of the same opinion, I told him to stand there, and keep the dog quiet, while I went to see what it was. Cautiously treading only on logs, and other places where the bears had scratched the leaves off the ground, I moved forward until I discovered the bear, behind a large fallen spruce pine, eating nuts as fast as he could find them. I waited some time to get a shot at his side, but as he still kept his head toward me, I took aim at him while his head was down, and shot him. Down he went, and in a twinkling the dog was on him, and I followed, of course.

Friend, being a great coward, kept himself at a good distance, calling to me to keep out of the bear's reach. The dog was fighting desperately, and the bear was constantly rising and falling. Seeing that he was getting better of his wound, as he made a push at the dog I seized his hind foot, and jerked him sideways. Being weak from the effects of the shot, he fell, and the dog seized him by the ear, whereupon I plunged my knife deep into his lights, and he soon fell dead. Mr. Friend came up, and scolded me for acting so foolishly, saying that I would certainly be killed some day or other, if I did not quit that foolish practice of fighting with my knife.

The sun was then shining warmly, and it was a fine morning for a bear to feed. We took out the entrails of our prize, started off again, and walked about half a mile, when I saw another bear travelling from us. I made a noise, and he stopped to see what it meant, when I shot him; but off he ran, as if he was not hurt. He crossed a small creek, and I followed. Friend kept on his own side, and the dog with him, fighting all he could. I got into a thick swamp of laurel, and presently heard Friend's gun go off, when the fight ceased. I scrambled through the thicket, and joined him, when I found he had laid the bear dead, by shooting him through the brain. The dog had run him up a tree while Friend stood at a safe distance, and made an excellent shot. I had shot him through the body. Being a small animal, we carried him to the other two, and then went home.

By this time the wind had raised to almost a hurricane, and as we passed out of the beech into the chestnut ground, we encountered a large flock of turkeys. Friend proposed that we should kill a turkey a-piece for our little wives, and shoot off-hand, to try our skill. He fired first, and down came a turkey. They were all on the trees, and he had taken the nearest one.

"Now," said he, "beat that if you can." I then took the next best chance, fired, and down came another turkey. "Well," said he, "if Clark and Dewitt don't do better than I ever knew them to do heretofore, the buckskin will be ours."

We left the high ground, fearing that some of the trees would be blown down on us; and as we were making all speed toward a shelter, we met a fine buck, running to get out of the storm. As he was within ten steps of us, I aimed my gun at him, and fired, after which he made but a few jumps, and fell dead. We took out his entrails, carried him to the place where the horses would have to pass in going for the bears, and pushed for Dr. Brooke's as fast as we could walk, where we arrived about noon. Clark and Dewitt were waiting for us, and they had killed one doe, all told.

They seemed surprised to hear that we had killed three bears, one buck, and two turkeys. The Doctor treated us to as much good whiskey as we wanted to drink, and gave us our dinner. After dinner, we all took a shot at a small paper, when Friend and I beat them at that also. We were well able to do that; for Friend was a good shot, and there were few to be found anywhere who could beat me. We then all went home, and hunted no more together during that fall.

[1] To hoot like an owl is a hunter's signal. Being accustomed to the sound, it does not alarm the game, like the human voice.

Chapter Five

The hunting season being over, its limit usually being the first day of January, Hugh and I having concluded to go to the Big Gap, we went to our camp within three miles of the rocks where the bears had previously been so plenty; but our attack had so scared them, that only one holed there during the winter just mentioned, and he was deep under the rocks. My dog ran into the hole, and attacked the bear in his own house, where I could hear him yelping every minute, but could do nothing to relieve him, nor would he come out when called. There were three places of egress for the bear, but he would not leave his den,

I had given Hugh a bayonet, fixed on a handle like a pitchfork, with directions to run it through the bear if he came out by him, and I guarded the hole at which the bear was most likely to come out. After fighting for half an hour, through a small crack in the rock I spied some part of the bear. I put the gun in the crack, and fired, when out he came. I called to Hugh to run his bayonet into him, but he being too timid to make the attempt, as quick as possible I rammed a naked ball into my rifle, and as the bear was leaving the place, I fired again, and broke his thigh. The snow being very deep, before he got a hundred yards away he received another shot in the head, that decided the matter.

There were six inches thick of solid fat on the carcass, which weighed three hundred pounds. We skinned and quartered it, carried it to our camp, went for a horse, and brought it safely home. But the poor dog had suffered sorely in the fight; for, somehow or other, he had seized the bear by the snout, and had held on to him all the time I heard him crying, while the bear had so torn his head with his claws, that there seemed to be no hair left on it, and his eyes were so much injured, that I really thought he would never see again. But he recovered, and became as well as ever.

That winter passed over without anything worth recording, until some time in March. During the winter, the turkeys used to leave the glades, and go to the Potomac and Cheat rivers, to feed on the steep hills, where the ground was less covered with snow; and as soon as the snow melted, they returned to the glades in immense numbers. There they remained, and fed on the grasshoppers until cold weather came on again.

Turkeys having been seen in the glades, Hugh and I went out to hunt them, but without success. This occurred in the early part of April, and a little snow had fallen the night before. As we returned in the evening, the movements of Watch showed that he winded game. Hugh was picking up chestnuts, for the woods having been burnt, the snow had melted off, and left the nuts exposed. I spoke low to Hugh, and told him that the dog winded something, which I knew was either a bear or a coon. I kept a good look out among the trees and rocks, when directly out walked a large and very pretty bear. He was behind a large rock, that hid him from us, and when he came out he was within twenty steps of us. I turned my gun on him, and sent a ball whizzing through his heart. He made a few jumps, and fell dead. Being within half a mile of home, we had but little trouble with him, and he furnished us as much meat as was wanted for that spring.

In a week or two there fell another light snow; and there being at my house a young man who made his home some part of the time with us, and was very fond of scouring the woods with me, I told Mary that I would try to get a turkey in the morning, while I could track them in the snow.

"Well," said Sam Vansickle, "I will go with you, and help carry the game."

So off we went in the morning, and hunted a long time without success; but by-and-by we heard an old fellow gobbling on the other side of Deep Creek, which had overflowed all the bottoms and glades — from hill to hill being covered with a sheet of water.

Going to the narrowest place we could find, we sat down, and called like a hen turkey. This being their mating season, if the gobbler has no hen with him, he will come running at the call, and only stop long enough to strut, and show the female his beautiful plumage; or until the crack of the rifle informs him of his mistake.

Sam and I seated ourselves, and I commenced talking the turkey language. A gobbler heard me, and answered by a continued gobble after gobble. I told Sam that he would fly ever to us if he had no hen with him; and directly over he came, alighting within a rod or two of us. The moment he touched the ground he saw us, and wheeled around to fly back; but I shot him as he turned, and broke his wing; yet, notwithstanding, he flounced into the water, and swam to the other side of the deep channel, and made off into a thick alder swamp.

"Well, Sam," said I, "is not that a pity? We will now lose him, and he will starve to death."

"Oh no," said Sam; "I will bring him back."

"How will you get to him?" said I; for we could see him sitting in the bushes. Sam said he would swim the creek, and catch him; and as there was snow hanging on the alders in every direction, I tried to prevent him from doing so; but he stripped off his clothes, and, as naked as he was born, he plunged into the water, and swam to the other side. In a minute the chase began. Off went the turkey, with Sam close behind him; and when Sam would stop to take hold of the turkey's tail, the latter would slip under the alders. Whenever Sam gained on him, the same dodge would be resorted to. I had a full view of the race; and sometimes, when Sam would head him and turn him toward me, I had a front view of Sam, and when the turkey would turn from me, I had a back view of him. I never laughed more at anything I ever met with, than I did at that chase. At last they both got out of sight in the thick bushes, when I heard the turkey cry out, "Quit! quit!"

"No, no," said Sam, "I'll be — if it ain't too late to say 'quit' now, after you have run me so long in these — briers. My hide is torn to giblets, and I am tired to death."

THE TURKEY-RACE.

He now reappeared, holding the turkey by the neck, and leading him along, telling him at the same time what he might depend on, till he came to the deep channel, when in he plunged again, and swam over to me, holding the turkey with one hand and swimming with the other, through a sheet of water thirty or forty feet wide, and twelve to twenty feet deep. He brought the turkey to me, and told me to hold his little horse while he dressed, when he would attend to him himself. He soon put his clothes on again; but his skin was so torn with briers and bushes, that he was bloody all over, and he was as red as a goose's foot during a cold day in winter. He then cut off the turkey's head, and we went home. He received no more injury from his swim and race than what he experienced from a sore and much scratched skin, and from his feet being torn with snags and sharp stones. So ended the turkey race.

Sam being now most anxious to see a bear killed, we set out for the beech ground, and arrived there in good time to hunt that evening. As we entered the outskirts, I saw an old bear and three yearlings feeding on nuts, when I pointed to a large lynn tree within ten steps of the bears, and told Sam that if he would keep the dogs quiet, I would go to that tree and kill the old one, after which it would be an easy matter to kill the young ones. I got very close to the tree, when the old bear moved somewhat nearer, and, as she approached at one side, I stepped back to hide myself behind the tree again; but setting my foot on a high hellebore, which fell, she raised her head to look, and as she thus stood, her nose ranging in a line with her body, I aimed at the end of her nose, and fired, when down she fell. I immediately ran up and stabbed her to the heart. Sam and the dogs were soon on hand. I sent the dogs after the young ones, two of which then ran up a tree, when Sam shot one and I shot the other. The third ran to a large spruce-pine, that had a hole in it, in which they had lain all winter, and there we left him.

We went to another bottom of beech, where the dogs started up another small bear. He had climbed a tree before we saw him; therefore we had no fight, and consequently but little sport. We then returned for assistance to take our bears home, where we got them all in good time.

Sam having agreed to help me to make hay, while we were eating our dinner we heard another hog squealing in the same place where I had killed a bear on one the previous summer. I ran to the spot, and there found another bear on one of Col. Lynn's hogs. He lay on the ground in the same manner that the other did. Getting a fair view of his head, his nose being toward me, I aimed a little above his eyes, and let drive at him. Down fell his head, and I went to him; but having run from the house, I had left my knife behind; though, as he lay still, and I saw the bullet hole in his forehead, I was sure he was dead. Presently he began to wink his eyes, and as I commenced reloading, up he bounded, and made off. He ran till he butted himself against a tree, when he fell clear over, with his head toward me. He raised quickly, and came running back to me as straight as he could come, till he got very near me, when he turned a little, and I shot him through the body, killing him.

This story seems strange, and, without some explanation, might be thought untrue. It is my opinion that the first ball glanced on his skull, the bone of which was blue with the lead, and when he butted the tree, he was not sensible that he had turned a somerset, but thought he was running in the direction he first started to go. I examined the skull, and found that his head had been raised up high enough to bring his skull in a slanting position with the course of the ball, which did not enter it, but so stunned him that he did not know what he was doing; and when his head was turned, he ran any way which seemed the most likely one for escape.

About this time my step-father and my mother, who lived in Ohio, came to visit us. After staying a month or two, during which time they had been persuading me to Bell out and go with them to Ohio, I at length agreed to do so. Accordingly I sold all my cattle, twelve in number, six hogs, and such other things as I could not take with me, to Dr. Brooke, for the sum of one hundred and seventy-five dollars, bargaining to receive the money when I was ready to start. I had five head of horses, two of which were valuable — one three-year old, one two-year old, and a sucking colt. The best mare, which was suckling the colt, got into the stable with mother's mare, and was kicked so badly, that she died the second day after. The three-year old colt had an operation performed on him, and bled to death the same night; and the two-year old colt took the yellow water, and died the same night on which the other bled to death; so I had but one left, and she was sick. My mother traded her large mare to Col. Lynn for two small ones, in order to help move me out to Ohio; but when the time came to start I could not get a dollar of my money; and there I was, with not a living beast but that sick mare and one dog, for Watch had died of the distemper.

Mother was almost crazy, but poor little Mary stood firm, saying: "God was able to save us, as He had done before." My mother departed as soon as she saw that I could not accompany her, and left Mary and myself to do the best we could. I was completely ruined, not having even a cow, nor would the Doctor give me one back for what he bought them. I cannot remember how we got our children along without their milk and butter, which they had always been used to having in plenty. I became so dejected and out of heart, that I could do nothing but sit and fret, and I did not pretend to hunt or do anything for a week or two.

Mary went into Mr. Friend's neighborhood, which was five miles distant, and there she found a pedlar selling gunpowder and lead, which the hunters said were the best they ever had. Mary bought two pounds of powder and four pounds of lead, which she brought home, and gave me, saying: "Here, Meshach, is powder and lead enough to last you all the fall. Now do let me beg of you to cheer up, take your gun, and try your luck. You have been very successful in all your hunting; and if you give up this way, what will become of us all? You know that all depends on you, for I have no way of doing anything; and if you give up to your feelings, you may get out of your mind."

I asked her how she obtained the powder and lead. She replied that the pedlar had trusted her, and that he would wait till Christmas, and take skins or hams in payment. So I set about making ready to try my luck next day. After running as many balls as were necessary, and filling my powder-horn, we retired to rest, and Mary said:

"Now, when morning comes, I will awaken you early, and I hope you will cheer up. Don't give way to your feelings. Remember what you told me when we began to keep house. You told me you were strong, and could make a living in any place; and that, if we would trust in God, we would never be left to starve."

I shall always remember her saying that poverty was not treason, and that we could not be hung for being poor. "Well," said I, "my dear Mary, I will from this time again try to make a raise, and while you retain your health, I will consider myself rich."

When daylight came, I rose and started for the woods. I hunted with all ray judgment till in the afternoon, but saw nothing except a pheasant, which I shot, made a little fire, broiled it, and ate it for my dinner that day. After dinner I went into the beech ground, and there saw a deer, and soon after two more. I commenced to creep toward them, and having got as close as I wanted to be, was waiting to get a shot at the side of one, when another at a little distance snorted and ran, and as they all followed, I got no shot after all. I then went to my old camp, where I made a fire, in order to have it ready at night, and then started out for a hunt.

I had gone but a short distance, when I missed my dog. I knew that he had followed the track of either a bear or a coon, and presently I heard him in full chase, coming towards me. I made up my mind to shoot running or standing, as I thought it was a deer. I looked for the tail, but saw neither deer nor tail, though directly a bear came running toward me at full speed. I stood still till he came within seven steps of me, when I took no sight, but held the gun against him, and fired. The bear never stopped, though I saw the ball strike, but too far forward to kill him. I reloaded as soon as possible, and ran out of the laurel, and knowing there was a path made by the bears, which I also knew he would keep, as it led into a great swamp, I ran on the clear ground till I got below him, and then going into the path, I soon saw him coming toward mc, fighting the dog off as lie walked along. When he had approached quite near enough, I hissed at him, upon which he looked at me, laid back his ears, and came faster toward me. I knew that he intended to make a fight; and taking aim at his head, I held on till he was within five steps, when I was certain my aim would send the ball into his body if I should miss his head, and I was also satisfied that my lock would not miss firing. When he arrived at the place I desired him to be in, I fired, and down he dropped, as flat as a bullock would have fallen. I mounted him in a moment, and drove my knife into him up to the handle, after which he never drew another breath. He weighed fully three hundred pounds. I took out his entrails; and finding him to be a fine fat fellow, I felt as if Mary's faith had surpassed mine, and in my heart I thanked God for the gift.

I then opened his stomach, to see what he had been feeding on; and finding that he was full of red-oak acorns, I knew where to hunt for others. Accordingly, I went out to the top of a hill covered with red-oaks, and saw where a very large bear had been that morning. He had made a road from his feeding-ground down to the great swamp.

I walked out of the feeding-ground, in order not to scare him, and had gone but a short distance, when I observed something far down towards the laurel, which, as the last glimmer of the setting sun shone upon it, looked white. I soon saw that it was an enormous bear; and as he came into view, I was greatly astonished at his size. I found he was going to the feeding-ground I had just left, and I waited for him to come to me. As I stood looking at him, I prayed God to let me get him; saying to myself, "If I don't kill another this fall, I will not murmur; for if I get that fellow, the meat will keep my family till next spring."

Presently he turned his course; which made it necessary for me to move as he did, in order to gain on him. He heard me, and stopped to listen; but as there were many squirrels running through the leaves, he gave it up, and went on. When he walked, I walked too, so that his steps would drown the noise of mine; and on I went, till he heard me again; when I was still too far off to shoot. Then he sat himself down like a dog, looking right at the spot where I was; and there I had to remain, as still as a stump, till my legs and knees got so weak that I could not stand without trembling.

After looking some time at the squirrels, he started off again for his feeding-ground; when I moved also, and was drawing near enough to shoot, as he heard me a second time. He turned to run. I saw a small log lying before him, and expected he would stop and look before he started off in earnest. Sure enough, he shuffled along to the log, put his two fore-feet on it, and turned to look at me.

Then, if ever, I did my duty in shooting; for I thought it was no use to supplicate the Good Being to let me have the bear, and then take no pains to sight straight at him.

SHOOTING A LARGE BEAR.

So I took the best aim I knew how, and fired. Off went the bear, by a circui-
tous route; but I crossed him, and ran so close after him, that I saw him turn
a somerset, and fall with his head toward me.

I went up to him, though I was really afraid; and he was, of all the bears I
ever saw, before or since, much the largest. I took hold of him; but, as I could
not pull him out of the place he lay in, I took out his entrails, and rolled him
over till the blood had drained out; when I put sticks across his body, to let
the cool air in, as the day was warm. I found I had sent the ball through the
middle of his heart.

By this time, it being too dark to shoot, I left him, determined to return
home as soon as possible; and I would have gone home that night, though it
was ten miles.

The moon gave no light, and I was forced to go to my camp, where I had
already made a fire. As I was passing through a thick laurel, my dog ran off in
great haste; and soon after I heard him fighting with great fury. Finding that
it was a running fight, I left the laurel, and ran up the swamp, to a clear place;
where the dog and bear arrived just as I did. I could not see either; but I
heard a scuffle, and found the bear was going up a tree. When he was high
enough, I saw him against the clouds, fired at random, and down he came. He
was a two-year old, and as good as one of that age usually is.

So Mary's hopes were fully realized in this hunt; I having killed three bears
in about four hours,

I went to the camp, roasted the liver of the last bear I had killed, and ate
my supper. As soon as it was daylight I started for home, and arrived there in
time to get Mr. Hoye's two horses and his negro man to help me bring in the
bears.

The following morning, the black man and I were off betimes; and we
found the meat in good order, for the weather had got cooler. We skinned all
the bears, but we were not able to lift I lie large one; and having nothing to
quarter him with but ray big knife, I look it and commenced splitting him;
leaving all the back -bone on one side. When I got past the shoulder, I left all
the neck on the side with the back-bone. I then tied the two large quarters
together, and then the two small ones, and so laid them across the saddle;
putting the large bear on the strongest horse, and the two smaller ones on
the other. We then sat out for home, the two horses bending under their burdens; and when we reached our destination, a little after dark, I never saw a
more broken-down pair of horses than they were.

I sent Mr. Hoye a quarter of each bear. The quarter of the big one, having
no back-bone in it, was the lightest; but it weighed ninety-six pounds; and we
estimated the whole animal to weigh four hundred and twenty-five pounds.
The other two probably weighed three hundred pounds each.

This was the first hunt I had made that fall; and I continued on till I killed
seventeen bears. I then abandoned the bear-grounds; and, going into the
glades to hunt for deer, I killed eighteen head.

By this time the first of January had arrived, and the hunting season closed. During that fall, I saw twenty bears; of which I killed seventeen, and wounded one, that got off, having been shot a little before dark. I left him, thinking I could take him the next day; but in the morning there was a foot deep of snow on the ground.

The extraordinary success which I had in bear-hunting requires some explanation, which I will endeavor to give. I always kept two good dogs; one of which walked before me, and the other behind. The one in front would wind the bear, and lead me up to him on that side on which he could not smell me, and I would come on him unexpectedly. If, by chance, he found us coming on him, and ran, the dogs would overtake him before he would be out of sight. The moment I would see one run, I would send the dogs after him; and as I could run almost as fast as any bear could, when the fight began I was close up, and a shot was certain death. In many cases, however, I killed them with my knife; but only when the fight was so close that I was afraid to shoot, lest I should kill a dog; which has often been done. I never in my life shot a dog in a fight; for I always took the knife in a close contest.

Now this, together with my having made it my study for many years, gave me an accurate knowledge of the disposition, habits, feeding-grounds, etc., of bears, and also of the hours and days when they did feed; all of which it is necessary for a successful hunter, of either bears or deer, to know. I began to hunt in 1795, and pursued the chase every fall till 1839 — a period of forty-four years — and in a country where game was exceedingly plenty. During this time, I think I found out as much about the nature and habits of the wild animals of the Alleganies as any other man, white, red, or black, who ever hunted in those regions.

Chapter Six

The hunting season being over, and the bears having retired to their holes, Mr. William Hoye proposed that we should go the Big Gap and rout some of them out. Accordingly, we sat out for the rocks, but got no farther than the house which had been put up for the preacher. It was called Wirsing's house; but he was afraid to occupy it, on account of so many wild beasts being in the neighborhood. Being a fine place for hunters to sleep in, we took our things inside and made a fire, around which we seated ourselves — the night being cold.

Just as it was getting dusk, a wolf howled very near the house. I told Hoye to keep all the dogs in, and I would go and have a shot at him. I had gone but a short distance from the house when all the dogs came after me at full speed, passed me, and jumped at the wolves; though not one, except my old dog, would fight. Almost immediately, five worthless dogs came running back for life, with six wolves in full chase after them. One old one ran so near to me that I shot at him; but I was iu such a hurry that I only wounded him. He separated from the others, but my old dog followed and fought him well; though it was so dark that I could not see to take part in the combat, and therefore returned to the house.

As I went back, the other wolves met me, some on one side and some on the other, and growled at me. I held my gun in my hand; being determined that if they did attack me I would put it against one of them, kill him, and then beat it to pieces over any one that would attack me afterwards. I have since thought it was the smell of the recently-discharged gun that kept them from me, as they dislike the smell of gunpowder.

During the whole night, our dogs could not go out of the house without being pursued back to the door; though it was so dark that I could not see one of the wolves. As the day began to break, I took my old dog, stole around the wolves, and placed myself between them and a swamp which I knew they would enter, and there seated myself, to await their coming.

While I was waiting for them they commenced howling; during which time I ran up close to them. But as it was not light enough to see, I sat down a minute or two in concealment; when I saw a large fellow coming towards me. I let him come as near as I wished, when, as I fired on him, the others ran towards the house, and my dog pursued the wounded wolf. I ran after my dog and the wolf, till I saw the latter lay down under a pine-tree; when I loaded my gun, and made ready to shoot him in the head. But Mr. Hoy, having seen the other wolves coming toward the house, had set the dogs on them, and they came scampering back by me again. I fired at them as they passed, when my dog left the wounded wolf, and ran after the other dogs and wolves. We saw nothing of the dogs from that time until afternoon; when only my old dog and one other returned; the latter not being worth as much rope as would hang him. The old dog was so cut and tired that he was not able to trace the wounded wolf, and the other would not try to do it; so I lost him. But Dr. Brooke's sugar-camp hands found him lying dead near the pine-tree where I had last seen him.

Mr. Hoy and myself went to the old camp, and stopped there for that evening. In the morning we started for the rocks, and then separated, to look for such holes as might have bears in them. Hoy soon called me; but when I joined him I found that he had only discovered a hole into which a bear had carried broken laurel, and then deserted it. We started out again, when I found a hole into which a bear had been carrying moss. I called for Hoy, who joined me; but we could not determine whether there was a bear in the hole or not.

At length I cut a long pole, which I poked into the hole, and with it felt the bear very plainly. Hoy disputed the fact, when, to prove the truth of my assertion, I gave the bear a hard punch with the pole, and then told Hoy to take it and feel for himself. I knew the bear would be ready. Hoye took the pole, and, standing on a sloping rock, gave the bear a hard punch; when the latter laid hold of the pole, and gave it such a sudden pull, that Hoy was drawn headlong down to the mouth of the hole. He made great efforts to get out, but did not succeed until I reached down, caught him by one hand, and raised him from his fearful position. However, I do not think that the bear was sufficiently angry, or he would have taken hold of him, as they were within six or eight feet of each other when Hoy was in the mouth of the hole.

After Hoye's escape, we took the pole by turns, and punched the bear till he got furious, and tried to run out at us; but as he put his head out of the hole, I took a deliberate aim at him, and blew his brains out. It was a hard task to get him out of the hole, but we succeeded at last, skinned and quartered him, and each carried a quarter to the camp. We went back for the other two the same evening, which we again spent at the camp, returning home the next day. We then sent for our meat, and got it home in fine order.

This was the last hunt I made in 1804, while I lived at Bear Creek Glades. Having sold all my property to Dr. Brooke, and failing to get one dollar in money from him, he offered me a lot of ground containing fifty acres, which was originally granted to a soldier of the Revolution, but had been sold for the taxes, amounting to two dollars and a few cents. He charged me thirty dollars for it, which I agreed to give, and prepared to move into a little settlement, in order that I might be able to procure a horse to bring my bread home, as I could get none nearer than ten miles.

This lot was entirely under timber, and I had neither property nor money. In a word, I had a wife and four children; but having neither horse, cow, sheep, nor hog, I was obliged to maintain my family as I best could. In February, 1807, I went to work on my lot, cutting timber with which to build a house; and as I had either to walk five miles to my home, or stay from home, and leave Mary and the children by themselves, she proposed that I should try to procure a house in the neighborhood, and thus save myself many a long walk. I went into the settlement, procured a small house ten feet by twelve in size, and soon moved Mary and her four little children into it; after which I went to grubbing, in order to get some corn planted.

The time for sugar making having arrived, and every family preparing to make their own sugar, Mary asked me if I could not get her a camp, and let her make some sugar also. I enquired where I could find a small lot of trees for Mary's use, when I was told that about a mile off there were eighty or a

hundred trees, which number was sufficient for our purpose. I stopped grubbing, and set about opening a sugar-camp for poor Mary to work at; while I
tilled the ground, and endeavored to raise enough grain to supply us with
bread.

As soon as the weather became warm enough, I tapped the trees, and
Mary carried the sap to the fire. When she could not boil it during the day, I
would help her to boil it at night. She would attend to the kettles one-half the
night, and I the other. When day-light appeared, I would go to my grubbing
again. Whenever the sap did not run well, she would help me to pick brush
and burn it; and so we worked on till we get out of meal, which could only be
procured at the mill, distant ten miles. Mary spoke to a friend to take care of
her children, while she went there in my place, and let me work at my clearing. Off she started for the mill; and as the day was very warm, and the horse
heavily loaded, she pitied him, and walked more than half the way. When she
reached the mill, being exceedingly warm, she pulled off her shoes and stockings, and, wading into the cold water, she washed her hands, face, and feet;
but she remained so long in the water, that when she got home she could
scarcely walk.

This occurred about the last of May, and she continued to grow worse and
worse, till I was compelled to send for Dr. Brooke. He pronounced it to be a
paralytic stroke, and gave medicine for it, but without effect. Finally, the little
crease on her face below the nose was turned to the corner of her mouth, and
the eye on the same side projected so far that it looked as if it was stuck on
the face, and all the white was distinctly visible. Her beauty was destroyed;
but that was a small loss compared with her health, which I had always
prized so highly.

Having killed a wolf early in the season, I gave the scalp to John McMullen
(Mary's second brother) for one month's work; and between us we managed
to get in five acres of corn, which we dressed once through, and were crossing, when John left. I had a house to build, and when John departed I was
obliged to do everything myself, beside taking care of my wife and children.

Mary still grew worse, and the Doctor decided that hers was a desperate
case, which took all my hope from me; but I kept on working at my house till
the last of October. One day, when I was busily employed at the inside of my
house, up came my old friend Col. Lynn. After a hearty shake of the hand, he
said: "How is your wife. Browning?"

I could scarcely answer him, for my feelings were worked up to the highest pitch; but knowing his disposition, I summoned up all my fortitude, and
told him all, without shedding a tear, and that Dr. Brooke said she must die.

"Oh!" said he, "Brooke was never a skilful man, and I should not depend on
his judgment. But," added he, "I am going to Frederick, where Dr. Thomas
lives, who can cure her if she is to be cured. "

"But," said I, "Colonel, I have not a dollar in the world, to send so far."

"Never mind that," said he. "I have money, and will bring you medicine, if you say so."

Gratitude for such kindness left me speechless for a moment; but at length I told him to bring the medicine, and if I could ever get the money, that should be the first debt I would pay. He asked for a description of her case, and as soon as he had written it down, he galloped off like the wind.

I still continued to work at my house, and before the Colonel returned I had Mary and my children in a good cabin. About the time the Colonel said he would return, he came to see me again, and seemed really rejoiced to find Mary still living, exclaiming, as he entered, "I thank God to see you still with your family." He opened his stuck of medicines, which comprised fifty-two pills, and blister plasters enough to keep up a continual running, till she got relief. We commenced with the pills and plasters, together with cold bathing, rubbing her well with a coarse towel, as directed; and she began to mend, her face and eye gradually assuming their natural appearance. On Christmas day I rose early, made a fire, and attended to other things I had to do. When I came in, I found Mary was up and dressing herself.

"Well, Meshach," she said, "I feel as well as ever I did in ray life."

I looked at her, and thought she appeared more beautiful than I had ever seen her look before. She had yet three pills to take, and as she felt so well, she consulted me as to whether she should take the other pills or not. I remarked that, as the medicine had done her so much good, and as the Doctor had directed all the pills to be taken, perhaps the cure would not be perfect unless his directions were complied with. So she continued taking the pills until they were all used, when her face was drawn a little to the other side, and her eye sunk, and remained for the rest of her life smaller than the other.

In about eighteen months she presented me with a second son, whom I called John Lynn, because that good man had been instrumental in saving the life of my beloved Mary. I cannot take leave of this benevolent and charitable man, without saying a word or two in relation to his deeds of charity. A man named Charles James (who held different political views from those of the Colonel) had said that he would rather shoot that old rascal Lynn than kill the best buck in the woods. Shortly after, James had his leg broken, and was without the means of securing his crops. The Colonel, happening to be in the neighborhood of James, visited him; when the latter complained to him that his grain would all rot in the field for want of means to have it cut; whereupon the old gentleman took out a ten-dollar note and gave it to him, to enable him to have his grain cut — thus furnishing bread to the family of his bitter enemy.

This, and many other like charitable acts, coming under my immediate notice, aroused feelings of love towards him in my heart that will never be eradicated while I live; and, moreover, it proves to me that there are good men to be found in all parties. Colonel Lynn was an old Federalist; and little as I like that old party, I still will say, that a better heart never beat in any man's breast than throbbed in his. He lived till a squabble arose between the United States and England about our ship Chesapeake, which was seized, and her crew impressed on board English ships-of-war, which were sent out to fight the French. This quarrel terminated in a declaration of war by the United States. My old friend died while the dispute was going on; but in a conversation with him on the subject of the war, he said to me: "Browning, do all you can to prevent the war; but if it comes, do all you can to bring it to an honorable and speedy close; after which, continue to advocate your old political principles." And although I long since ceased to support his political principles, I do know that a better patriot and a truer man to his country never lived.

That fall I did not make much of a hunt, only killing two bears and sixteen deer. By this time I had become renowned as a great bear hunter, and there were some who envied me for my skill. Having no time to hunt that season, I told Mary I would take a day, and set a beartrap, or pen, as it is called. So one morning I set out before day, in order that no person should know where I had gone, telling Mary that, if any one inquired for me, to say only that I had gone out with my gun. I made a whole pen, set in, and came home during the night, so that no person had tiny knowledge of my day's work. It is a good day's work for two men; but its effect was felt for many weeks.

In good time, I again slipped out before day to hunt, went to my pen, there found a fine fat bear of middle size, shot him in the head, took him on my back, and carried him home by nine o'clock. There being but few acorns that year, bears were scarce; and when I was asked how I found the bear I killed, I told them that my old dog having winded, I saw the bear very near me, between two fallen logs. This was all true; for the pen was made of logs, and the dog did smell him before I saw him. Thus I kept up my name as a great bear hunter, and left no clue to those who might be ill-disposed, to look for the trap, and either throw it down, or take the game.

At the proper time, I again went out before day, and finding another small bear in my pen, killed him as before. By skinning the bear's legs, and tying the skins together I formed a strong loop, and then laying him on my back, I put my head through the loop, which passed over my left shoulder and under my right arm, and thus conveyed my prize home. I have carried so much meat in this way, that if I should name the amount, probably I would not be believed. Suffice it to say, however, that, for two or three years, I so carried home, for the use of my family, all the meat I killed within from one to six miles of home.

As I was walking home with my second, and, I believe, the last bear I ever caught there, when within a mile of the house, I saw a fine young buck, which was as red as a calf It was the first red deer I had seen that spring. He had been to the river, and was then returning to the mountain. I had plenty of time to lay down my bear and get ready for him; and, when he came to the right place, I fired at him. He ran but a few jumps, and fell dead. I dressed him, walked home, and returned as soon as possible for my little buck. lie was a two-year old, and, with the bear, furnished us a good supply of meat for a while.

During that summer, I was attacked with rheumatic pains in my hips, thighs, knees, and ankles. I laid three months on my bed, and never left it except when lifted off; even that slight motion putting me in agony. When I recovered so that I could move about the house, I was so lame in my right hip, and down that leg to ray heel, that I thought I never should walk straight again. The lameness seemed confined principally to the hip, and thence extended down to my heel, causing me the severest suffering. So I continued, with slight changes for the better, till October; when I could walk a little, but not enough to venture far out.

One evening a young friend of mine called on me. His name was John House, and he was the only man I ever met who could run in the woods with me, and keep up in a chase. He had been out hunting, and told me that, in the grounds he frequented, he had observed the tracks of a very large bear --in fact, one of immense size. He offered, if I would travel slowly, and reach his camp, to make all the fires, and do all the cooking, for the sake of my company.

Mary feared that I would get so far from the camp that I would not be able to get back; and so would lay out all night and freeze to death. I promised her not to travel out of hearing of the young man's rifle; and if any accident of that kind happened, he would attend to me.

It was agreed that I should meet him at his camp the following Monday; and during the interval I should walk out and try my joints, to see whether I would be able to stand the trip.

One morning, before the time specified, one of the children came in and told me there was a flock of wild turkeys in the corn-field. I took ray rifle, crept slyly round till I got the fence between them and myself; when, lying down on the ground, I crawled to the fence, and there waited to make a selection. One of the turkeys had assumed the control of all the corn-shocks; and if, while he was picking an ear at one side of a shock, he heard another turkey on the other side, he would run round and drive him off. lie would not allow any gobbler to pick at the same shock with himself.

After he had driven three or four away, and they all seemed in dread of him, I called to him, in a low tone, "You are a fierce old tyrant, and it won't last you long." This I knew would cause him to stand still, so that I could have a fair shot at him.

When he heard my voice, he could not tell where it came from; and straightening himself up, he stood as still as he could, looking for the cause of the noise I then fired at him, and over and over he went. I started to rub, but made such a poor attempt that I got ashamed, as I saw Mary and the children looking at me. I hobbled along to him, and, finding that he was dead, I took him to the house and helped Mary to clean him. After he was cleaned, he weighed twenty-six pounds; being the largest turkey I ever killed.

On Monday, all being ready for the hunt at young Mr. House's camp, I sat off early, as I had about nine miles to travel. I proceeded slowly, resting occasionally, until the afternoon; when a heavy fall of snow came on. It was not very cold and, as I was walking in a public road, — for the camp was close to the road, — I did not hurry myself.

I had just crossed Deep Creek, when, in a thick grove of pines, I saw the tracks of the big bear, where he had just crossed the road. As it appeared that he had not passed there more than ten minutes before, I followed after him, scarcely feeling my lameness. I followed him perhaps a quarter of a mile, keeping a very sharp look-out, as the snow had covered everything over, and was hanging thick on all the underbrush, when I discovered a black-looking object through the snow-covered brush. I was within thirty steps of it, but was afraid to shoot, lest it might prove to be the end of an old black log; in which case, if I shot, the bear would hear the report of the rifle, and make off; and I might as well set my old dog to stop a heavily-loaded wagon when it was going down a steep hill, as to send him after that beast to stop him. So I watched the black lump till I saw it move; when I aimed at the middle of it, fired, and down went the gentleman bear. I ran up; but, knowing my inability to cope with him, I left the battle to him and the old dog; who knew, by long experience, that if he wished to keep whole bones he must remain at a safe distance from such a foe; particularly when, as he and I both saw, the bear was in no humor for soft dealing; but intended, to the utmost of his power, to sell his life as dearly as possible to those who had made such a cowardly attack on him, without giving him the least notice of their bloody intentions.

I think he was the most vicious beast I ever saw; and though he had his back broken so that he could not stand up, yet he would strike the most terrible blows at the dog, and try in every way to get hold of him. If he had got him within his big paws, he would have killed him as easily as a cat would kill a mouse. But the dog kept out of reach until I had loaded my rifle and poured in a second fire, which finished the contest.

When I saw him laid out at my feet, and thought how manfully he had fought in his own defence, and also how unfairly he had been taken, without the least notice of the onset, it destroyed all the pleasure of the fight. But then It occurred to me that, if he had escaped at this time, he would perhaps have killed a dozen hogs for some of my friends; and that if he had received the least notice of the attack, he could not have been taken by all the dogs in the neighborhood.

100

This reasoning having satisfied my scruples, I dressed him and left him, with his hide on, till I could come for him another day. I then went to the camp; but, as Mr. House did not arrive that night, I had to pick up such sticks as I could carry, and make a fire; which, not being sufficient, I suffered much from cold.

Daylight came at last, and with it the promise of a fine day. After eating a cold breakfast, I sat off for a hunt; and in a short time I found some deer, shot one, and broke its shoulder. I readily traced it by the blood on the snow, and was following after it, when two wolves entered the track before me. As I had sent my dog after the deer, I began to fear the wolves would find him with it, fall on him, and kill him. I pushed on a little faster, in order to be up in time to help the dog if they should attack him, when presently a middle-sized bear also took the track behind the dog and the wolves.

I saw they were all drawn there by the smell of the blood, and I was afraid that, among them, they would kill my dog. But in a little while the dog returned to me; when I directed my steps homeward, as evening was coming on. I pushed for the camp on the same track by which I had gone out, and found that the bear had just preceded me. But I cared not, as I was too tired to follow him. I kept on, and he left the track. In a short time I saw the bear's tracks again; and they were so fresh, that I determined to try him at all hazards. On I went, after his tracks, and in a little time the dog winded him to my left. I looked that way, and saw the bear sneaking along as if he was afraid of something, and thought he was aware of my presence. As soon as I saw a spot between the pine-trees big enough to shoot through, I made a slight noise; when he stopped between two trees, I fired, and off he went. I followed, in a sort of run; and going by where he stood at the time I shot, I saw a great deal more blood on the ground than I knew could have come from him. But I passed on till I came to his track; and seeing quantities of blood after him, I followed carefully on. A large hemlock-tree, having a great many limbs, had fallen in such a manner that it did not come to the ground by two or three feet; and, the bear having gone under it near the butt-end, the snow had so completely covered all over that I could see nothing of him. I walked round the whole tree, and found that he had not come out after entering; when I sent the dog in, and hearing him pulling at the bear, I crawled under and dragged him out. Taking out his entrails, I left him for another day, and started for the camp. But when I arrived there, I found neither man nor fire.

This was very trying to me, as I was tired, hungry, and cold. "Well," said I, "this is enough to kill any man; and I will go home, if it takes me till daylight tomorrow."

Off I started; and after travelling about a mile, I got so tired that I thought I would go to Mrs. Lynn's, the widow of my old friend Colonel Lynn. I had then about two miles to go; and as I was making my way as I best could on the top of a high mountain, my dog ran off at full speed, and presently I heard him barking. Feeling confident that he had a coon, I went to him, and found him looking under a large rock.

The dog was old, and had been so severely bitten by coons, that he had become afraid of them; and as he stood barking outside, thinking it was surely a coon under the rock, I urged him to take hold of him.

He went in, and did take hold of the animal; but I soon found that it was not a coon, but a bear. I called off the dog, and going close to the hole, waited for the bear to come out, intending to have a good shot at him, but he would not stir. I then commenced building a fire, in order that I might see him; and as I was gathering sticks with which to make a light, I heard a rush at the other side of the rock; and, looking around, I saw the bear running off.

I could get no sight on my gun, but fired at random, as he ran, with the dog in full pursuit. They were soon out of sight; but finding, by the noise, that they were making a turn, I ran across and met them; when, seeing me before, and the dog behind him, the bear climbed a tree; but as he came out against the light of the sky, I fired, and down he dropped, dead. I took his entrails out and left him, to be carried home with the other two. I then continued my course for Mrs. Lynn's, where I arrived at nine o'clock, and the following morning I went home.

After getting my bears home, three or four hunters and myself agreed to go to the glades to hunt deer. We all started for what was called the piney cabin, and met at the place; but it was too late to hunt that evening, and there was no snow on the ground.

A light snow having fallen during the night, I said in the morning that I would bet any man a gallon of whiskey I would kill two deer that day.

"I'll take that bet," said a man by the name of James.

It was agreed on; and I told them to pick their course, and I would take the ground that was left. So they all made choice of a locality for that day, leaving me the very ground I wished for.

Every one sat out in great spirits; but while going to the place assigned me, I heard a buck bleat; which they will do in mating-time when they smell other deer. I walked quickly to the leeward side of him, in order that he should not smell me; in doing which, I crossed a number of deer-tracks. Knowing that the buck was after them, I stood close to the tracks, where I could still hear him bleating, and every time the sound was nearer. In a short time I saw him following the tracks, sure enough. I let him come within eight steps, and then stopped him by bleating as he did; when I shot him in his tracks. I skinned him very rapidly, and went on; but I had proceeded only a short distance, when I saw a small buck trot along the top of a steep hill, and disappear down the opposite side.

I ran to the top, and looking down, saw him going leisurely along; whereupon I snorted like a deer, which I could do very naturally. As soon as he heard the snort, thinking it came from the other deer, which he expected to see, he stopped to look round for them.

I had with me a deer's tail, which I showed him from behind a tree, and then exposed a small portion of my clothes, which were about the color of a deer. Uncertain what to do, lie stood there, occasionally stamping his foot on the ground, all the while holding his head as high as he could. Then I would show the tail quietly, and as if I was not scared; and at last seeing him lick his mouth, [knew he would come to ascertain what was there. He came on little by little, still stamping his feet on the ground, until he came within range of my rifle, when I shot at his breast, and broke his shoulder. I set my dog on him, but he soon turned to make fight, when I shot him again. I then skinned him, and as I was in the glades without a hat, and it was blowing and snowing as fast as the snow could fall, I started to run across a glade, out of the storm. As I ran through the fern, about half leg high, up sprang a large buck, which, after making two or three jumps, stopped in the middle of the open glade. He had scarcely stopped, before my rifle sent a ball through him, when he jumped forward a few yards, and fell over dead.

The storm was so severe, that I was obliged to seek shelter in a grove of thick pines; but after it abated, I started for the camp again, still looking for deer. I was about half way in, when I saw approaching what I took to be another buck. I stood still, but the deer saw me too, though it could not make out what I was. Each stood perfectly still, looking at the other, until I became tired. There was between us a large fallen tree, which hid the body of the deer, so that I could see nothing but the head; and finding there was no other chance, I raised my gun and fired at the head. After the report, seeing nothing of the deer, I hurried forward, and there lay as fine a doe as I ever killed, with her brains blown out. I commenced skinning her as fast as possible, as it was getting late, and I was quite ready to leave for the camp, when I saw on the entrails so much tallow, that I stopped to save it. As I was sitting picking off the tallow, it occurred to me that it was a wonder a buck had not been on her track, for she was in that peculiar condition when the males will follow them, wherever they find their track.

So I raised my head to look, and there stood a stout buck within ten steps, staring at myself and the dog, as I was sitting at my work, and the dog licking up the blood and eating the small pieces which fell to his share. I dared not rise to get my gun, which was standing against a tree, out of my reach; but I began to creep towards it, all the time being afraid to look at the deer, lest a sight of my face should scare him, for I knew it was not pretty.

When I had secured my gun, I looked around, and saw him walking off, and as I did not wish to spoil his saddle, I delayed shooting until I could get his side toward me; but all of a sudden he stopped, turned round, and came walking back to look for the doe, stopping at the same place where I first saw lrim. That moment I pulled my trigger, and the ball, striking in the middle of the breast, killed him at once. He never attempted to jump, but reared up so high, that he fell flat on his back. I skinned him, put him on the same pole with the other, and then started off for the camp.

When I arrived there, all hands seemed astonished at my good luck; but James disputed the fact, saying that I had been there the week previous, and had hid those skins in the woods. But a Mr. Frazee, who had hunted with me all the previous week, during which time I had killed some eight or ten deer, told James that my boys and his had come out the last of the week with horses, and carried in all the meat both of us had killed, together with the skins; and thus satisfied him that there was no foul play in the matter. I told James that I could kill a deer yet that night. He was anxious to take another bet, and in order to give him a chance for his whiskey, I closed with him; for, as I left the camp in the morning, I had observed a spot where a great many deer had been feeding on thorn-berries, and I knew that they would be there again at dusk after the berries.

Seizing my gun, I made for the thorn nursery, on the leeward side, in order that the deer should not smell me. The dog beginning to wind, I knew that he scented the deer, and therefore I crept along very cautiously, though I could see no game. Presently a very large buck made his appearance, when I said to myself: "That will make the sixth deer, beside two gallons of whiskey, and the reputation of being the best hunter in the woods."

It will be seen that my vanity began to rise. The buck gradually drew nearer, but the pine-trees stood so close together, that it was a hard matter to secure a good aim, and beside, I found I was becoming so much excited, that my hand was growing unsteady. So I waited till the buck came opposite the space between two trees, when I called to him to stop, which he did, but not until he had so far passed the open space, that his ribs were hid from my view. I tried to take aim; but as I could not hold my rifle steady, I waited to get rid of the shakes, though to no purpose; for the longer I delayed the worse I became, till at last, observing the buck's tail begin to spread, I knew he was about to make off. As this was the last chance, I put my gun against a tree, thinking thus to brace myself; but my gun absolutely knocked against the tree. As I was then compelled to shoot, or to let the buck run off unharmed, I fired at his whole hips, at a distance of not more than twenty steps, without ever touching either hide or hair of him.

At any other time, I could have sent twenty shots into a space the size of a dollar; but the idea of a great reputation gave me the ague; and through my vanity I lost both the buck and the whiskey. When the report of my gun was heard at the camp, Mr. Frazee exclaimed: "There, James, you have another gallon of whiskey to pay for, as Browning never misses." But when I returned empty-handed, the whole company enjoyed a hearty laugh at my expense.

Chapter Seven

When the autumn hunt was nearly over, it was agreed, between the two brothers John and Charles Friend, and myself, that we should go to the glades called "The land flowing with milk and honey," and there finish the season. Accordingly, we all met at our camp, and in two or three days killed seven or eight deer — four of which, I think, were despatched by myself; when there fell a pretty heavy snow. We all turned out to try the new snow, but it was so cold that we killed nothing the first day. Charles discovered the trail of a large bear, which he said was looking for a hole, as he had followed his tracks, and observed where he had tried to make himself a shelter from the storm, but had abandoned it, and proceeded further on. He enquired if either of us would assist him in hunting that bear John refused at once, saying that it was not only too cold for him, but he also wanted to go home and Bcc his little woman; whereupon Charles turned to me, remarking: "What say you, Browning? Will you go with me in search of the bear, or will you go with John after the women?"

"Well, Charles," said I, "as I think the women will not run away, and the bear may, I will go with you after the bear to-day, and leave the women till to-morrow."

We then all ate breakfast together, and after it was over started off; John to see his wife, and Charley and I to seek the bear; Charley carrying with him a long rope and a wax candle, for use in case of emergency. We soon found the bear's track at the place where Charles had left it the evening before, and pursued it about a mile to a deep, muddy spring, into which the bear had plunged, throwing the mud around all over the snow. He had done this to cool himself, for he was so fat that he was too warm for comfort; and subsequently he had walked off to a large ledge of rocks and laurel, where he entered a hole. The hole was about seven feet deep, at the bottom of a wide seam in the rocks, and extended under the main ledge.

The question now arose, how we were to get him out. I had never entered the den of a sleeping bear, nor had Charles; but one of us must do it now, or we would be compelled to leave the bear in quiet possession of his residence.

"Well, Charley," said I, "as you are a much smaller man than myself, I can pull you out more easily than you could me; and therefore you must try it."

"No! no!" said he, "if I never eat a piece of bear meat in my life, I will not go into such a place as that is."

"Well," said I, "do you think you can draw me out after I shoot, if I should only wound him, before he can tear me to pieces?"

"Oh yes! I can — I know I can," he replied

"Well, Charley," I remarked, "I will try it, at all hazards."

So Charley tied his rope to my ankles, so that he could pull me out when I shot, and I went down to the mouth of the hole, the entrance to which turned to my right, through a narrow aperture, which I was barely able to squeeze myself through. I then entered a large room, with my wax candle on the end of a pole before me. I had to crawl on my hands and feet, while I held the pole in my left hand, and the gun in my right. I crawled along till I saw in one corner of the room a black lump, which resembled a large sugar-kettle turned bottom upwards. This I knew to be the bear.

I held my gun ready, and called to him, telling him that I had come to see him in his own house, and to rise up, so that I could see what he looked like. I thought that the sound of the human voice would rouse him, and that, when he got frightened and attempted to leave the room, I would kick the rope for Charley to pull me out, and as I would be out before the bear, I could shoot him as he came out. But he would not raise his head, and when I spoke to him he would only shudder. Finding that I could not rouse him, I passed the pole over him to see how I could shoot so as to make sure work of it, for otherwise I might have got myself into a scrape which it would not be very easy to get out of again.

I put the candle close to him, when he snuffed the fumes of the burning wax, and wanted to know what it was. He raised his head, and attempted to smell at the candle, which I was going to let him do, when it occurred to me that if the blaze of the candle touched his nose, and burnt him, which it surely would do, he would become furious, and I might look out for breakers. So I quickly drew back the candle, and kept him in a good humor.

I was still in hopes to coax him out of his dwelling. and kill him outside, for he seemed to be in a perfectly good humor; for I knew that the moment he was hurt, everything would depend on hard fighting. I tried to draw him out with the candle, which smelled like honey, of which bears are exceedingly fond. I would put the candle near his nose, and when he would reach after it, I would pull it from him; and in that way I succeeded in raising him upon his feet. Then I kicked the rope, and Charley tried to pull me out; but being not only too far from him, but also around a corner, he could not succeed. What was worse, when I would get on my knees to shove myself backwards, he would pull at the rope, and down I would fall again; so I shouted to him not to pull the rope, and succeeded in getting out without his help,

I waited for the bear to follow; but as he did not appear inclined to do so, I relighted my candle and again entered the hole; where I found my old friend seated precisely in the place he had occupied when I first went in. I passed the light of my candle over him; and finding how his body lay, I thought I could send a ball to his heart. Looking closely how and where to put the ball, I levelled my rifle, and let fly; when such a stunning report never before rang in my ears. My candle was put out, I was enveloped in midnight darkness, and I heard a snorting and thundering around me such as I had never heard before. Scrambling back, as best I could, till I reached the mouth of the hole, I made my way out safe. We waited a long time; and, though we could hear the bear making a great fuss, he would not come out.

At length, all having again become quiet, I went down, and found him still alive, but so badly wounded that he took no notice of me; so I put the gun to his head and finished him.

But the worst job yet remained to be done; and that was, to get him out of the den. We took our rope and tied it round the bear's neck; when Charley pulled at his head, and I pushed behind, till we got him to the mouth of the hole; which, being seven or eight feet perpendicularly, we could not pull him up to the top. But at last I thought of a plan by which we could effect it; and taking my tomahawk, I cut down a sapling which had a limb projecting far out from the trunk. This sapling we placed over the seam in the rock; and tying one end of the rope to the bear's neck, and the other round the sapling, we took hold of the limb and turned the sapling round till we raised the bear's head up to the top of the rock; when we tied the limb fast, to keep it in place while we pulled the hind-parts up. In this way we got the carcass on the surface of the ground.

We then made a fire, to keep ourselves from freezing while we skinned him; after which, we each carried a quarter to the camp. The remainder we carried to the camp the next morning, when Charley started off to procure a horse and boy to take the meat home. I continued hunting till the horse ar-rived; when, having loaded him, and sent him off, I hunted through the woods on my way home, but without success.

Reaching home after night, I found the bear lying in the middle of the floor; for, when the horse arrived with his load, Mary and the children being unable to take it off, and having no help, she led the horse into the house, cut the strings that tied the meat together, and let it fall; but first she laid skins on the floor, to keep the grease off the boards; and there I found it when I came in

After a few days, I met Mr. John Friend; and when he heard of our having gone into the hole, and of our there killing such a fine bear, he said he knew of a hole in which bears frequently wintered, and asked me if I would go with him to see if there was not one in it now. I agreed to accompany him the next day; and in the morning we sat out for the bear-hole.

When we drew near the place, he said that I should go before, as I was a better shot; but I thought it was because he felt afraid to be the foremost. However, I took the lead, and we went on till we got in sight of the hole; where I saw that a bear had been scratching in the rubbish to make a bed.

I said, in a low tone, "Look, John, how a bear has been at work;" and walk-ing up quietly to the mouth of the hole, we found there was one in it then, sure enough.

The wax candle was lighted; and, as it had been agreed on before we left home that I should be the one to enter and do all the shooting, I of course said nothing to him about going into the den, but prepared to descend and shoot the bear myself.

When I got about my own length into the hole, I found it turned to the right, and continued on, very narrow, about eight or ten feet. At the farthest end lay the bear, sound asleep, or apparently so. I was in such a tight place that I could not put my gun to my face, but was compelled to level it as well as I could; and in laying my face to it, to see that it was pointed right, my head was brought close to the lock. I then reached back, and with my thumb fired off the gun. I was stunned; my ears rang with the noise, and the flash from the lock set the heavy mop of hair on one side of my head in a blaze. I shuffled out of the hole with all my head on fire; but by beating it with my hands, and rubbing it with handfuls of snow, I soon put it out.

All being again quiet, I loaded ray gun, went in, and found the bear's under-jaw hanging down, and broken to pieces close to her ears. She was in such pain that she was tearing at her own jaw-bone, trying her best to pull it off.

With as little noise as possible, I crept in as near as I flare go to her; for I thought that if she should notice me she would at once jump at me. I then took the best aim I could, shot her in the right place, and instantly killed her.

During a long life devoted to the chase, these were the only holes that I ever went into beyond the reach of daylight. I now know, and I knew then, that there was great danger in doing so; but if I undertook anything, I thought it must be accomplished; and if I got into a dangerous scrape, the greater the danger appeared, the more anxious I was to win the fight. I feel perfectly assured that if a man undertakes a dangerous enterprise, with a determination to succeed or to lose his life in the attempt, he will do many things with ease, and unharmed, which a smaller degree of energy never could or would have accomplished.

This adventure ended that autumn hunt, and winter closed in on us with heavy snows and very cold and hard weather. I was again attacked with the rheumatic pains and sciatica, so that, during three months, I was not able to walk from my bed to the fire. But when the warm days of May returned, I began to mend, and was again able to walk.

In 1812, our Government proclaimed war against Great Britain. At that time. Levin Winder was Governor of Maryland, and James Madison President of the United States, and it became necessary to draft men from Maryland to repel British invasion, as a large English force lay in Chesapeake Bay, threatening an attack every hour.

There were two requisitions for men; and I am not certain which was to be supplied from the company at Selby's Port. This occurred at the time the National turnpike was being made through that neighborhood; and every man who had resided ten days in the vicinity was drafted and enrolled by order of the Colonel of our regiment. I think the President called for thirty men, or more, from our county; and in a few days a call arrived from Governor Winder, for eighteen privates and one sergeant. The commander of our company, Captain A. Beall, having been appointed Clerk of the County Court, had gone to Cumberland to attend to the duties of his office; and every other officer, both commissioned and non-commissioned, had left the place, except two — Robinson Savage and myself, who were sergeants.

When the major came to make the draft for the eighteen privates and one sergeant, tickets were prepared, and disinterested persons selected to conduct the drawing. This, being but a small job was soon over, and Mr. Savage and myself were required to draw; when he, being called first, drew his ticket, and left mine the draft.

I then went up to the colonel and asked him how I would be situated. He told me that I could not be turned into the ranks as a private; but that I should serve as a second sergeant, who was entitled to double rations and twelve dollars a month.

"Well, Colonel," said I, "that is all I could ask; and I will be at the rendezvous in Cumberland at the proper time."

I went home and prepared two pairs of new, strong buckskin moccasins, saying to my wife, "I can, with these on, outrun any British devil that has crossed the sea; and if I have to run after him, I can catch him; but if he chases me, he never can overhaul me. So I am ready for a race either way, according as either offers the best chances."

"Well," said she, never disgrace yourself by running while you have a chance to fight."

I assured her that I should be among the last who would run; and that, if I had an equal chance, I feared no Englishman who had landed on our shore.

Mary made me a new knapsack, into which she stowed my clothes; and, as we had secured a little property, and had saved some money, she begged me to take some of it with me; "For," said she, "if you should get sick, you may need it; and we are all at home, where we can do better without it than you can." So I took fifty dollars, which left her but little.

In the morning I bade her and the children farewell, took the road for Cumberland, and arrived there the second day. Captain Blair was the commander of the company; and a finer little fellow never lived than he was. He paraded in the evening, and called the roll; before which, I went to him, and reported myself in readiness; stating to him the promise made to me by Colonel Greenwell, that I was to be the second sergeant.

The captain answered me pleasantly, that the colonel had nothing to do with the appointment of his sergeants, as that was his own business. Said he, "Browning, you know I command a company of volunteers, and my officers are all in their places. If I should turn one of them out to make room for you, the men would rebel against me; so I cannot do it."

"Then," said I, "I'll be --- if I go one step."

The captain turned from me, saying, "As you please, I suppose, about that."

I walked off; and, as I had been brought up in the old Federal school, which taught that the British, then fighting against the great Napoleon, who was, it was rumored, preparing to make an attack on America, and to treat us as he had treated Italy, were our only safeguard against the encroachments of France, I had an invitation to spend that night at the house of a gentleman who was a member of that party.

When I went to my friend's house, I found there two or three other very influential gentlemen, and politics were being vigorously discussed.

I had been in but a few minutes when I was asked what had brought me to town. I told them that I had been drafted to go to Baltimore with the rest.

"Have you turned fool," was the rejoinder, "to go and fight against the only people who dare to resist the greatest tyrant with which the earth was ever cursed?" Then they said to me, "Go you home, and attend to your own business; and let those who declared the war fight the battles of their own making."

"But," said I, "gentlemen, I have but little property; and after the troops return there will be courts-martial held, and I will be fined, and at a high rate, too; for I have reported myself to Captain Blair as being ready to march; though I told him I would not go a step unless I got the place I was drafted for; that I had been drafted as one out of two, and the privates were eighteen out of two hundred and forty; and now to be turned into the ranks as a private, was treatment I did not like to put up with."

But I had still determined to go and stay sixty days with them, as that was the time I had to serve.

"Well," said one of the men, "I know all about the courts-martial; and I promise to pay every dollar they will ever make off any man who refuses to go."

I said little more; but after I went to bed, I considered that it would be of service to me to stay my time out in the army, as I had been notified that a commission would be sent to me as captain of the Selby's Port company, and f could thereby learn everything necessary for me to know in order to fill that station.

I rose the following morning, and going to the camp, told the boys that I would accompany them; and we all ate our breakfast together. As the Captain was taking his place at the head of his men, and all were waiting the order to march, a man informed me that a friend wished to speak to me. I hurriedly accompanied him into a house very near the place, and upstairs, where I found two of my friends, as I then thought, but whom my better judgment has since taught me were the worst enemies I ever had. They said that I should not go if they could prevent it; and one of them told me that he was in the council-chamber at Annapolis the previous week, and had then been promised that a commission should be sent up for me as soon as possible. He said that if I did go down to Baltimore, he would send immediately for me to return, and attend to the business of the company.

In a few minutes the word "march" sounded through the streets, when off the company went, while I foolishly remained behind — an act which has caused me more sincere, heartfelt grief, than any other; yes, than all the acts which I have committed during the course of a long life. But the deed was done, from no want of love of my country; neither was it occasioned by cowardice, but by the operation of the two causes above stated; and ever since I have longed for an opportunity to repair that much-lamented act. And although I am now an old man, and may never, perhaps, have an opportunity to retrieve that misstep, yet, if an occasion should offer, I would freely enter into any fort, and do all in my power to make ample reparation. If I could not do much in a fight, I could stop a ball that might kill a more useful man, though if could not rob me of many days. If I never have the opportunity of doing that which it is my desire to do, I yet have the satisfaction of leaving in my place six sons, forty-four grandsons, and seventeen great-grandsons, making in all sixty-seven males: thirty-two grand-daughters, eighteen great-grand-daughters, and five of my own daughters; together summing up one hundred and twenty two descendants, sixty-seven of whom (all good, healthy people) will serve as soldiers for the defence of their country. I hope that whenever it is necessary, in the defence of their native land, to repel any foreign enemy, no matter who they may be, nor whence they come, every man who has one drop of my blood in his veins will never refuse his assistance to drive all enemies from the soil of their and my beloved country.

Thus I leave as a legacy to all my relations, the injunction that, above all duties, next to that which they owe their God, they must regard as of paramount importance their duty to their own country; for I am exceedingly proud of it, and I thank God, from the inmost recesses of my heart, that I can in good faith claim for myself, and for all my descendants, the glorious name of American citizen. My humble prayer is now, and shall ever be, that Divine Providence will at all times so guide the councils of our nation, that all the laws may tend to the preservation of our peaceful habits and fair fame, and to the perpetuation of our equal rights and liberties; and continue to preserve us from all evils, till this glorious country arrives at its highest glory and renown, and is fully competent to enforce every just demand it may have on every other nation and people.

Not long after I returned home, a commission as captain came to me from the Governor; and although I had determined not to accept it, I was urged by my Federal friends to be sworn in, and take the command of the company. I agreed, and received an order from the Colonel to call the company together, and have them divided into classes; so that, in case of necessity, they could be mustered into service oy their numbers, from one to the last number.

As this order required that I should attend to it in a given time, I immediately sent out two sergeants, to give notice that, on a certain day, all who had been enrolled in the company should attend at Selby's Port. The Democrats, or Republicans, sent me word by the sergeants, that if I appeared there on that day, they would not only whip me, but take my commission from me, and that they never would suffer me to command them.

Here was an unforeseen difficulty to contend with, which entirely occupied my thoughts. My old friend Lynn being in his grave, I had no adviser; and more the pity, for, had he been alive, I feel certain that I should have gone on to Baltimore with the rest of the draft, and thus kept out of trouble. But being the captain, duly commissioned, I was not to be frightened in that way; and both they and I knew that there was not a man among them who could make anything in a fight with me, whatever he might lose; though I really had no apprehension of a fight occurring. But on the evening before the parade, a friend came to me, and told me that my enemies had sent to Smithfield, in Pennsylvania, for a bully, who was there engaged in butchering for the hands who were building the bridge across the Yough river; and that he had agreed to come, and give me such a whipping that I would never come there again, to trouble them any more.

Still, I thought they would not attempt to do what they threatened; and the following day I set out for the parade, and when I came to the ground, I found a great many men gathered — among the rest Mr. Shannon, the butcher and bully. I then began to see that there was some reality in what I had heard, and concluded that I had better settle the matter at once. I took a good view of the man, and found that he was truly as dangerous-looking a man as I had ever seen; but though I had just recovered from another attack of rheumatism, I was determined to bring the difficulty to a close as soon as possible.

Having spoken to my three brothers-in-law, Hugh, John, and Thomas McMullen, to stand by me, we went to Shannon, and I asked him if his name was Mr. Shannon. He said that was his name. I remarked that I was informed he had come there to give me a whipping. He said that was his business there.

"Well," said I, "if you don't do it, it is not because you are not big enough, for you are a great deal larger man than I am; but I never will acknowledge it till it is done. At the same time remember, sir, I shall not stand idle while you are at it. But before I am whipped, I wish to know what I am to be whipped for?"

"Well," said he, "I have been told that you said you could whip any man who worked on the turnpike, and you ought to remember that there are a great many good men on that road, and I am one of them; and we don't take banters without a trial."

"Well, Shannon, I do not intend to make any apology; but in justice to myself, I say it is a falsehood, and that such a word never escaped my mouth, nor did such a thought ever even enter my mind. Now, sir, do your own will: I don't crave a light with you, nor will I go one step to escape it."

He seemed at a loss what to do, but said that if I had not used such language, he could not see anything to fight about. I told him that any man who would say to me that I had ever used such language, would not be long telling the lie till I would stop him short.

"Well, Browning," said he, "I think the fight might as well be let alone."

"Very well, Shannon," said I, "I am sure it suits me; and if you are satisfied, I am too."

"Well," said he, "let us take a glass of whiskey, drop all, and be friends."

This being agreed on, he called for a glass, and offered it to me; when, still keeping a close look out, I called for another glass, and offered it to him. He took it, and I believe if he had been let alone he would never have said anything more about it. After we parted, I mustered the company, and called the roll, when some twenty, refusing to answer to their names, were marked down as delinquents.

While I was engaged with the affairs of the company, the opposition were endeavoring to raise another company. When I got through my business, I went to them, and told them I was pleased to see them making up another company, for there were men enough to fill three companies, and that, in this way, every man could be commanded to his satisfaction; that it was what I really wished to see, and anything that I could, I would cheerfully do for them. To this I received no answer.

My company having been dismissed, the people had mostly gone away, with the exception of those who were trying to raise the opposition company. These all came marching by where I was preparing to go home, and formed into two lines, on both sides of a tail-race belonging to Hoffman's mill, about twenty on each side, determined to attack and beat me as I should pass the bridge. A friend came and told me that they had adopted that plan to get hold of me before I would know of their design; and he begged me to take the other end of the road, and thus disappoint them. John McMullen objected to the other end of the road, saying that he never would be driven out of his way one step. I mounted my horse, which was a strong, spirited animal, and moved towards the two lines. The end of the bridge being clear, I gained it; and when my horse was about to step on it. Shannon reached out his hand to take the rem of my bridle, but I struck the horse so quickly that he sprang across the bridge, and carried me safely to the other side, entirely out of their reach.

Shannon called to me to stop till he would give me a whipping; but I told him that he was a blackguard, and that I was not coming back to let him and those around him beat me as they pleased; that I believed he was not able in a fair fight to whip me; and that I knew, and they knew, there was not a man among them who would dare to attempt it, unless they could have two or three on me at the same time.

But when they saw that I understood what they were at, they fell on the McMullens. I immediately jumped off my horse, and ran in, when I found that John had been knocked down with a club. I raised him to his feet, and hearing a great fuss in the crowd, I went in, beating my way with my fist. Thomas was down, and all hands were pelting him with their fists. I soon knocked them in every direction, till I got him up, and ready for action again. Many passes were made at me, but the cowards would run as soon as they struck. After I had set Tom upon his feet, I knocked one fellow down, and as I looked around, another struck at me. I threw off his blow, returned it, and at it we went. He fended off very well, when, finding that I was doing nothing, I sprang at him, caught him, and threw him on the saw-mill. As quick as thought, he slipped himself through an open place, and down we both went. We were no sooner down than a dozen more were around us; and let me turn my face which way I would, it met somebody's fist. But I kept striking till I hit one chap on the loins, and down he went. I saw that his head was black, and I knew he was not the man I fell through the mill with, for he had a red head; but I saw no more of red-head that day.

Then they fell on me so fast, that I thought I would Dot contend any longer, but say that I had enough. It then occurred to me that if I yielded they would not stop till they killed me; when they would say that I died bawling "enough." So I concluded to go on, fight all I could, and sell my life as dearly as possible.

I let them beat away; but once in a while I would get a chance at one who would be exposed, and give him a good send.

In the midst of this struggle, old Mr. Hoffman ran in with a dirk; and making a furious attack on them, took some of them off, while the others took hold of me, and passed me up, feet foremost, to those on the top of the mill; who, reaching down, caught me by the feet and legs, and pulled me up by the same road I had fallen down.

Shannon stood by, and, as I came up, kicked me in the side, leaving not a speck of breath in me. They dragged me off the mill by the legs, and I thought I would feign to be dead.

I lay a considerable time before I got my breath; and when I recovered my wind a little I was afraid to breathe, for fear they would fall on me again. After I had drawn two or three breaths, and found that I could rise, I made a sudden bound; but they saw me move, and kicked and struck me till they hurled me away out of the crowd.

Meantime, the three McMullens were busy, and the crowd left me to go to them; for they were too hard for their men. This gave me time to draw a few more good breaths. I rushed in again to assist my three friends; striking every man in my way, till I got to where they had Thomas down, with a little fellow on him.

As soon as Tom would throw the man off, they would put him on again. I hit one of the principal ones in the head, and knocked him clear off, when I stooped down to help Tom up. As I took hold of him I was struck by Shannon.

I do not know whether I fell or not; but the first thing I recollected was finding Shannon's right arm round my neck, and myself about half-way up, while he was striking me very heavy blows in the side.

As I found that it was useless to try to pull ray head from him, I commenced climbing up, and succeeded in getting on my feet. He was a left-handed man; and as I raised up he kept striking round, endeavoring to hit me on the kidneys; but, being up to that, I would throw my body out of his reach. In the meantime, I caught at his arm, to keep him from striking; but I could not hold it, and in the attempt, my hand slipped into his shirt-sleeve, which he had rolled up above his elbow, to keep it out of his way. That stopped him from striking; and as I then had all his front exposed to me, his right arm be-

114

ing over ray left shoulder, I told him that it was now my turn. Oh! but I was glad that I had a chance; for he had beaten me unmercifully.

I laid one blow into him after another, in the pit of his stomach; and with every blow I found him growing weaker. But, neglecting to keep close to him, with one desperate effort he drew his right arm off my shoulder, and, seizing my right hand with both his, put my forefinger between his strong jaws.

I was really furious at that act; and, in my anger and desperation, I pushed my hand into his mouth, with the object of poking it down his throat, and, by choking him, cause him to release it. In that attempt, finding that my knuckles came against his nose and upper lip, I began to job them with all my strength; raising myself up, and pitching my whole weight on my arm. After two or three blows, I saw the blood pouring down; when he began to lean his head back, to escape the severe thumps I was giving him.

Finding the grip of his teeth began to relax, I made a desperate jerk, and pulled my finger out of his mouth; when, without knowing whether it was off or on, I clenched my fist and struck him in the head. He would have fallen had not his friends held him up. I repeated the blow, and he fell hack; but they caught him again; when I gave him a third and last blow, fair on the temple, and he fell hack stunned.

Finding myself failing, and expecting that they would set a fresh man on me, and knowing that I could stand it no longer, as I had been beaten incessantly for at least half an hour, I wheeled round, and attempted to leave the ground.

I heard them say, "Follow him, Shannon; for you can whip him."

But he replied, "If you want any more fighting done, you may do it yourselves."

This was the best news I ever heard; for I could do no more, though they did not know it. I called him whipped, and hurrying to my horse, I mounted him, with not a stitch of clothes on, except my pants and the coat I had left across his back; my waistcoat and shirt lying in scattered fragments all over the battle-ground.

It was getting dark when I rode up to a friend's house, ten miles distant; till when, I did not feel my hurts. But when I went to get off" my horse, I was not able to do so without help. I could not hold a knife to cut my food, which had to be all cut for me; and it was three weeks before I could wear a hat; my head being so swollen and sore from the beating I had received.

This happened about the middle of November, and I was not able to carry a stick of firewood till the first of May following; as I had three ribs broken, besides being badly beaten about the body also. Lest the news of my being so ill should reach my enemies, I took a friend with me, and went to the hunting-ground, where I staid a week; meanwhile causing the report to be circulated that I was so little the worse of my injuries that I was hunting as usual; and that if Shannon would put up fifty dollars I would cover it, when we would .see who should take the hundred. But that was the last I ever heard of Shannon.

During that week I killed four deer and two bears. The first day we went out, I took my friend to the old beech ground; and when we came fully into the place, I saw a pretty stout bear, which was standing looking around Raising my gun, I fired; when he started off, followed by the two dogs in full chase. I could not run a step; but my friend followed them into a large laurel-swamp. I seated myself on a log, and listened to the chase. Presently they took a turn, and came back. I stood still; and, as they passed within close range of my rifle, I shot at and killed the bear.

We killed one more bear, and I think the other man killed as many or more deer than I did; for we made a good hunt of it.

This was about the last hunting I was able to do; and, indeed, though I was not able to do that, I was determined that they should not have the gratification of knowing that they had hurt me. When the cold weather of winter set in, I was not able to do anything, and ray wife and children had everything to attend to. My oldest daughter was obliged to thresh every day, cold or otherwise, in order to provide straw to feed half a dozen or more cattle, as they needed it.

In that condition I remained till the following May; when I so far recovered as to be able to work a little. But my beating, together with the rheumatic pains, had so broken down my strength, that it was three years before I was able to do more than half a day's work at a time; yet, by economy and perseverance, we not only secured a living, but also saved a little money. Still having a notion of removing to Ohio, I went out with a friend to look at the country. But it not suiting my ideas, Mary persuaded me to buy a little farm adjoining the fifty acres I lived on. I promised to pay four hundred dollars for it; one hundred and fifty dollars of which was to be cash in hand. I borrowed forty dollars, paid down the money, and gave my note for the balance, to be paid in two years. Everything possible was done to raise the balance of the money, in order to save the interest. I moved on the new place, worked night and day to maintain my family (which had now increased to seven children), and to raise money with which to pay for our land. When the first note fell due, every child that had fifty cents loaned it to me to aid in the payment of the note for one hundred and twenty dollars; which was paid, and the note taken up.

I attended to my farm as well as I could with my little means; but when the warm weather returned, I was again attacked with the rheumatic pains, and laid until July as helpless as a child, and my body became so crooked that I thought I would be a complete cripple. After the pain left me, I could not stand straight; so one morning I tried to lay myself on my face, thinking the weight of my back would press my back-bone and hips straight. But it was like pulling the joints out of place, and I could not lay that way any longer than I could hold ray breath; when I would be compelled to turn on my side and rest. I tried it again and again, until it became less painful, and I could lay in that position with very little trouble. From that time I continued to lay that way, till I became as straight and as strong as I was before.

I exerted myself in every way that I could to make a dollar and, the same old peddler from whom Mary had bought the powder having come into the neighborhood, it was agreed that he and I should buy up a load of venison and take it to the Federal City

I collected all my venison, and he bought all he could get, until we bad a respectable load of fine, fat, and fresh deer-meat; when off we started for the city. We got on very well, selling some of it along the road. At Hagerstown it met a ready sale, and in Frederick City we disposed of over eighty dollars' worth, all for cash, at twelve and a half cents a pound. We then went on to Georgetown, where we sold out without trouble, and I loaded up with salt and groceries; for, as there was no license to take out, I could sell anything I chose, free of any duty whatever. By this means I raised money, paid for my land, and had something left for the family, besides being able to hire a hand in a pinch of work.

It always appears that, when a man begins to rise, the more he makes the more industriously he will work. So it was with me in those times: I tilled my farm industriously until the leaves had fallen; when I would go to the woods and hunt till a little before Christmas, and then set off to market with all I could take.

The following fall I set five or six traps for bears; and, with what I caught in the traps, and those that I killed besides, I secured fourteen bears and twenty-two deer. With the exception of one, I do not remember how I killed those I took outside of the traps.

One day, as I was walking rapidly through the feeding ground, seeing a she-bear running, I let the dog slip at her, and he soon put her up a tree, where I shot her without any fight.

I know I killed fourteen, by the load of meat and skins I took that fall to Baltimore.

When the hunting season was coming to a close, I prepared to take my load to the National Road; and the roads from my farm to the pike were so bad that we only took half a load out at a time. I hired a team, and sending my own with sleds, accompanied them into the hunting-ground After starting them toward the pike, I told them that, if they found any deer hung up along the road on their return, to throw them into the sleds and carry them home.

We parted, and I went into the woods; where, at length, I found a buck lying down, and shot him dead the first fire. I took him to the road, hung him up for the boys, and hunted till evening, but found no more. I then started for the nearest house, to stay overnight; but when within sight of the fence, four deer sprang up, ran a short distance, and then stood still. I could not see the sights of my gun, but levelled the best I could, and fired. I took good notice where they were; but when they stopped again, one, which stood in an open place, was the only deer I could see. I fired again, when I could see only two run. After they stopped, though I could see nothing but a white tail, I fired again, and this time only one ran away.

I went to where they had stood when I shot, and found that I had killed three deer at three shots: I had missed the body of one, but a random shot at his tail struck him in the head and killed him. I took the carcasses to the road, hung them up, and got into my neighbor's house before bedtime.

The load being ready, I took the wagon and that part of the meat which yet remained behind, and started for Baltimore. I had eighty-seven saddles of venison, and three whole deer, with the skins on; which were frozen so stiff that they would stand up in the street as though they were alive. I had also with me seven saddles of bear meat, together with butter, beeswax, and furs of different kinds.

I travelled on till I reached a small village in Frederick County, called Newmarket, and put up at a tavern kept by Mr. Dunham; where I met with a gentleman whose name was Chambers.

While living at Bear Creek Glades, we heard that my brother Jeremiah, whom my mother left behind when she moved to Allegany, had been in the employ of a widow, as overseer of her negroes; that she had moved to Mississippi, and that Jeremiah had gone with her. That news had prevented me from making any inquiries about him; but in the course of conversation with Mr. Chambers, finding that he lived in the same neighborhood where my mother had left Jeremiah, I began to inquire of him concerning the family of Brownings.

He said he was acquainted with several families of that name, and that the head of one of them was a house-carpenter, whose Christian name was Jeremiah. From all I could learn from Mr. Chambers, it was reasonable to believe that the person he spoke of was my brother, whom I had not seen for more than thirty years.

After making arrangements with Mr. Chambers to deliver a letter to Jeremiah Browning, I wrote one to him, as nearly as I can recollect, in the following language:

"Newmarket, *December* 22d, 1823.

"Dear Sir: — From a conversation with your neighbor, Mr. Edward Chambers, it seems likely that you are my brother; and I hope and feel sure that you will excuse me if I should be mistaken.

"Whether I am right in my opinion, you will be able to judge by the following statement. I am the youngest son of Joshua and Nancy Browning; and after the loss of our father, my mother took her oldest son, Joshua, and myself, and moved to Allegany county, in this State; leaving the second son, Jeremiah, with the family of Aaron Lee. I had only one sister, called Dorcas, who married ver* young, and much against the will of my mother. If we are brothers, as I have reason to believe, you will do me a great favor by meeting me at this place on Wednesday next, as I am now on my way to Baltimore, but expect to return on that day.

"Should you not be my brother, please answer this; and if you can furnish any information of the whereabouts of Jeremiah Browning, you will confer a great favor on

"Your most obd't servant,
"Meshach Browning.

This letter Mr. Chambers promised should be immediately sent to Mr. Browning. Having settled everything, I bade farewell to Mr. Chambers (whom I have never seen since), and pushed off for Baltimore, where I arrived with as good a load of venison as ever went into that market. I sold out at good prices, took in my return load, and started for Newmarket again. I drove hard that day, but I did not reach Newmarket till about eight o'clock; and when I arrived, there was a great shout, and running to and fro, for my brother, having put up at another tavern, had young men out waiting for me. When they were assured of my identity, they became very noisy; and in ten or fifteen minutes from twenty to thirty persons arrived, mostly men, accompanied by five or more ladies of my brother's acquaintance. Some of his friends introduced him to me as "Jeremiah Browning, your brother."

On this occasion my feelings were indescribable: I was at a loss for utterance, and he likewise seemed embarrassed for a few minutes. The company were all highly interested; and what with questions asked and answers given, the time passed rapidly until we were summoned to a good supper. Many of the company joined in a conversation round the table, when the landlord spoke of the load of bears and deer that I had carried down in my wagon, saying that it was the largest he had ever seen, and that I must have been with the Indians to learn how to kill wild animals This gave rise to many questions on the subject of hunting; and, listening to the sporting tales of some of our company, I found that their exploits were confined to the killing of two or three rabbits; ten, twelve, or twenty partridges; two, three, or four squirrels; and so on.

At last my brother said, that on one cold, frosty morning, he went out to hunt rabbits, when he caught two in a short time, and was on his way home before breakfast, when he found the tracks of a third, and followed them on towards his house, to a small stable, under which the rabbit had gone. He gathered all the dogs, as well as all the hands about the place, and tore up the floor; when out darted the rabbit toward the woods, amidst yelling dogs and shouting boys; but one dog being more fleet than the rest, the poor rabbit was fairly run down, and thus he obtained three fine rabbits before breakfast.

This being the best hunt described, among a good many, it seemed to meet with such marked attention, that I felt afraid to speak of some of my adventures in that line, lest the company might think I intended to turn their sporting into ridicule, by telling the greatest lies I could invent; consequently, I

119

told but few, and those only such as I thought they could easily believe, and which would at least give no offence to my sporting friends.

The night being far advanced, the company retired; when my brother and I occupied the same bed, where we talked the whole night, and until it was broad day-light. It was necessary for me, however, to attend to my horses; so we rose, dressed, and went out to the team. On our return to the room, as there were many persons taking their bitters, I asked my brother what we should drink. He said that he seldom used spirits of any kind, but with me he would take whatever I chose. So we took a glass of brandy, and then ate our breakfast, by which time the ostler had my ream geared, and ready to hitch up.

After breakfast, our bills being settled, and all right, it was agreed that my brother should accompany me as far as the Monocacy. I had one of my little sons to drive the team; and we traveled on together so comfortably, that it seemed but a short time until we came to the place of parting, where we spent one more hour in affectionate and brotherly intercourse; and then parted, with promises to see each other as often as our circumstances would admit. I then went home with my load, sold it out, and cleared three hundred dollars by my trip.

Having discovered that I had a good site for a mill on my farm, I undertook to build a grist-mill, which was much needed. By this time we had several new neighbors — Captain Campbell, from Frederick county, with his family, and son-in-law, James Cunningham: as also Dr. James McHenry, of Baltimore, and John McHenry, who settled at the Buffalo Marsh, and still live in the same place. Captain Campbell agreed to build a saw-mill, if I would build a grist-mill. He had a pair of country millstones, but as he did not wish to start them, he proposed to let me have them at cost, and take the pay in work; so I agreed to take them. I consulted one of my best friends as to the cost of the mill, who told me that, with my own labor and boarding the hands, it would cost at least four hundred dollars. This alarmed me, but having got myself into it, I determined to go on; and within six months I had my mill running, and grinding all the grain raised in the neighborhood. This was a great convenience to the people, whose children had formerly to go ten miles to mill, in all weathers.

In the year 1826, I was notified to attend at Annapolis on the 11th day of June, 1827, when a caveat case would be heard between James Cunningham and myself I was prepared with everything necessary for my trial. This caveat was issued to prevent me from obtaining a patent for a certain tract of land in Allegany county.

When I was nearly ready to leave, Mary asked me to take her with me as far as Montgomery county, where I had a brother living, with whom she would stay until I returned from Annapolis. I at once agreed, and was much pleased to do so, as this was the first time she had ever made such a request of me. We made our preparations, and took leave of our children, the youngest being a very interesting little boy, just weaned. Mary parted from them with tears in her eyes, but soon became cheerful again.

We performed the journey without any difficulty, except considerable fatigue, and arrived at my brother's, where we were cordially welcomed by the family, who were delighted with their new aunt. When the 11th day of June drew near (for I had allowed myself ample time to meet the trial), I left Mary, and went on to Annapolis, where I arrived on Saturday evening.

Having taken lodgings at Mr. Isaac Holland's hotel, I ate my dinner, and was resting myself after my ride, when a fine-looking man, dressed in regimentals, handed me a letter from Captain Archer, who commanded a company of soldiers stationed at the barracks. He had been in Allegany, with Captain Shriver, and other engineers, taking the grade of the different watercourses running through the Glades, with the view of extending the canal to the Ohio; and had seen me in his travels, though I had forgotten him.

When I was preparing to go to Annapolis, I told Mary to make me as nice a hunting-shirt as she could; and she did make as handsome a one as I had ever seen. Dressed in this, and a neat pair of moccasins, I appeared in the city, where I excited some curiosity; for every one who saw me stared as if looking at an Indian chief.

The Captain's letter contained a polite invitation for me to attend his parade that evening, and the sergeant who brought it waited for me, and conducted me to the barracks, where I was so politely received that I felt out of place. But the easy manners of the Captain made me feel much more at ease myself, and I was soon quite relieved from my first embarrassment. I was then shown all the different places and apartments, and everything that was interesting. After I had seen all those accommodations for the comfort of the soldiers, the company was called out, and drilled in the most orderly and officer like manner by the First Lieutenant, whose name I am sorry I have forgotten.

When the drill was over, I took my leave of the Captain, as well as all the others who were near me, and returned to my lodging. Mr. Holland was a kind, good man, and seemed desirous to make me comfortable. He had everything provided that I wished, yet he appeared desirous to furnish me a treat that was entirely new to me. He proposed a supper of oysters; but I told him that I had never tasted them except once, in Georgetown, when I could not say that I was pleased with the taste. He said he thought they had not been cooked properly, and soon had some prepared as they should be. Supper being ready, and all seated, I was abundantly helped to oysters. All eyes fastened on me as I tried to make free with them, swallowing down several mouths full, until my stomach became so much offended that I could not conceal my disgust. Fearing that the company would notice my restive situation, I took the opportunity to remark that I could not say I admired oysters, although perhaps after eating them frequently I might become more partial to them.

Things went on very well until next day, when, before dinner was served, Mr. Holland asked me if I was fond of crabs. I told him that I had never seen one.

"Well," said he, "we will have one for dinner, as I am very fond of them."

When dinner was ready, as I walked into the room I saw a great thing standing on all fours on a dish, looking as gaudy as a sunflower, and about the size of a half-grown snapping-turtle. "Well," thinks I to myself, "old fellow, I reckon I shall have to try your queer-looking body next; though, if you are no better than the oysters, I shall wish you as far in the sea as a humming-bird can fly in a month; but here is at you, anyhow."

In my turn I was helped to a choice piece of the crab, which I tried, but found to be little better than the oysters. "Well," thinks I, "as the man has done all in his power to treat me well, I must go into the crab, like it or not. Confound it! other people eat it, and I will eat it, let it taste as it may."

So into it I went, and kept on eating, but with very little appetite; for when I wished to swallow, it was with great difficulty that I could perform the act. I was soon asked how I liked the crab; when I replied that I could get along better with him than I did with the oysters, though I could not say that I was fond of either; but if ever Mr. Holland should visit Allegany, I would take great pleasure in treating him to a fine piece of a bear, or of a fat buck, which I thought, if he could divest himself of prejudice, he would find to be preferable to anything that could be taken out of the salt water.

When dinner was over, Mr. Holland proposed a walk down to the wharf; asking me if I had ever seen a steamboat. I told him that I had not, and that I would be pleased to look at one. We then walked down to the wharf, where the boat lay, with a great number of persons, looking as though, like myself, they had never seen a steamer before.

Mr, Holland and myself went on board, and he showed me many things in different places about the boat. But presently Mr. H. and I got separated, when I heard a great rush in the end of the boat next to the shore, and found the people were going off in haste. By the time I could see what was going on, the crowd was off, and the planks drawn in; when I had either to get off or be taken to Baltimore; which last I was not willing should be done.

As quick as thought I determined to jump for the wharf; knowing that if I fell into the water I could easily swim out; which would be better than to be carried to Baltimore. But I had no time to lose. Being at the farther end of the boat, which gave me a good starting-distance, I took a main-send for the wharf, and succeeded in reaching it, amid roars of laughter on all sides.

Captain Archer, who was present, congratulated me on being safe, and declared that he would bet I could jump farther than any man in Maryland. The distance, I think, was about twenty-five feet; but I had often cleared twenty-three feet, on level ground, in a running jump; and the boat, being higher than the wharf, gave me an advantage. I feel certain that, under like circumstances, I could easily jump from twenty-five to twenty-seven feet.

I disposed of my business in Annapolis on Monday, and set out for Montgomery; where I joined my brother's family and Mary, who was in the highest spirits, and enjoying herself among the neighbors; most of whom seemed to vie with each other as to who should show her the greatest courtesy. I, who had made such a favorable impression among the same people only a year previous, was now but little noticed when she appeared in company; and it made me feel very proud of her, to see her so highly complimented by strangers.

After spending a month with our friends, we took cur leave, and returned home, where we found the children all well.

Chapter Eight

My mill being in full operation, and having grain and many other things for sale, I amassed a considerable sum of money, and began to buy land adjoining my little farm. There was a fine block of soldiers' lots that were liable to an escheat warrant, on one of which lived a man by the name of Henry Lewis, who, hearing that I was going to Annapolis, came to me to know if I intended to take those lots. I told him that I did. He then asked me to loan him the money to secure one hundred acres. I told him that I could not lend him the money, but that I would willingly do anything I could to help him to secure the land.

"Then," said he, "you take all the land, and I will buy one hundred acres from you."

"What will you give me," I asked, "if I take it, pay for it, take out the patent, and make you such a deed as I have?"

He replied, "I will give you two hundred dollars."

"Lewis," said I, "that is more than I will ask. You shall have a hundred acres for fifty dollars; and that will pay me for my trouble. But you must pay twenty-five dollars in twelve months after the warrant issues."

To this he agreed with the greatest pleasure; saying that it was the greatest favor any man had ever done for him in all his life.

I accordingly went to Annapolis, took out the warrant, and then pursued my other business until the twelve months were drawing to a close. I saw Mr. Lewis, and called his attention to the payment he had promised. He seemed lukewarm, and did not appear to wish to talk about it. I asked him if he could advance his twenty-five dollars, when he replied coolly that he could not. I told him that we must execute our survey before the warrant expired, or we would lose money, land, and all.

Finding that he could not, or would not, do anything. I proposed to send down five dollars more, and take out another warrant; which I did, and also procured an additional twelve months to pay in. Then I rested easy until another twelve months had nearly expired; when I saw Mr. Lewis again, and asked him for the twenty-five dollars.

He told me he had been informed that he had a better right to the land than I had; that Colonel Ashby and William Hoye had both advised him not to pay me a cent, as his title was better than mine; and that he did not intend to pay me one penny.

With all the moderation I could assume, I told him that Mr. Hoye and Mr. Ashby had given him bad counsel, and that if he did not comply with his promise to me he would lose the land; for, as I was now in for all the money, if he did not pay his share I would pay all, and keep the land.

He said that he knew I would do so if I could, but he thanked God that I was not able.

I then sent for the county surveyor, and went to Lewis again with the same officer; but still he would neither pay any money nor give up the land; whereupon, I had the land surveyed, returned ray certificate, with the money due on it, and in six months took out a patent. I then wrote to Lewis, and informed him of what I had done; telling him that if he would give me the fifty dollars I would make him a deed for his hundred acres. Bat still he would do nothing.

Finding that I must enter on a troublesome law-suit, I made him yet another offer — that if he would bring me two two-year old steers I would make him the deed. But it was all in vain: he would not even do that.

I waited two years, in hopes that, through the influence of his wife and family, he would come to terms. But, finding him deaf to all, and determined to keep possession, I sued out a writ of ejectment. He hired a lawyer, who entertained a great hatred for me, and kept me seven years in court, paying fees and costs. But as I had undertaken to eject him, I was bound to succeed, at any cost; and at last I outgeneralled Lewis's lawyer, and obtained judgment against his client. Then I put the sheriff on him and took possession of the land.

One of his sons then rented it from me for one year, at twenty dollars; of which they swore me out of every cent. I could not get a tenant to keep possession for me; every one being afraid to live so near them. My dear Mary, having been thrown from a horse, was laboring under the effects of the injuries she received, when I rented out my farm, took possession of the disputed land, and built a new house on it. During this time my wife suffered such great pain that she was compelled to have some person continually with her; and as Mrs. Lewis was very kind to her, and attended to her wants at all times, I told her that I would give her fifty acres of the improved land as long aa she lived.

I was obliged to return to ray old home again, on account of ray wife's ill-health; leaving the fifty acres in possession of the same persons with whom I had been at law to gain the ownership. The agreement made between *Mrs. Lewis* and myself was, that *she* was to hold the land as long as she lived; when it was to be mine again. This agreement was entered into with the full knowledge of the whole family.

124

Mrs. Lewis died within two years after she obtained the land, and I allowed the family to live two years on it before I again demanded it; when I was compelled to sue them a second time, and go through a tedious law-suit, to gain the possession which the sheriff had given me before. This was the most costly land that I ever owned. I mention this circumstance in order to set public opinion right, as much has been said about my cruel treatment of Lewis. Having now made a true statement of all the facts in that case, I will return again to my old subject of hunting.

My eldest son, when about sixteen years of age, being anxious to hunt a bear in the holes, in the month of January we sat out for the Big Gap of Meadow Mountain, where we seldom failed to have good luck.

We reached the rocks early in the day; but before we got to the bears' holes we found in the deep snow what we took to be the tracks of a wolf, which had apparently just passed along before us. We slipped the dogs, and, soon hearing them barking at a great rate, we ran to them; when, to our surprise, instead of a wolf, we found a panther, upon a tree. I took a fair shot at him, and killed him without any fight.

We then went to the holes, when the dogs soon found a large bear in one of them. They ran in, commenced the attack, and fought desperately until we came up. We pulled one dog out, and held him, though the other would not budge, but kept up the fight a long lime, until my boy saw a part of the bear through a crack in the rock. I saw it also; and, firing at a venture, I gave him a severe wound, which made him mad, and out he came, full drive A.S he was leaving the hole, I sent a bullet through him, which decided the battle in our favor, and the bear was ours.

As we went home, I remembered a hole on the route, which we agreed to visit. As we came near the rock, we heard dogs barking in the direction of the hole, and thought that our dogs had sneaked off, and got into the hole with a bear. Without looking behind us, we ran toward the place; but when we arrived there we were in advance of our dogs. We then discovered that two other hunters had found a bear in another hole, and, having let him get out, he whipped them and their dogs, and ran off.

When we arrived at the rock, and I looked down at the mouth of the hole, I saw that a bear had been there, but that he had gone off. I thought, however, that I would go down and look in; but as I turned my eyes below, to see where to jump, the head of a very large bear became slowly visible. I immediately shot him in the head; and, fearing that the wound might not prove fatal, I took William's gun, and gave him the contents of that also. We then both loaded our guns again, and, knowing where the other hunters' dogs would run, we set out to head them off, leaving our bear as he was.

We proceeded at full speed till we came to the place to which I knew they would run; but we arrived just after the bear had passed. We saw two of the dogs; and had we been a quarter of a minute sooner, we would have had a shot at that fellow also.

In a short time the other hunters came up, and proved to be two of the Davises; the father being an older man than myself, and one who had killed many bears. He and his son accompanied us to where I had killed the bear, and helped us to pull him out of the hole. He told me he had not seen such a fat bear during the last ten years. We carried home the meat, which weighed nearly three hundred pounds; and a piece of it, which was cut in a square form, after it was salted, and raised out of the brine, measured six inches of clear fat on every side, with not a speck of lean in it.

This bear and I had been in a fight before, during the previous summer. I fixed up a canoe in the following manner, for the purpose of shooting deer along Deep Creek by candle-light: I took a sheet of maple-bark, doubled it into the form of a half-square, and secured it in place with a forked stick; after which, I arranged a position for the candle in the flat side of the bark. The flat surface of the bark formed a shed-like covering over the back part of the canoe, while the perpendicular side, being placed toward the front, entirely hid any object which might be behind it, in the canoe. Two cross-laths were nailed on the canoe — one across the top of it, and the other inside; and each of these was pierced with an auger-hole, to receive the upright pole that held up the bark shed, and the candle; which, being a large wax one, lighted up the creek to a considerable distance.

The deer used to come into the creek to drink, and to eat the moss, which grows on the bottom. I would take the canoe up the creek in the evening, and be ready to drift down as soon as the deer entered the water; all the time sitting unobserved under the shade of the bark, though I could in that position see to shoot by the light of the candle.

One night I took William with me, to steer the canoe; and as we were paddling it up the creek, we found a deer, which had been killed by wolves; and I told William that as we passed down we should find the wolves feeding on the carcass.

After dark, we set out down the stream, but saw no game until we drew near the dead deer, when I heard something running. We proceeded on; and as I could hear the animal running through the grass in the glades, and the moon was shining brightly, I thought that I could see him in the open ground. I went into the glades and hunted around; but finding nothing, I returned to my canoe, and was in the act of pushing off, when I heard the wolf, as I took it to be, coming back.

Our canoe was lying in deep water, in a place wider than the natural stream; and the unknown animal ran out on the high bank of the creek, whence he made a tremendous leap towards our canoe, and struck the water a little before us. The force with which he jumped, and the weight of his body, drove up such a heavy wave of water in front of our canoe, and gave her such a sudden send backwards, that I came very near falling headlong into the water with him; and had that been the case, I should have fallen on him, or very nearly so.

126

On recovering my balance again, seeing that he was determined to fight, I stood a moment, and as he rose a little, and began to touch bottom, I levelled my musket, loaded with eighteen large shot, which I had myself manufactured out of a bar of lead, in a very rough manner, and fired at the unknown animal, at the distance of only ten feet. He was rising out of the water, no doubt with the intention of rushing into the canoe, to attack me; but the heavy load of coarse shot striking him in the shoulder, though too far forward to kill, put him out of the notion of fighting, and as soon as he could he gained the shore, when a noble young, high-blooded dog sprang at him, and into the high weeds and bushes they went, fighting desperately.

We had left our moccasins and leggings close to our fire, where we intended to end the hunt for deer; because, as we were often obliged to get out of the canoe into the water, the less clothes we had on the better. As the rattlesnakes were very numerous on the shore, we dare not venture in our bare feet to the assistance of the dog, or to see what kind of animal it was. On lighting our candle, which had been extinguished during the bustle, we discovered his tracks in the mud, which proved to be those of the largest kind of bear; but we left him and Bosin to fight as best they could. Bosin did not return to us until near day-light, when we found that he was considerably hurt, and greatly fatigued.

While William Browning, the Davises, and myself were skinning the fine bear that we took out of his hole, we found the whole load of those rough shot lodged in his shoulder, though not deep enough to kill him. This proved to myself and old Mr. Dayis, that it was the very same fellow which wanted to drive me from his prey, in Deep Creek.

After the flurry occasioned by the bear in the Creek had subsided a little, William and I again started down the stream after deer, discovering along the route otter, muskrats, ducks, and even hundreds of trout, as they jumped out of the water. At length, hearing a great splashing and bubbling, we saw a fine deer standing nearly to his belly in the water, with his head entirely under it, feeding on the moss which grew on the bottom of the creek. We pushed our canoe so near, that we could hear the noise of his teeth cutting and chewing the moss. Levelling my musket, I put the whole load into his side, and he dropped dead in the creek. Taking the deer into the canoe, we paddled to our fire, where we had our horses hobbled, eating grass; made up a good fire, roasted and ate some of our venison, and then laid ourselves down to sleep. As the day broke, my famous dog Bosin returned to us; but I shall speak of him in another place.

Having overlooked one circumstance, it will not be amiss to mention it here. Hugh McMullen and myself having been far in the woods for some time, we were without bread for two or three days, during which time we lived on meat, without either bread or salt. Wo started for home early one morning, and as we traveled along discovered the tracks of a panther, which had been pursuing some deer. I told Hugh that though we were hungry and weak, I would like to follow that fellow, and stop him from killing any more deer. Hugh at first refused, saying that he was so weak and hungry that he could not stand it.

"Well," said I, "you may go on home, and I will give him a trial for if we let him slip now, we may not see his tracks again this winter, and he will in a year kill fifty deer. It is enough for us to kill them; but as this d — I kills more deer every year than I do, I will try my best to finish him this day, hungry as I am."

"Well," replied Hugh, "if you are determined to attack him, I will see you out."

Following his tracks, we pursued him vigorously for a mile or two, when we discovered a fine large buck covered up with snow and leaves, like a large heap of potatoes, his feet alone sticking out. We pulled him out, and found him quite warm. There was but a small place torn in his side, through which his entrails had been pulled out by the panther, which had eaten nothing but the liver, covered up the carcass, and departed. We skinned the buck, and hung up the meat, which was well bled, and the entrails taken out as well as any hunter could have done it. Indeed, it was a hunter that had done it, for that fellow killed more deer in a year than any hunter, because he was all the time, both night and day, in the best hunting ground, where he was killing game at every chance; but after the first of January, the hunter hunts but little more till the following fall.

This fellow had placed himself near where the buck was feeding, and when the buck changed his position, he crawled on his belly in the snow, until he got before him again At last he placed himself behind the limb of a tree which had fallen, but was raised a little off the ground. There he had lain flat on the ground until the buck came within his reach; when he sprang on him, threw him down, turned him on his back, and bit him across the brisket until he crushed his heart. The buck, though so strong and active, had not so much as kicked in the snow.

After we had hung up the venison, we again followed the panther's tracks, which soon entered a dense laurel swamp We had traveled but a short distance in the laurel, when my dog showing signs of the presence of game, we let him off, and in two or three minutes we heard him in full cry. We ran to him, and there found the panther standing on the limb of a pine-tree, but high enough to be out of reach of the dog. When we came near, he crouched down, wagged his tail, and prepared for a jump at us, his eyes flashing with fury. I took care to keep at a safe distance, and taking good aim, I sent a ball whizzing through his brains, which put an end to a wild and furious monster. Being faint and hungry, we skinned the panther in as little time as possible, and set out for home, having six or eight miles to travel.

We trudged along together until we came to the road that led to our home. There was a near way across a steep hill, which Hugh said he was too weak to climb, and he would follow the road. So we separated; and I crossed the hill, and got home before him, where I found old Uncle Spurgin, who had come to see us with the intention of hunting a day or two. He had killed an opossum, which Mary, having heard me say that I would not eat them, and being bent on having some fun, had cooked, knowing that we would be here that day, as it was Saturday,

When I came in, I told her that I was almost starved. She replied that she had my dinner waiting for me, and setting it on the table, I commenced eating without asking any questions, till I was nearly done, when I inquired what it was I was eating. Mary replied that it was a duck, which Uncle Spurgin had shot on the pond; so I continued eating until one of my little daughters came to me with the tail of the opossum, saying, "Father, here is the duck's tail."

Mary was greatly amused with the trick she had played off on me, and begged me to let her fix Hugh in the same way. I promised to keep dark, and let her carry out her fun with him also. Presently in came Hugh, tired enough, and as his dinner was waiting on the table for him, without loss of time he went at it; but coming to the neckbone, he said: "Polly, what is this?"

"It is a duck, which Uncle Spurgin killed on the pond."

"Well," said Hugh, "it has a — big neck-bone."

Then the little girl showed him the tail, but, notwithstanding, Hugh would not stop until he had finished the last piece of the opossum. That was the first and last piece of opossum I ever ate; and were it not for my prejudice against his rat-looking ears and tail, I could find no fault with the taste of his flesh.

Here ends this story; and now I will relate another, which I had previously overlooked. John McMullen, Sam Vansickle (the man who had the race with the turkey gobbler), and myself, went to the Meadow Mountain to hunt; taking with us five dogs, in order to be able to cope with the strongest bear we might chance to meet. When we arrived at the hunting-ground, there was no snow on the ground, but that very evening a slight snow fell. In the morning, as we were all anxious for fun, we started into the woods, the dogs being keen for the chase. We had traveled but a short distance, when we found the tracks of a bear, which we were sure was a tremendous big animal, but in reality it was quite a small one. Our mistake was caused by the snow being dry, and the leaves under it frozen; so that, when the bear put his foot down, the frozen leaves were moved to a considerable distance, making the track very large. This mistake raised our expectations to the highest pitch, as we anticipated much fun, and a great fight.

We sent off all the dogs, and such a noise as they all made, is seldom heard. "Now, boys," cried I, "let us see who will have the first shot at the bear;" and off we started like so many wild bucks, and in a short time I distanced both John and Sam. On I went, leaping every old log, until at last having to jump a high log, and seeing a small tree on the other side of it, I made a spring, in order to clear the large log, let one foot strike the small one, and then pass on. But the small log being very smooth and icy, the moment my left foot touched it, up went my heels as high as my head, and down I came with my whole weight across my fine rifle, which was broken off in my hand.

When I rose, my rifle was in two pieces, and the lock hanging by one screw I stopped about a minute, until the others came up, when we set off at a more moderate gait, and soon came up to the dogs, expecting to find a huge bear; but we could see no bear at all. I looked high up in the tree which the dogs were barking under, and there sat a two-year old bear, hid among the limbs of the spruce-pine. One of the boys shot it; and while they were taking out the entrails, I sat down on a log, and tied up my broken gun with a coarse tow string. It was completely ruined, though the lock stuck to its place, and the gun would fire every time it was tried.

After they had got the little bear ready, I took the first turn, shouldered him, and, picking up my broken gun, set off for the camp. We walked on half a mile or so, when looking up to the right, on a high bluff, I there saw a very large buck, which was staring steadily at us. I laid down the bear, without thinking of my gun being broken, and slipped up the steep hill, by which time the buck had walked out of sight. When I came to the top of the bill, I looked after him, and saw him standing fair, and at a good distance,

I raised my gun, but the string around it prevented me from taking sight; yet, knowing that I must shoot quick or not at all, I levelled the barrel as well as I could, and fired, when the buck made a few jumps, and fell dead. We carried the bear to where the buck was, hung them up together, and left them until we could get horses to bring them in. That evening turning out to be very stormy, with hail and snow, we started for our homes.

It continued stormy for some days, and the snow fell to a considerable depth. John McMullen went home; and after the storm had passed over, Vansickle and myself went for our game, taking with us both my dogs. Finding our meat all safe, we loaded it; and as we were on our way home, we saw the tracks of four bears, which had crossed the road while we had been gone. I told Sam to attend to the horse, and take the meat home, while I would try to kill the old she-bear and her cubs. So off he started for home, and I followed after the bears, taking the dogs with me.

When I came to the Little Crossings, I found that the water was deep; but, discovering a tree that had fallen across the stream, I got safely over, and pursued the bears into a thick laurel-swamp. It was then raining fast, and was very bad weather for hunting in the thicket; so I sent the dogs in, and after some time, hearing them in full chase, I followed them; when presently something came rushing through the laurels, which I suspected was one of the bears, taking the back track, as they often will do. I stood still, and saw the old bear coming toward me at full leap. The laurel was so thick that I could not see any open place to shoot through; yet, knowing that I had no other chance, I fired at random, but without stopping her. I saw that my ball had passed through a large laurel-bush, and supposed that it had done nothing more; but on approaching the track, there was so much blood on it, that I concluded she was shot through the ribs. I loaded again and still heard the dogs barking in the swamp. I followed the old bear to the creek, and on the opposite bank, there she lay, on her back, now and then moving one foot a little. I looked at her, and, thinking she was breathing her last breath, I turned to go to the dogs, when it struck me that I had known bears to act in that way, and then get up and clear themselves. I turned back; and as she still lay in the same position, I took good aim, at a distance of not more than twenty steps, and fired at her heart; when she sprang up on her feet, and ran off out of sight. I told her to go; being satisfied that if my last shot had not fixed her nothing would.

I then went to the dogs, which had two of the young ones up a tree. These I soon shot, hung them up, and went back to see what had become of the old one. I crossed on the same log, and found her lying on the ground dead.

On examination, I discovered that the ball which passed through the laurel had struck her on the big joint of the fore-leg, on the bone of which it had made a broad wound, and had then fallen out. The wound being painful from contact with the cold water, she laid down to wait until the pain would cease; and if I had gone to the dogs before I shot her the second time, I should never have seen her again.

I then started for home, but did not reach it until a late hour in the night. The next day, Vansickle and I went for the bears, which we loaded on a horse, and brought home in good order. They were fine and fat, and an excellent addition to our stock of winter provisions.

Soon after this time, there was a fine warm spell of weather; during which four friends came to my house to stay all night, who told me that they had started to go to the Little Crossings to hunt. They seemed — or I thought so fit least — as if they did not care whether I went with them or not. But though that did not seem pleasant, I told Mary to get me some bread ready, and in the morning early off we all started for the hunting-ground, which I knew well, though they did not. We reached there in time for the evening hunt, which was intended to be especially for bears.

They chose to couple without making choice of me. I said to myself, "Boys, you made a poor selection of a dunce when you took me to be one; and now you shall find that I will not act by you as I see you wish to do by me." I then remarked aloud, "Boys, this is a fine evening for a bear; and some of us will see a few, or I am much mistaken. Now, as you are all coupled, and I have only my old pup for my helper, you may take your choice of the ground; after which there will be room enough left for me."

They made their selections, and left me the place I wanted. This they did from want of judgment.

Off we all started, in the highest spirits; but I had decidedly the best ground by half, and more too.

I had not proceeded more than half a mile, when, precisely where I had killed the big bear before mentioned, I saw an old she-bear and two cubs coming directly towards me.

"Well," said I, "some of you, if not all, are surely my meat."

I waited until the old one came within shooting-distance, the little fellows, meantime, playing all sorts of capers among the trees. They would chase each other round and round a tree; off one would jump, to keep the other from catching him; then off would go the other, on top of the first one down; when they would get into a scuffle, and tumble over and over. They were considerably behind their mother; which had, in the meantime, come very close, and stood looking towards me. Being so near, I sent a ball into her breast, which tore a hole through her heart lengthwise and killed her instantly. The dog caught one of the little play-lads, and held on until I killed it with my knife; but the other cub cleared himself.

I dressed the two bears, and, the sun being low, I went into the feeding-ground, where the dog soon began to show signs of game. I followed him slowly, and saw a little bear eating chestnuts; but, as there were many signs of bears thereabouts, I did not wish to shoot at it, lest I should scare some larger ones.

I crept softly towards it, thinking that I would get near enough for the dog to lay hold of it, when I could kill it without noise. I crept on until within a few steps of where I intended to let the dog slip, when the bear got alarmed, stopped eating, took a look all round, and sat down to watch; so I thought that I would stand so still that the little fellow could not distinguish me from a stump. There he sat, while I remained in my place as quietly as I could stand, until I happened to turn my eyes to the left. There stood the old one, and two more young ones; the former being within ten steps of me, and presenting as fair a mark as could be desired.

I instantly turned my gun on the old bear, and shot her dead; when the dog, which had been long watching the cub, at the crack of the gun, sprang on it, while the other two ran up a tree. Loading quickly, I shot one of them, and then ran to help the dog, and keep the other from scratching his eyes out. I stabbed this one, and then took the dog to the tree where I had left the remaining one; but it was gone. However, the dog followed his trail, and soon had him up another tree, when I went to it and shot him; thus killing five bears in about three hours. I walked into camp with a good grace, and I thought ray companions would rather I had staid at home. They kept quiet, however, and treated me respectfully.

I went home for help to bring in my game, but the others staid two or three days longer. They killed no bears, and, as well as I can remember, they secured but few deer, if any at all.

Chapter Nine

In the year 1829, on the 10th day of May, that being about the usual time to find the first bears feeding, I took my son William with me to Meadow Mountain to have a bear-hunt. Being too late to hunt that evening, we made a fire under a large tree, and, as the evening was warm and pleasant, we hobbled our horse in a glade of fine grass, then took our suppers, laid down by our fire, and slept soundly till morning.

When we awoke, the birds on every side were singing in the liveliest strains; and, being in good health, it seemed to me to be one of the sweetest mornings that had ever dawned on me during my whole life. I left William to attend to the horse, and started away in search of my choice game — bears.

I went from place to place without finding the trace of a single bear, and hunted until I became tired; when, being three or four miles from my boy and the horse, I began to direct my course toward the camp. On my way in, I found where a bear had that morning commenced to feed on acorns; and, being certain he would return again in the evening, for there were plenty of acorns on the ground, I went to the camp, where I found the boy and horse all right.

Telling William that we would move our camp nearer to the place where the bear would come to feed, we led our horse to within half a mile of the feeding-ground, hobbled him in another fine patch of grass, made a fire under a great spreading hemlock, and laid ourselves down to await the approach of evening.

The desired hour having at last arrived, we went to the ground; and as we entered it, I saw a bear coming to his feeding-place, and such a looking animal I had never in my life seen. He was long and tall, and his back bowed up like a fighting hog; his legs looked like a naked man's arms, and he walked along as if he scarcely felt the ground — in fact, he was the poorest-looking beast I had ever seen.

He came on until he reached the tracks which I had made in the fore-part of the day, when off he broke. I sent two good dogs after him, and in a few minutes they were out of hearing; but in an hour or two the dogs returned, completely tired.

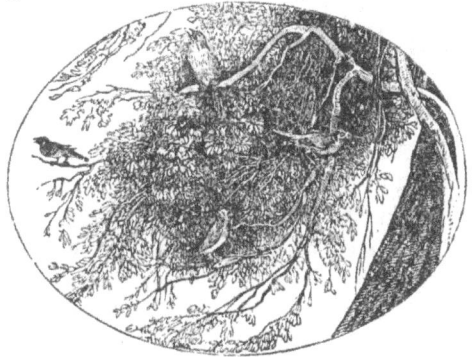

The sun being still high, we went to another part of the feeding-ground, and sat down to watch the bears as they came to feed. We sat a long time, when by and by I heard something at a great distance walking over the dry leaves; and the noise becoming still plainer, I knew it was certainly a bear. I could not get near enough to shoot him, because, the leaves being dry, he could hear me walking; but seeing a small stream of water running towards him, I got into it, and was proceeding along finely, when I heard a noise directly behind me.

Supposing that William had let the dogs out, I turned to stop them, when I saw a stout bear coming toward me at full gallop; and he ran on until he was within five steps of the place where I stood in the branch. As he reached the high bank, he stopped and looked back, as if something behind had alarmed him; and this being just what I wished, I took good aim, and drove a ball through his heart; when he fell down the bank into a quagmire up to his belly.

The dogs and William came running to my assistance, but he was mortally wounded, and could not make any resistance. We then dressed him, and went to our camp; where, finding the horse safe, and in the best of pasture, we remained that night. The next day we took our prizes home, and then went to work on the farm.

On the corresponding day of the following week, I took my two dogs, went to the same place, and sat on the identical log on which William and I had sat before; when in a short time I heard a bear pawing up the leaves, in search of acorns. I had a blanket, with my bread and meat rolled up in it, which I laid down, told the dogs to stay by it, and started in the direction of the noise. I soon discovered a very large bear, but as he was standing with his head towards me, I was afraid to shoot him in the shoulders; the bones being so strong, that a ball will not sink deep enough to kill him. I waited for him to turn his side toward me, so that I could get at his heart; but while I was waiting, one of the dogs left his place, and came walking up to me, when I beckoned to him to lay down, and he stood still. I then looked for the bear, and finding that he was staring at myself and the dog, I knew that he would make off. I shot at him in a hurry, when down he fell, and the two dogs sprang on him like mad tigers. The very worst kind of fighting then took place. I had one young dog, which would seize the bear by the head, but the latter always knocked him off, mashed him to the ground, and bit him desperately.

I ran up and shot the bear a second time, but too far back to kill him. When I fired, the bear let the dog go; but as soon as he got loose, he again seized the bear by the ear. The bear dashed him on the ground with one blow, and was again biting him, when I drew out my knife, and, putting my thumb on the end of the handle, I held the blade behind, placed my eye on the spot where I knew I could send it to his heart, and, running past him, gave him a backhanded blow, which sank the whole blade into his body. He let the dog go (which they will always do when a knife strikes them), but as soon as the dog

134

got loose, he again took the same hold. The bear threw him and bit him as before, when I again stabbed him; but in passing him the second time, the bear made a grab at me, caught my right leg, tilted me over a fallen tree, and heels overhead I went, his nails tearing out of my pants a piece the size of his huge foot. The bear was in the act of springing on me when I fell; but the two faithful dogs, seeing my danger, seized him by the hams, and as he could not bear to have *his* breeches torn, he turned to defend himself When I got up, I found the same dog was down, and the bear again biting him. I repeated my thrusts with the knife, and thus relieved the dog; and so I continued to give one stab after another, till I had driven my knife into him seven times. All these severe cuts were made in a space the size of a large dinner-plate — four of them touching his heart, and the others cutting his lights.

Although it may appear improbable, yet it is not the less true, that a hunter may steal on a bear, and shoot him through the lungs, when he will die in three minutes; but if the dogs attack him, and worry him until he becomes reckless and furious, he will live and fight for fifteen minutes, and perhaps

DESPERATE FIGHT WITH A BEAR.

longer, though wounded in the same manner. After I had given him the first five cuts, he would not let the dog loose, and I suppose that he was not then sensible of his wounds. Seeing that he was still biting the dog severely, and that I could effect nothing with the knife, I ran up suddenly, seized him by the wool on his hips, and gave him a hard jerk, which, as he was very weak, threw him flat on the ground. He then gave a long groan, which was so much like that of a human being, that it made me feel as though I had been dealing foully with the beast; but there I had to stand, and hear his heavy groans, which no person could have distinguished from those of a strong man in the last agonies of death.

135

I stood loosing calmly at him, until the sport was marred by the thought of the brave manner in which he had defended himself against such unequal numbers, and it really seemed to me that I had committed a crime against an unoffending animal. But when I turned to look for my dog, and found that he was laid out on the battle-ground, I felt very sorry. As he was not able to rise, I helped him up, but he could not stand; and though I offered him food, he refused it. He could stand on his forelegs, but had no use of his hind parts. I then went to attend to the bear, which the other dog was still pulling at, when the young dog commenced whining, and dragging himself down towards myself and the bear, I thought that the pain he felt caused him to be so uneasy, but he pulled himself along until he came within reach of the bear, which he laid hold of, and began to shake and worry as if nothing was the matter with him.

After I had dressed the bear, and ray dog had become quiet, I took my gun and walked into the feeding ground, just out of sight of the sick dog and the bear, when I saw another bear moving in the opposite direction. I followed after him, but the leaves were so dry that I could not gain on him. After I had pursued him for some time, still not being within shooting distance, he suddenly turned round, and returned towards me, on his own tracks, as I believe, until he came as close as I wished him to be. I was prepared for him, and told him to stop, which he did, when I took a fair aim at him, and fired. He ran but a few steps, and fell dead. By the time I had dressed him it was getting dark, when I returned to the place where my first bear was, made a fire, and slept there all night.

Some time late in the night, I was awakened by the most frightful noise I ever heard in my life. It was as loud and harsh as the lowing of an ox, and seemed to echo from the other side of the hill on which I was camped, and the whole space above seemed to resound with the noise. It continued for twenty minutes, as near as I could judge, and seemed to die away by degrees, until all was again quiet. I supposed then, and yet think, that it was caused by two old male panthers, which had met and got into a fight; and being of the cat species, they make a similar noise, only much stronger and coarser. But I cannot say for certain what animal made the noise, because, having but one dog fit for action in the morning, and the place where the fight occurred the previous night being in a dense laurel thicket, I concluded to let the beasts alone, if they would keep away from me; so I did not attempt to investigate the matter.

My dog being still unable to stand, when I was ready to start home for help, I ate my breakfast, and started off, leaving him with the bear. He cried piteously when I left him, which made me feel sorry for him; but I walked fast, and presently heard a turkey gobbler, when I imitated the cackle of a hen turkey, and as he came running to find her, I shot him. As soon as I fired, the lame dog came to where I was, but as he refused to follow me, I left him again by himself, to do the best he could.

136

I picked up the gobbler and went home, and in the afternoon the dog returned. He was bitten from the loins to the neck, and would have been killed had he not been very fat; for when the bear tried to bite him, the hide and fat would slip from between his tusks, and they would pass over the back-bone without injuring it. In that way he escaped being killed. It was a full mouth before he could hunt again, by which time my attention was directed entirely to the deer.

In those days I lived some eight or ten miles from the Green Glades, the grass of which I used to cut and make into hay on the ground, take my cattle to it in the fail, and leave them there until spring, by which time they would be in good order; and the cutting and curing of the hay afforded is a fine frolic. I used to take two sons with me, and also one of my daughters to cook for us; and having two scythes, we would mow enough grass in the evening of the day we first went out, to make a good stack the next morning.

As about this time the deer began to feed, I used to walk into the clear glades and hunt them, frequently seeing ten or twelve during one morning and evening. As the grass was very high, I could see nothing of them but their heads; and taking a bush in my hand, to hide me from their view, when they would be feeding I would cautiously advance till I got as near as I wished, often having to shoot through the grass, and guess at the position of the body of the deer; though I do not recollect ever having on any occasion missed my mark; for I would be so close that I was nearly always certain of the position of the deer, and the grass could not stop or turn the course of the ball.

I seldom killed less than from four to six deer during one hay-making trip; and when I obtained a load, I sent a boy home with it and the horse, as we at all times kept one with us for that purpose. Frequently, while I would be hunting, the boys would be fishing for trout, and take from fifty to a hundred, to send home to their mother, who would send us, in return, all the best things she had. So we "fared sumptuously every day," having the best of venison fried in butter, and trout, also fried in the fresh and sweet butter which we kept in one of the many fine springs found in that vicinity, which bubble up through beautiful white sand, in half-a-dozen places — the water being so clear and cold, that it will make a man's arm pain him to the elbow, if he holds his hand in it a few minutes.

In this way we used to spend a week or ten days every rear in hay-making, and in the fall we took our cattle to the hay, and kept them there all winter; but as they wasted too much hay, by eating from the stacks, I had a long rack made, which would hold hay enough to last them two weeks. I also kept there a yoke of oxen and a sled, on which we would haul hay to the rack, until it was full, when we would leave the cattle to eat it as they pleased. When they wanted water, it was within ten steps of the rack; and if the wind blew from the east, they could get shelter on the west side of the rack, but when it shifted to the west, they could change their position to the other side.

Having got through the winter, we all went to work on the farm, and in the mill, until about the end of the following May, when I took my third son, James, and started off to hunt a bear. We searched all the beech grounds, but found not a single bear, and I despaired of finding any; but as we were walking on the outskirts of the beech land, I saw a bear rising up to look for us. Having got some notice of our approach, she stood up like a man, to reconnoitre. I fired at her in a hurry, and down she fell; but her ladyship was not much hurt. I had only one dog, a tine old fellow, which was a cripple, from a wound received in one foot during a hard fight; but he was strong, and willing to do all he was able. James was holding him when I shot, but he then let him go, and at the bear be went, in good earnest, when a very fair tight took place. James and I ran up to see the fun, and it was hard to tell which had the best of the fight; for when the bear seemed to be in a fair way of getting the dog in her arms, he would let go his hold, and run off out of her reach, but when she attempted to run, he would seize her by the hams, and run round and round, until she would be forced to stand and fight again. In this way the fight was kept up, until it became so close that I concluded lo put an end to it, for I feared that the bear might get hold of the dog, and wound him. So I waited until I saw a fair chance, when I drove my knife so deep into her lungs, that it ended the battle, and left old Gunner in the full enjoyment of a victory over his adversary.

I will now relate an adventure which I had on one occasion with a male bear, about three or four years old. Having set a steel trap for wolves, I had appointed iv certain day to go and see whether or not a wolf had been caught. The day arrived, and with it a friend of mine, named George Knox, who called to spend a few days with me in hunting; so we started off together to see my trap. We went to the place where the trap had been set, but it was gone; and we soon discovered that it was a hem which had taken it away. With eager steps we pursued the trail, until by-and-by we found him, with the trap fast to an old root. Knox was afraid of the bear, but I laughed at his fears, and told him that a man as big as he was, should not hesitate to fight that bear with his naked hands. lie swore he would like to see me fight him naked-handed.

"Well," said I, "Knox, "I believe he could make but little to brag of, in such a fight with me."

"Well," replied he, "I have never seen you in a fight with either man or beast, but I have heard people say that you are not slow at it. Now, if you were to let that fellow out of the trap, and undertake to fight him nakedhanded, if you wouldn't meet —, I am no judge of such things."

I then walked up on the other side of the root, and found that the trap had the bear's fore-foot fast, and lying upon the root. I took hold of the chain, and pulled him; when, though he grumbled a little, he seemed unwilling to fight. His foot was only hanging by a small portion of the skin.

I told Knox to hold the dog, and keep him ready to help, in case the bear should get the better of me. Ha made some objections, saying that he did not wish to see me engage in such a foolish undertaking; but I had got the idea into my head that I could box him off, so that he could not come to me. Knox agreed to hold the dog, while I tried what the bear could do in a fair fight. All being ready, a strap was passed round the dog's neck, of which Knox held the other end; and arrangements were made as to the time he might let the dog slip, in case of necessity.

The bear was on the side of a steep bluff, from which there was only a short descent to a pretty stretch of bottom land. I went up to the bear, and with my knife cut off the small piece of skin that held him in the trap. As I knew that he would want to go down the hill, I waited until he found that he was free from the trap, and attempted to go off, when I made at him. He rushed at me with a snort that made Knox shriek like a woman; but as he came toward me, I ran down the hill into the bottom. As he did not seem disposed to try to catch me, I again faced about to receive him; Knox all the while screaming at me to leave. But being determined to give him a crack or two, at all hazards, I stood till he came within reach, when I struck him in the ear as hard as I could, and turned his head round. He then became mad, and rose on his hind-feet to make for my face or neck; but I struck him in the pit of his stomach, which seemed to double him up. He made another sudden attempt to run under at my legs, when, seeing that he would get hold of me if I stood still, I made a leap, and, as he came on, landed in his rear.

He was now getting in earnest, and did not try to run from me at all; but when he found me behind him, he wheeled around, and again came up to the attack. I gave him another fair stroke under the butt of his ear, which made him stagger; but still he aimed at my legs, and I jumped over him the second time; when Knox, being uneasy for my safety, let the dog go, which took my place, and the fight continued for several minutes on pretty equal terms. After awhile, finding that the dog began to grow tired, and the contest becoming close, I took my knife, and with one stab put an end to the fight, to the great astonishment of Mr. Knox, who told that story to many people, with great interest.

Things went on snugly until the hunting season returned, when I took ray gun, and a fine hunting dog (for I never kept one that I could not risk my life on), and went to the Meadow Mountain, just as the chestnuts were falling. I traveled until about four o'clock, but found nothing except chestnuts. At last, being a little tired, I set my gun against a tree, laid down ray blanket and provisions, and commenced gathering nuts. I shuffled round and round, until I filled all my pockets; when, being satisfied with what I had secured, I rose up to leave the place. As I did so, however, I saw a full-grown bear on the other side of the same tree under which I was gathering nuts, picking up and eating them also. It being but a step to my gun, I soon had it in my possession, and fired at him as quickly as possible. The bear fell, when I leaped on him like a panther, and drove my knife deep into his side before he had time to recover. This bear could certainly not have been under the tree when I arrived, or I surely would have seen him; but he must have come while I was busy looking for the nuts. He must also have been fully engaged in looking for and eating nuts; for neither he, nor the dog, nor myself, had any knowledge of each other's presence, until, being ready to leave, I rose up on my feet, when I saw him within five steps of me.

I took out his entrails, hung up the carcass, and set off again on the route that I had planned for my hunt before leaving home, which was to scour the south side of the mountain going out, and the north side coming home. I continued on down the south side, when up bounced a fine buck, which ran up the steep hill until he was almost out of reach of my ball; but he stopped at last, and turned to look at me. As he did so, I took good aim, and fired, when he came running toward me, and fell dead. I dressed the carcass, hung it up, and then crossed the mountain to the north side, where I found the woods had been all burnt over; but the nuts were plenty, and there being many signs of deer and bears, I kept on my course, though then not less than fifteen miles from home, looking for the best places to camp and hunt.

At last my dog found a middle-sized track, and as it was late, I let him off at once. In a few minutes, hearing him in full cry, I ran to where he was, and found that he had a bear up a tree. I shot the bear, dressed his carcass, and hung it up, as I had done the rest of my game; after which I had five miles to travel to the nearest house, and was then eight miles from home.

After this time, I have no recollection how the hunt turned out; but in May of the following year, I went to the house which the neighbors had raised for the Methodist preacher, Wirsing, and which was then a hunting-camp, taking a good dog with me. I hunted the first evening, but not seeing any bears, and very few signs of any, I stayed all night, and took an early start in the morning. It was likely to be a fine day for my purpose, as it was raining a little, and bears like to feed in damp weather. I had been out but a short time, when the rain poured down so rapidly, that I sought shelter under a large tree, and sat down close to it. While there, my dog showed signs of game being near; but I remained in my place, in hope, it might be a bear coming toward me. Presently a tremendous buck appeared, with his old coat of hair on, and looking long, lank, and shabby. I thought that to kill him would be to destroy a valuable animal to no purpose, and I determined not to shoot him, as I knew he was not fit for use. On he came, until I could have touched him with a ten-foot pole; but he fed unmolested, and passed by without noticing me at all.

I remained under the tree, keeping my gun dry, until the shower passed over, when I walked out to examine one place which I had not seen the night before, and the only hope I had of finding a bear. I took the leeward side of the ground, and when I came to it, saw an old bear and two young ones. Between us, and near to the bears, was a fall of timber. I took good notice that they were feeding near a black tree, so that I should not be mistaken as to the place where to look for them again; for I was compelled to lose sight of them, while I went upon the fallen timber. I soon arrived at the fallen trees, and easily climbed to the highest place, where I could obtain a fair view of my game, which were feeding quietly, without any idea of approaching danger.

"Well," said I to myself, "is not this a cruel act, to steal in this way on a mother and her little helpless family, and put them to death? But," said I again to myself, "we do the same with our hogs, cattle, and sheep; therefore you have no right to complain, and you will have to take it."

All this time they were busily engaged, and my nerves were as firm as possible. I took a steady aim at the old one, and killed her instantly; whereupon I immediately reloaded my rifle, and rammed down a naked ball as quick as possible. The dog caught one young one, and the other ran up a tree; but as he was coming down, I shot and wounded him in the shoulder; yet down he came, and made for a swamp. As I had no time to load again, I dropped my gun, went after and overtook him. But the question was how to get at him; for I knew he would be a very unhandy customer to work with, as he would bite and scratch severely. So I ran close to him, and kicked him behind, hut he still kept on. I ran at him again, and gave him a thundering kick in the hind end, which raised him up with such force, that he turned a somerset, and fell with his head toward me. I jumped on him with my feet, expecting that he would seize me by the legs, but that, as they were thickly clothed, before he could do me any injury, I could run my knife into him. So it happened, for the moment I jumped on him, he laid hold of one of my legs, and although one of his fore-legs was much injured by the shot, yet he held me with his sharp nails, and bit with all his strength, until I put my knife through his heart. This done, I went to see what had become of my dog and the other bear.

As soon as I came within hearing, I found that they were still fighting, and when I came up, they were both so tired that they would stand and rest between whiles. When the dog would get the bear by the throat, the latter would scratch him in the eyes with his hind-feet, until the dog would let him go, when, after having rested, he would tackle on to him again.

I killed the bear, and relieved the dog; after which, I gathered my prizes together, dressed them, and hung them up, to keep other animals from eating them. I then went into my camp, or rather house, and laid down to wait for evening; when I intended to give the bears another trial, in a different feeding-ground.

In the evening, a man by the name of Enlow, who was married to my wife's sister, joined me. Hearing of the route I intended to take next, he advised me to bring in the three bears I had killed that evening, and leave the proposed hunt until the next morning. This being agreed to, when morning came, we started off early, and hunted from one place to another, until Mr. Enlow became tired and hopeless. I told him that I knew of one more place, and if he would go with me to it, and we found no bears there, I would then agree to go home with him.

He consented to go; and as we approached the spot, we saw the foot-prints of a very large bear, leading directly to the ground. I told Enlow that a bear was surely in that place, as it had just gone by, and, with good management, he would be our prize without fail.

As the wind was blowing from us, we ran round to the other side of the ground; but by the time we arrived there, the wind had changed, and blew wrong again.

"Well, Enlow," said I, "if we go in at this side the bear will certainly smell us, and we will lose him."

He said that he would not be fooled in that way, but advised that we should go in there; and if the bear ran, the dogs would stop him.

This did not suit me; so I told him that we might certainly count on losing the bear if he smelled us; and that I would turn as often as the wind did, until it would be right. Whereupon, he agreed to go round again to the place where we saw the track.

The wind remaining in the same quarter, we entered the ground; and about midway I saw the bear going off, and pointed him out to Enlow, telling him to stand and keep the dogs quiet, and I would show him how to shoot him. He agreed, and I set off to exhibit my skill in bear hunting.

The bear was travelling out of the ground, and I did not gain much on him; but after a little while he turned his course, so that I could cut across, and double my gain on him. I soon got to a place where, if he continued his course, he would be as near as I wished him. On he came, until he was right opposite me, but crossing my track. I spoke to him, and he stopped, when I sent a ball through his lungs. He ran but a short distance, and fell dead.

Enlow was much gratified at what had been done, and helped to secure the meat; after which we set off for home; but we had not traveled more than a mile or two when I found a place where something had scratched up the leaves. At first sight, I supposed it was done by a turkey; but on a close examination, I found it had been a bear, and a very large one, too; and that he had been there very recently. I told Enlow to keep the dogs quiet while I followed his trail a short distance, and perhaps I could see him.

The ground being soft, and clear of bushes, I hurried after him, and had not got out of sight of Enlow, when I saw the bear walking slowly down a hill.

142

The leaves being so dry that they rattled as I walked over them, I could gain but little, if anything, on him. I had lost sight of him, and expected I should see him no more, when presently he made a great noise in breaking through the brush; and as I knew that he could not hear me while he was making such a racket himself, I ran after him till I got within sight, and discovered that he was playing among the dry limbs of a fallen tree.

Hellebore is the first weed that shoots up in the spring, and it grows to the height of two feet, with a stalk somewhat resembling that of corn, and a strong, broad leaf. It grows in marshy ground; and this place, being a narrow, muddy branch, was full of it. The bear had got into the mud, and was amusing himself by biting off the hellebores and slinging them out of his way.

This he continued to do until I was on the bank of the run, and within thirty steps of him. I then knew that he was my prize, and I stood quietly looking at him playing; for I had never before seen a grown bear play. I stood until he stopped his gambolling, went to the water, and took a drink.

All this time his stern was toward me, and I was afraid to shoot, lest the ball should not sink deep enough to kill him. But I knew that, as he mounted the hill on the opposite bank, he would turn either one side or the other to me, as he would not go straight up such a steep bluff.

After he had drank, he walked in a diagonal direction up the steep bank, and turned his side to me; but not until he had got under the branches of a spruce-pine, when I could see nothing but his legs. However, I had to shoot then or not at all, as I knew that would be the last chance I should get; so I took aim through the limbs, as if there was nothing in the way, and fired.

Down tumbled the bear, and over and over lie rolled, into the rand, when the dogs jumped in also, and at it they went, for life and death. I saw that he would kill some of the dogs if I did not help them; so I drew ray knife, and, as he was trying to catch the dogs, I struck him. But the knife turned in my hand, and hung fast in his side; and, as I was not able to draw it out, I left it there, with only the handle projecting. I immediately commenced loading ray rifle, while the dogs and the bear were doing all they could to overcome each other. In the meantime, Enlow came up with his rifle and shot the bear in the Head, and the fight was ended without any one of us being hurt.

In the autumn of 1825, about the last of October, I commenced building a barn without other help than that of my oldest son, William. However, we went to work; and the first day, though it stormed hard, with wind, rain, and snow, I kept on cutting timber, and the boy hauling, until he was so chilled that he had to quit. But I wanted to get the barn done, as I had no shelter for ray horses or other stock, and I was anxious to get into the woods. I stopped for no kind of weather, nor did I stop even at night, as long as I could find anything that I could do after dark that would forward my work the next day. I worked by moonlight until nine, or even ten o'clock at night; and by this means I was, in a little over a week, ready to raise my building.

The barn was to be forty-eight feet by twenty-five, and built of round logs. I collected twenty-two hands, who were two days in raising the walls, and left the roof untouched. I had two rounds of rafters to put up myself, for it was a cabin-shaped roof. We had ropes to raise them with, and I would help William and his mother to raise each log upon the skids, and prop it up until I mounted to the top of the wall and let down the rope, which they would tie round the log, when I would pull out, cud up as high as I could, and hitch it fast, and then let down another rope, with which I would draw the other end of the log up still higher than the first. Thus, with great labor and difficulty, all the logs and boards which covered the barn were properly placed, and we had it under cover in less than three weeks. We finished on Saturday evening, at ten o'clock, and rested finely on Sunday. All the time we had fine weather, and the moon gave sufficient light for me to finish my work and prepare to go into the woods.

On Monday morning, I took my gun and set out for the Little Crossings. When I got into the hunting-ground, I perceived something as white as snow lying at the foot of a tree, which, as I came nearer, I saw was a large rabbit. As I did not wish to fire my gun at him, I took a club, and went round the tree, thinking to kill him by striking at him from behind it. But I missed him, and out he flew, like a streak of lightning, with the dog after him, yelping at every jump.

The dog was soon left so far behind that he got ashamed, and gave up the chase; though it was not an unprofitable one, for they started up a fine buck, which, as he ran within gunshot of me, I shot through the ribs, when he made but a few jumps, and fell dead. I dressed him, and took all one side of his ribs to roast that night; but, in hanging him up, I got a great deal of blood on me.

After having put his carcass away, I started off on my intended course, and was walking through a clear piece of ground, when, while looking at a small patch of fallen timber, in which a thicket of briars had grown up, out bounced a pretty little buck.

He had a steep hill to run up, and I knew he would stop before he reached the top. I stood ready, and when he did stop, I fired my gun as soon as possible; whereupon, the back wheeled, came running back, and fell nearer to me than he was when I shot him. I loaded again, and started toward my deer, when out came another fine big fellow, which ran up nearly to the same place where the first one stood, and there stopped also, when I fired again, and down he came. "Well," thought I, "this is certainly the best kind of luck indeed."

I laid my gun on my shoulder, and walked on again, when up jumped another very large buck, which ran up to the same place, and there stopped, as the other two had done. But this time I had an empty gun; and before I could load it, he ran off.

I then dressed the two I had killed, hung them up high, and pursued my course for the Little Crossings. I hunted all day, and saw but four deer, of which I killed three; and if I had promptly loaded after my second fire, and had been ready for the last fellow, I would have killed the whole four. But at first I thought there was but one, and by chance loaded before I moved from the place; and then when the second came out, I was sure that was all, and did not load as before, or I would surely have had them all.

I pushed on, and got to my desired ground, where I found a small bear eating hickory-nuts. The dog put him up a tree, and the little fellow was shot without any chance of defence.

By this time I was tired, and it was nearly night. I found two old trees lying across each other; and, seeing no chance of better accommodations, I peeled bark off them to lay over me, made a fire, and sat down to rest. While sitting thus, I heard a wolf howl; but as that was a common occurrence, I took no notice of him, especially as he was far off. When it became dark, I set my buck's ribs before the fire to roast; and when they were ready, I made a hearty supper, not having eaten anything since daylight. I then laid down to sleep; but late in the night I heard my dog growling, as I lay with ray head on him. Being sound asleep, I did not become conscious of danger until his repeated growlings fully aroused me; when I heard something coming up to my fire. To my surprise, it came up right in the smoke, when I was sure it knew I was there, and could smell me; for it came quite near, and commenced growling at me.

The old dog was so frightened that he lay close to me for protection. I would not shoot by guess, and it was so dark that I could not have seen an ox if he had been there. As I found I had no chance of shooting to any certainty, I thought I would try to provoke the wolf to jump on the old dog; which I knew he would do if the dog was only out of my reach.

There being a high log lying before me, I took the dog, and held him up so that the wolf could see him, but kept myself out of view, with my knife ready in my hand. If the wolf jumped on the dog, I intended to catch him by the leg, and let him bite all he could until I got my knife into him. But, though I could not tempt him to come over to me, he kept round me until daylight began to appear; when he went off about a hundred yards, and gave a long howl, to which no answer was returned.

As he was going down the Crossings, into a thick swamp, I got out and went below, between him and the laurel, and sitting down, howled like a wolf, which I could imitate very well. I did so twice or three times; but, getting no reply, I despaired of hearing from him; and, as it was yet too dark to see to shoot, I sat still until I heard something moving towards me through the dry leaves; and, notwithstanding I could partially see it as it ran, yet I could not tell whether it was a deer or a wolf.

On It came, until about to pass me; when, finding it was a wolf, I spoke easily to him, and held my gun ready. He heard me, and flopped, when I fired at him. He gave a stout grunt, and ran off, over a small stream, on to the hill on the other side, where he howled again. I again ran below him and howled, but got no answer. I howled until, having no more hope of seeing or hearing him again, I turned toward my fire, and moved along until I approached the place where I heard him last.

I had noticed that the howling seemed to proceed from a pine-tree which had a very large top; and, as I returned, I saw a hawk going from the top of a tall poplar, and making a noise as if he saw something. When I observed him, I saw that he was gazing at the spot where the wolf had given his last howl; so I turned and went toward the big pine, and there found the wolf, as dead as a herring.

This greedy animal had smelled the blood on my clothes, as also the roasting venison; and if his associates had been within hearing, and had come to his assistance when he was howling for them, I have no doubt that his intention was to attack me. But he was afraid to tackle me by himself, lest I should be too hard to get through with; and therefore he was willing to let me alone.

In October of the year 1819, I set a trap for bears, which I examined one evening, and found untouched. That night it rained; and the following day being a fine one for hunting, I started off for the same ground in which the trap was set; and in passing by, I thought I would look at it again.

The trap being laid at the side of a high rook, I could stand on the top of the rock and examine it without making any tracks about it to scare the game. So I went on the top of the rock, and saw that the trap was down, and that a small bear had his head under the fore-part of it. On going down from the rock, I saw that the head of the bear was flattened out by the weight of the trap; but, there being a crack left, through which I could see in, I saw another bear inside the trap. I did not want to shoot into the trap, as the smell of the powder would scare the other bears from going in. I then laid down far enough away to keep the smoke of the powder from the trap, and when the old bear looked at me I shot her in the head. I then stepped on the trap, to go to the lever which rai-ed up its top, when I heard a scuffle inside. I thought it might be possible that I had not killed the old one; so I went back, looked in, and saw the bullet-hole in the bear's head, and, slipping my hand in through the crack, I put my finger into the hole, and felt that the bullet had gone into the brain. Thereupon, I stepped on the trap again to pass over to the lever, when, hearing the same noise again, I went to the front, and on looking in, discovered another young bear in the trap with his mother. I then shot him, and thus secured the whole family.

I suppose the old bear and one of the cubs entered and took hold of the bait, and as the other cub was in the act of coming in also, the trap fell on his head.

After cleaning and securing them, I turned into the hunting-ground, and walked to a spot where I knew an old buck used to feed. I found his tracks, and, having a young dog with me, which was not trained, he was so eager to follow the buck that I could scarcely hold him back.

The buck had gone into a thicket to lay down, whither I followed him cautiously, and presently saw his horns sticking up like a grain-cradle. He was laying down looking at me, with his head over the bushes, but his whole body obscured.

I raised my rifle, sighted at the end of his nose, fired, and down went the horns. Then it was that my moccasins made tracks fast, for on him I sprang, and cut his throat without looking where the ball had struck; though I found afterwards that it had penetrated about three inches higher op than I had aimed it, and had dashed out the deer's brains. My spoils that morning were three tears, and a magnificent buck, all fat, cleanly handled, and taken in a very short time; for, at a little after nine o'clock I was at home, eating my breakfast.

Not long after this, a friend named George Riley, who had done a stout job of mason work for me, came to see us, with the view of taking a trip with me, and, as he said, of learning how to hunt. The following morning, we set out for the Little Crossings; and, as we proceeded thither, found the tracks of four deer, which we followed until we overtook them, before they got sight of us. I shot and wounded the leader; but as the others did not leave her, I fired a second time, killing one and again wounding a third, when the remaining deer ran off. We then hung up the carcass of the one we had killed, and afterwards followed the tracks of the two wounded ones, which, having gone different ways, I took one track and Riley the other. I had not gone far, when, discovering mine lying down, I killed it; and was cleaning the carcass, when Riley came to me, saying that he could not get a shot at his. I went with him to the spot where he had left it, and followed it until we overtook it, I shot and killed it. We stowed the meat carefully away, and went on to Mr. Cunningham's farm, at the Cherry-tree Meadows, where Colonel Lynn shot the bear which my dog had treed,

Mr. Cunningham and his family having gone to Frederick to spend the winter, there was no one there but Mr. George W. Drane, who was taking care of the premises. Drane being lonely, desired us to stay with him, to which we agreed; and while he and Riley were preparing supper, I turned out to hunt during the remainder of the evening. As I was walking lightly along, where I knew the deer were in the habit of feeding, I saw one peeping round a tree at me; when, without delay, I let fly at his head, and down he went. He proved to be a small one. and I carried his carcass to the house before they had supper ready.

We stayed with Drane all night; and in the morning there being a nice snow on the ground, as soon as breakfast was over, Riley and I went to the woods; but the wind being unfavorable for us, we scared several deer, without obtaining any shots; so I told Riley that we had better travel to the eastern side of the hunting ground, and then hunt up against the wind. "We traveled at least three miles, until we got the wind in our faces, when we went into the ground which I knew the deer frequented, and commenced looking for them. We had hunted but a short time, when I saw four deer lying down, though Riley could not see them, nor dare I call to him to tell him where they were. I fired at them, and killed one in its bed; when the others rose up, and not knowing from what direction the shot came, stood till I fired a second time, and killed another; when, seeing the others run off, we went to the two dead ones, and commenced dressing them. As I rose to look for a limb on which to hang them up, I saw one of the others, which had returned in search of its company. I shot that one also, hung it up alongside the other two, and then turned out to hunt for more.

I suppose we hunted over a mile of ground, and found the tracks of two deer, which we followed, and soon overtook. I shot both of them, without moving from my position; though Riley never saw them until they were down and kicking their last. After they were dressed, we started to return to Drane's again; and while on the way, I saw three deer quietly feeding in the deep snow, which had been falling nearly all the day, and was then half-leg deep. I crept up close, and shot the doe, when the fawns ran until they got beyond a fallen tree, where they stood huddled close together I sent Riley to kill one of them, for I knew they would stand there until they were again scared. On went Riley, but, forgetting where they stood, when he looked for them he could not see them; so he turned back. "When I saw him coming, and the two deer still standing in the same place, I ran up and asked him what he came back for? — to which he replied that the fawns had gone off. I then took his gun, went to the fallen tree, looked over, and seeing the two little fellows still standing side by side, I put the gun over the log, and took a good aim; but the gun, being a flint lock, burnt her priming, and missed Ore, or I would have killed eight deer that day.

We returned to Mr. Drane's that evening; and as the snow continued falling all night, in the morning it was nearly knee-deep, but the weather was soft and thawing. While breakfast was being prepared, I went out to try my luck once more; and traveled until I thought it was time to return, as Riley and I had agreed to go home that day. Coming to a road that led to the house, I took it, and was walking lightly along, when on my left I discovered a large buck quite near me, and lying down. Pointing my gun at him, I shot him dead in his bed; when, as the gun cracked, up jumped a fine doe, which bounded off a few steps, and then stopped. I put in a load as quickly as possible, shot her dead, and went in to breakfast.

Thus, in less than two days (for we left my house after dinner, lodged at Drane's the same evening, hunted during the following day, and on the third morning until breakfast time), we killed twelve deer, all full grown except one, which was a fawn. Riley has informed me, that, after that hunt with me, he killed many a fine deer, and considered himself a hunter.

After Riley (who lived twelve miles from me) had gone home, I went out to the woods with two horses and a boy, and gathered all the venison, which made a good sled-load for two horses.

But I have passed over one hunt, which I will here relate. It took place during the fore part of the same fall that Riley and I had our hunt. On the morning when the first snow fell that season, I rose early, intending to hunt on the west side of the Great Yough river. I went to the river, which, being pretty well up, the water reached about half-way up my thigh. I took off my pants and moccasins, waded over, and after again putting on my clothes, I felt first-rate. I had gone but a short distance, when I discovered the tracks of a very large buck, which had gone into a thicket, as I thought, in search of company, it being then in their mating season. As I concluded that he would not stop until he found what he was seeking, I did not think it worthwhile to follow him; so I passed on, and hunted until toward the close of the day, when, finding the tracks of a large bear, I followed them to a thick laurel swamp. It being very cold, and everything being frozen hard, I knew that he would not feed until the weather moderated; at which time I promised myself to meet him on the same ground, if he should think proper to come out.

With this on my mind, I left the feeding ground, and directed my course for home, until I came to the buck's track which I had seen on my way out. From what I had seen of the movements of the deer during the day, I knew that he was still in that thicket; of which I took advantage, as he could not run any other way than through the river, or out by me. I went on toward the spot where I thought he lay, when directly out he camo, within the range of my rifle. But as I saw I would have to fire at him while on the run, for he was badly frightened, I let him come as near as he would, when, as he was dashing on, I shot at him. He kept on for some distance, but at length stopped. As soon as I fired, I ran after him with all speed; and when he stopped, I was still within gun-shot. Before I could load, however, lie went into a thicket; and in following his trail, I found, by the quantity of blood after him, that he was badly wounded.

I had a first-rate half-breed greyhound dog with me, which, finding that I was going home, had crossed the river; but when he heard the report of the gun, he returned to me. I sent him into the thicket, when out came the buck, with the dog close at his heels. They passed me like a streak of lightning, and down a steep hill into the river, making such jumps as were really astonishing. When I reached the edge of the water, I could see neither dog nor deer; but, looking down the stream, I discovered them fighting with great desperation. The river was so deep that they could get no foothold, and they had floated down until they came to a ripple, at the head of a fall of at least ten feet. Immediately below where the dog and the deer were fighting, there was a hole in the river, about twenty feet deep, out of which it would be almost impossible to get the buck, if he once got into it; so I concluded to leave my gun on shore, wade in, and kill him with ray knife. I set my gun against a tree, and waded in — the water in some places being up to my belt, and in other places about half-thigh deep. On I went until I came within reach of the buck, which I seized by one of his horns; but as soon as I took hold, the dog let go, and struck out for the shore, when the buck made a main lunge at me. I then caught him by the other horn, though he very nearly threw me backwards into the river; but I held on to him, as I was afraid of our both being carried into the deep hole by the swift current. I dared not let him go; for if I did, I knew he would dart at me with his horns. I must kill him, or he would in all probability kill me; but whenever I let go with one hand, for the purpose of using my knife, he was ready to pitch at me. I called and called the dog, but he sat on the shore looking on, without attempting to move.

After awhile, it occurred to me to throw him under the water, and drown

FIGHT WITH A BUCK IN YOUGH. RIVER.

him; whereupon I braced my right leg against his left side, and with my arms jerked him suddenly, when down he came with his feet toward me. Then it was that my whole front paid for it, as his feet flew like drum-sticks, scraping my body and barking my shins, till ambition had to give in to necessity, and I was not only compelled to let him up, but even glad to help him to his feet again, though I still held on to his rough horns. From the long scuffle, my hands beginning to smart, and my arms to become weak, I took another plan.

I threw him again, and as he fell I twisted him around by his horns, so as to place his back toward me and his feet from me. Then came a desperate trial, for as this was the only hope I had of overcoming him, I laid all my strength and weight on him, to keep him from getting upon his feet again. This I found I could do, for the water was so deep that he had no chance of helping him-self, for want of a foothold. There we had it round and round, and in the struggle my left foot was accidentally placed on his lowermost horn, which was deep down in the water.

As soon as I felt my foot touch his horn, I threw my whole weight on it, and put his head under the water, deeper than I could reach with my arm. I thought that was the very thing I wanted; but then came the hardest part of the fight, for the buck exerted all his strength and activity against me, while I was in a situation from which I dare not attempt to retreat.

I was determined to keep his head under, although sometimes even my head and face were beneath the water; and if I had not been supported by his horns, which kept me from sinking down, and enabled me to stand firmer than if I had no support, that stream might have been called, with great truth, "the troubled water;" for I know that if it was not troubled, I was, for often I wished myself out of it. I know that the buck would have had no objection to my being out; though he probably thought that, as I had come in to help that savage dog, he would give me a punch or two with his sharp points, to remember him by. Indeed, that was what I most dreaded; and it was my full purpose to keep clear of them, if possible.

In about two minutes after I got my foot on his horn, and sank his head under water, things began to look a little more favorable; for I felt, his strength failing, which gave me hopes of getting through the worst fight I had ever been engaged in during all my hunting expeditions.

When his strength was but little. I held fast to his upper horn with my left hand, and keeping my foot firmly on his lower horn, I pressed it to the bottom of three feet water, and, taking out my knife, when his kicking was nearly over, I let his head come up high enough to be within reach, when at a single cut I laid open the one side of his neck, severing both blood-vessels. This relieved me from one of the most difficult positions in which during all my life, I bad been placed for the same length of time,

Chapter Ten

A SHORT time after the hunt detailed at the conclusion of the preceding chapter, a friend, named Daniel McHenry, living eight miles distant, sent for me to come to his house and join in a hunt with him; at the same time sending me some of Dupout's rifle-powder.

As my wife had some business in that direction, we agreed to meet the following day at Mr. McHenry's, and return home together.

We traveled in company until our roads parted, when I went towards the hunting-ground on Meadow Mountain, and found where a bear had been feeding. I stopped, and, intending to watch for him, took my station on a fallen tree, about eight or ten feet from the ground, and there sat till after sundown; when, hearing a noise of something coming in the dry leaves, I rose to my feet and made ready for action.

At last I saw the head of a fine doe over a large fallen tree. The moment it raised its head it saw me; when, knowing that she would be off, I took good aim at her neck, fired, and down she fell.

Having loaded my gun with the Dupont powder, it was so much stronger than mine, that I was very nearly knocked off my high stand; but a tree close to my back saved me from being thrown flat on the ground.

I went to the deer, the neck of which was broken, and a fine one it was. I soon made a fire and had some of the ribs before the coals, which is the best way that venison was over cooked. After supper, I lay down by my deer to sleep; but a light shower of rain falling in the night, I became anxious for the return of day.

As soon as it was daylight, I glided into the woods, and with a light foot penetrated deeper and deeper into the forest, until my dog gave me notice that game was near; but I kept him going on against the wind until he took a stand and refused to move farther. I then examined the locality closely, when I discovered a very large bear on the other side of a fallen tree, and as near as I wished, though I could see nothing but the top of his back, which I thought I could break.

As the wind was unfair, and I was afraid he would be off, I aimed to break his back; but being very fat, the ball passed over his back-bone, doing him but little, if any, injury.

When I saw my game run away, I was angry with myself for not going up to the fallen tree, when, by putting the gun against his side, I would have had a sure shot. On examination, I found my ball had carried some of the fat against a tree on the opposite side, and I came to the conclusion that it was a lost shot.

"Well, old fellow," said I, "it is in your favor this time; but take care if you ever meet with me again; for you may not be so lucky if I have as fair a chance at you the next time; and only let me see one more of your tribe this day, and I will show him how things will go." So Baying, off I started in search of other game,

I trudged on until I came to a fair-looking place, when, stopping to take a careful view, I saw the paws of a bear which was climbing a tree; but, the body being on the off side of the tree, I could see nothing but the paws. I kept quiet, and in a little time down she came, ran off a few yards, and then halted to see where I was; when, as I was ready, I fired, and off she scampered. Her two young ones, which were at some distance, were frightened by the report of the gun, and followed after their mother. The old bear soon dropped, and, when dying, groaned so terribly, that one of the young ones, being fright-ened, came running directly toward me. In the meantime, I had rammed down another load, and the cub ran so near to me that I could almost reach it with the gun. When it saw me, it rose up on its hind -feet to see what I was; whereupon, I shot the entire load into its breast, and killed it so dead that it never kicked.

Then I ran quickly and put my dog on the tracks of the other little one, which, in a few minutes, he chased up a tree, when I shot that one also; not leaving one of the family alive.

I then cleaned the carcasses, hung them up as usual, and steered my course for the house in which old Dr. McHenry lived, where my Mary had appointed to meet me.

I got to Mr. McHenry's after dark, and all were pleased to see me come to hunt with the young gentleman from Baltimore. The conversation throughout the evening was lively; many questions were asked about the probable events of the next day's hunt, and at a late hour we all retired to rest.

Before day, a messenger was sent to inform me that the appointee" hour was approaching, so I rose at once. Ae there was snow fulling, I knew that the game would be hid in the laurels out of the storm; but the young Baltimorean would not agree to wait until it blew over; so we got ready, and started for the woods.

We hunted all day without any luck, and in the evening came to the place where I had stowed my three bears. My companion asked me if we could not make a lire and lie down alongside of the bears. I told him I could take him to his home that evening before dark; but he said he was tired, and would like to have some of the bear-meat roasted for his supper.

"Well," said I, "if you wish to stay here, I will make the night as pleasant for you as I can; but I am afraid you will repent your choice before you see daylight again."

Notwithstanding, he decided to remain.

After laying down our blankets and provision, I scraped away the snow, collected enough wood to last during the night, laid spruce limbs thick on the ground, spread one blanket over them, and reserved the other to cover ourselves. This matter arranged, we roasted some of the young bear-meat, seasoned it well with salt and pepper, and then ate it for our supper.

The young man ate and joked, and was as good company as if he had been with me a lifetime. Whenever I asked him if he suffered, he would answer with a laugh, and say, "You need not trouble yourself about me; I am comfortable, and am looking for daylight to return, in order that I may kill a buck." Then he would commence joking again; and I never had a finer fellow with me in the woods than he was.

At last the sun rose; and, after making another meal on roasted bear-meat, we started off to hunt deer; for the day was too cold for bears to come out of the laurel.

We continued our hunt until the afternoon before we found any game. At last, seeing a herd of deer feeding, I crept within shooting distance, though at long range, and fired; when, instead of the rest standing until my young friend had a chance to try his skill, they all cleared cut.

We then took the track of the wounded buck, and soon discovered him, lying down. I took my friend up within a short distance, and told him to take good aim, when he shot at the deer's head, and killed him nicely. He was much pleased with his shot, but killed no more game that day.

On going home, he received business letters from Baltimore, which prevented us from hunting together any more that fall, and, indeed, for ever; for he never returned, as he was thrown from his horse, and died in a short time. If he had lived to come back to Allegany, he would have been a good hunter and an excellent neighbor. I considered him a highly honorable young man.

A short time after this, my second son, John Lynn, said to me, "If I had any one to accompany me, I would go to the head of the North Branch of the Potomac," (which was the greatest wilderness we were acquainted with,) "and seek some place which no hunter has ever yet trod."

I told him that I would go with him, though, as everybody called me "old man," it was thought that I was failing in strength and activity.

"Well," said he, "if you were able to walk with me, I would want no better fun than to travel through that wilderness; but, father, you cannot bear up to travel with me on so long a trip."

"Very well, John," I replied; "if I undertake it, and give out, you'll be glad to stop also, I can assure you; for I do not think I have a son who is yet able to tire me in the woods. So don't be afraid of your daddy being tired out. by a green boy."

"Well," said he, "it's all right; if you think you can go through with it, we will make the trial."

So we appointed a day to start on our trip; and when the time arrived, we took with us a horse, to carry our provisions as far as we would have a road to travel on. When we came to the outskirts of the settlement, we there left our horse, and entered the wilderness.

We traveled until evening, when we found ourselves in Virginia, far beyond our knowledge; but we also discovered fine hunting-ground along the river, on either side. Finding that the farther we went the less game was to be seen, we agreed to go back to the river, and accordingly turned our faces again in that direction.

Our purpose being not to kill game, but to find where it was, so that we might return and settle on a place to hunt for a month, we selected the locality along the river. As soon as we came to that conclusion, we began to look around for a deer, on which to make our supper; and at last we saw four; but they ran until they got almost out of sight. At length one stopped within range, which I shot, breaking its thigh; and night being near, we started our dog off to catch it. But it got into the river, and baffled him until it was so dark that we could not see to follow it.

We then built a fire in the thick laurel, and remained there till morning. During the night the dog returned to us, when we saw that he had killed the deer; but we were determined to lie there all night. We had a poor time of it; the ground being muddy, and the laurel so thick that we could not procure wood to keep us warm.

Morning came at last, and we were glad of it. After we had eaten a dry breakfast, we started the dog forward to show us where the deer was; and after traveling a mile or two, we found her; but she was an old doe, that had raised fawns, and was poor. We took only the skin and the hams, leaving the balance for the bears. We carried the hams out of the laurel, and hung them high up on a tree, intending to leave them there until we returned again to hunt; after which, we roasted some of the most tender pieces, and made a tolerable meal.

We then started for home as soon as we could, and traveled until we arrived at the place where we had left the horse; and, stopping there that night, we made an early start again the next morning.

I stopped as I went out at the house of one of my daughters, who resided on the road, at a distance of seven miles from my home. She had a very interesting little boy, who, when he heard I was going after bears, made me promise to stop as I returned, and tell him about my hunt.

As I drew near the place, I turned in to see the little fellow; when, behold, as I came in sight, there lay the house, which was one of the best in the neighborhood, now a pile of ruins, with the fire still burning, and bones white as chalk scattered around.

My feelings I cannot describe. There stood a table, with an article or two on it, which, together with several fine fat hogs in a pen, were the only living things to be seen.

I called again and again, until I heard an answer, and the eldest son made his appearance, to feed the hogs. He related to me the circumstances of the heart-rending occurrence, in substance as follows:

The workmen, having just finished the floor, with all pertaining to the house, had gone, and the family then seated themselves round a large fire. the small children played around on the new floor until all went to bed; and the whole family, old and young, had fallen into a profound sleep, when two of the oldest children, being awakened by the suffocating smoke, that came in at the door, which had been left open when they went to bed, saw the flames in the under part of the house.

The eldest child ran down stairs to rouse her father and mother; and as soon as she had done so, she returned upstairs again, to bring down two smaller ones. She entered the smoky room, and awakened her brother, who was smaller than herself, when each took a child in their arms, and ran for the door; but the flames met them there, and they could not get down. They then sought to extricate themselves by jumping out of the window; but the room was so full of smoke that they could not find it.

By this time they were suffocated with the hot smoke, and gave up; and as they then found that the two little ones were strangling, and nearly dead, they laid them on the bed. As the daughter turned from them, she saw, through the thick smoke, a spot which looked light; and, as a last effort, she ran to see what it was; when, finding the window, she called to her brother, and they both threw themselves out and escaped unhurt. All was bustle and dismay, the nearly distracted parents running helplessly round the burning building.

At length the roof fell in, the floor began to yield, and soon descended, carrying with it the two infants into the scorching flames. Oh! what a sight was that for a mother I and no means of relief at hand The ground was covered with snow, and all were without other clothes than those they had slept in. This was the most melancholy sight I ever met with during my life.

But to return to my story. At a suitable time I went home, and John L., and James, my third son, prepared for the hunt. We loaded one horse with provisions, and two others with other articles, such as an axe, a pot, a small griddle, potatoes, apples, etc.: when, all being ready to take up the line of march, after breakfast we set out for the Potomac.

We had traveled but a few miles, when rain commenced falling slowly, and continued all day. As we returned from the previous trip, we found a fine sugar-camp, at the foot of the Great Back-bone; and there we proposed to shelter ourselves that night. Late in the evening, we arrived at the camp, wet and tired; when the horses were unloaded, and a fire was made as soon as possible, for we were all cold, as well as wet. After feeding our horses, the boys proposed that we should eat our supper; but telling them that I would rather dry my clothes, and get warm before I ate, supper was put off for a short time, while we all placed ourselves so as to share the heat of the fire. After we became warm, we all fell into a sound sleep, which lasted until nearly day-light, when the hooting of an owl awakened me; and as I knew that day was near, I aroused the boys, who rose up quickly, and prepared for breakfast.

As it was too soon for me to breakfast, I fed the horses, in order to have them ready for two of the smaller boys to take home. Here John L., James, and myself, each packed up as much provision as we could carry over the mountain, as our horses could not accompany us any farther; so I postponed my breakfast, intending to eat it in the hunting ground, at another time.

After the horses were sent back, and our three loads tied up, including an axe, pot, griddle, and provision, we then took the provision which we could not carry with us, stowed it behind a log, and covered it over with puncheons, and cut pine and laurel bushes, which we strewed over the ground so thickly, that a passer-by could not discover that anything had ever been there. Then off we started for the hunting ground, and on the way saw different herds of deer; but being encumbered with our loads, we did not get a shot at them.

At last we discovered the saddle of venison which we had left when we were up before, and turned in to seek a situation for a camp, which took a couple of hours. Finding it clouding up, and threatening rain, I went to work in great haste to construct a shelter for our provision; and we worked with all our energy, until the boys said they were hungry, and would eat their dinner, camp or no camp. I then told them that I would go and look for a good tree, to split up into puncheons, and that they must come to me as soon as they could. I readily found a suitable tree, and felled it, when the lads coming to my assistance, we soon cut it up, split it into slabs, and commenced covering our cabin. The rain was then beginning to fall slowly, which was the time for the game to come from their hiding-places, and feed. We had our provision under cover, but there were three slabs yet lacking to complete the roof of our shelter. Though I had not eaten anything since the morning of the previous day, and night was near at hand, yet I determined not to eat until I had a little sport; so I took up my gun, and told the boys that I would go up the bottom, shoot a deer, and have a roast for my supper.

I had thrown off all my clothes, in order to be at full liberty to work, and had on only a thin linsey hunting shirt, together with a pair of new buckskin moccasins, without stockings; and in order that I should see my game more clearly, I left off my hat, as was always my practice when the sun did not shine. Thus accoutred, I started out, with the expectation of returning again within an hour or two, at farthest. Being keen for sport, I scarcely felt the ground under my feet; but poor sport it turned out to be in the end. I hunted with care and judgment, and presently my fine half-breed greyhound told me there was game near. I moved on until the dog took the tracks of a large herd of deer, which had so recently passed that I expected to see them every moment. I soon found that several old bucks were chasing a lot of small deer, and that the little ones were afraid of being overtaken by their pursuers. I increased my speed, to overtake them; but round and round they went, crossing my tracks twice or three times. By this time the rain had increased, until it began to run down my back plentifully, when I gave up the chase, and endeavored to return to the camp. Off I started at a fast walk, the rain still pouring down in torrents, and soon increased my speed to a running gait, looking for the camp all the time, but could see nothing of it. Still on I ran, until I thought that, in my hurry, I might have passed it, and was leaving it behind me. I then stood a moment to collect my thoughts, and shouted with all my strength, but received no answer. I turned back, and ran until I felt sure I had gone far enough, and shouted again at the top of my voice, but still could obtain no answer.

Then thinking the camp was behind me, after all, I turned again, but to no purpose. I now began to think seriously of laying out all night; and as it was then getting too dark to shoot, I deemed it prudent to begin to prepare a resting-place, while I could see to do so. I went in search of some place of shelter, but could find nothing better than a crooked old hemlock, which had been injured many years previously, and which the bears had gnawed so much, that there was a great quantity of rosin plastered over the whole side of the tree, which was much flattened by the injury it had received in years gone by. I chose that tree for my shelter, and set about building a fire, but the rain put it out as soon as I made it. I tried it again and again, until I saw that it was useless to try it any more, though I had wood in plenty. I then pulled off my hunting-shirt, spread it over two limbs that jutted out from the tree, and thus made a little place where the rain could not fall on my fire, until it got fairly started. Then I took a dry limb from the tree, split it fine, and kept it under the shelter until I struck fire again; when, having a large bundle of the splinters which contained a quantity of pitch, the fire took hold, and in a minute or two I had a high blaze among my pile of dry logs. In a few minutes more, I had a fire which gave light for some distance through the thick piny grove, so that I could see to prepare for the night.

It so happened that, under my fire, and also where I wished to lie down, there was a low hollow in the ground; and the rain, which was still falling rapidly, was ankle-deep in it. I looked around for something that I might at least sit on, to lay over the water, and found a very large hemlock stump, that was rotten inside, but surrounded by a shell of sound wood on the outside. I tore off a piece, and finding it to be the very thing I wanted, I soon made a good floor, and had a large piece left. This I also made use of; for, as it was long, I propped it up with the hollow side toward the fire, in a slanting position, so that I could creep under it. The rain could not then fall on me, and as the fire threw its heat under my shelter, I would turn first one side and then the other toward the blaze, which was continually increasing, until I smoked like a coal-pit; and as I had pulled off all my clothes, wrung the water out, and put them on again, they dried very fast. I turned round and round, until my fire got so strong, from the quantity of large logs I had piled on, that I had to creep from under my hollow tree, let it down, sit on it, and lean my head and shoulders against the hemlock.

The rain having ceased to fall so fast, I rested against the tree, and fell asleep. Being tired, I slept soundly until it ceased to rain, and commenced snowing and freezing; when the cold becoming severe, and the fire having died away, I grew chilly, and, awakening, attempted to mend the lire, but found the hair on one side of my head sticking fast to the tree.

At first, my temper being pretty well tried, and my patience (with which I was never overstocked) having failed me, I was as mad as a bear shot through the belly, and bawled out, as if twenty persons had been looking on:

"What other curse from --- is on me now?" I made the second trial to rise from my place. There I was, like Absalom in the oak, fast by my locks. I soon calmed my temper, and putting my hand up to find what held me, I discovered my hair fast in the pitch that had been heated by the fire. I had laid my head in it while it was soft and running, and had slept until the cold had chilled the pitch, with my hair sunk deep into it; and there I was, safe aa a mouse in a mill.

But when I discovered what was the cause of my confinement, I laughed to myself at the thought of the strange kind of fix I had got myself into. I then began to try to release my head, but not one lock would come out, except by pulling off the pitch, or pulling the hair out of my scalp; so I took sometimes the one and sometimes the other plan, as it happened, until at last I got my liberty. I then mended my fire, being still half-angry; though I could not help laughing to myself, when I thought that, if I could only see a fellow with his head fast to a tree, like a breachy dog which had been tied there for bad behavior, what fun it would be for me to help him out of such a scrape!

After I had gained my liberty, and the fire burned up lively, I reasoned thus: "What in the world is the use of my punishing myself thus? Now, I have not eaten one mouthful since the day before yesterday, and it was nothing but a foolish desire for sport that brought me here. This is certainly great sport, to have my head stuck fast to a tree; and, as like as not, I will have to cut all my hair off; for if I cut one-half off to get clear of the cursed pitch, the other half will have to come off also, or I may be mistaken for a convict escaped from the Penitentiary. However, this is all fudge. But what about eating? I am now in need of something to eat; for as soon as the fun fever leaves, which I think is fast going, I shall be weak, and perhaps sick into the bargain; and then God only knows when I shall find the camp again. Well, the first thing to be done is to kill a deer, and get something to eat. I have half a pound of powder in my horn, fifty balls in my pouch, and some salt; and I must have a deer soon. If I get one nearby, I will return here, to save making a fire in the snow."

At last the daylight appeared, when everything being covered and bent down with snow, I hunted for bushes that had leaves on, which I dried over the fire, and, putting some in my moccasins, I put my feet in on the leaves, crammed in leaves around them until I could get no more in, then tied them up, and was ready for the snow,

I started out from my warm fire into the snow, taking a course that I thought would bring me to some high ground, in order that I might form some idea of where I was. I soon scared up four deer, but did not see them until they ran off. Moving on, I saw a deer standing looking at me, and though it was a long shot and a bad chance, I cracked away at him. The snow was falling so fast, that it was difficult to see anything at any distance; and as I could not discover the deer after my gun was discharged, I went to examine what damage had been done. It seemed as if there had been twenty deer there, all running and fighting; for there was blood after several of the bucks, and so much hair torn off, that I could not arrive at any certain conclusion.

They all went off together, and as the fun fever began to rise high, I started off in a long trot after them, and had gone but a short distance, when my dog wheeled suddenly to my left, which told me that one was within shooting distance. I viewed the ground, and found that it must be behind a very large fallen tree; but to see it was impossible. I looked around for a means of raising myself up high enough to see over the log, when I discovered a tree which had fallen into the fork of another, and was considerably elevated. I went to it, and crawled up it side-ways, until I saw the horns of an old buck.

"Well, my fellow," said I, "you are my meat, or I am no judge of shooting."

Still, though I did not see his head, I could see very near to it; and I thought that if the snow was off the log his head would be a fair mark. So I guessed at his position, shot at him through the snow, and down fell the horns. I leaped off the tree like a panther, and with one jump was on him, cut his throat in the crack of a thumb, and commenced skinning him. If ever I skinned a deer quickly, then was the time; for the sight of all those deer in one gang had set my pulse up so high for sport, that I thought every minute was an hour; as I was sure that, if I could only overtake them in good ground, I could kill half a dozen of them before night.

The buck skinned, I cut off one whole side of the ribs, tied the meat up in the skin, and started off on the trail of the others.

I had not gone more than half a mile, when, hearing a halloo, I turned round and saw my two sons, who had heard me shoot, and, finding my tracks in the snow, were in full chase to overtake me. I could not prevail on them to follow my big gang of deer, as they were afraid I would faint with hunger; but I knew that I could have gone on until dark if I had once got a shot at those deer. They turned me toward the camp; and, as we passed by the place where I had killed the buck, we took his carcass with us. John Lynn baked buckwheat cakes, besides stewing a fat hen-turkey, with potatoes and turnips; and I really thought that was the best meal I ever tasted in all my life.

We had commenced this hunt too late, for the deer and bear were leaving those woods, which they always do as soon as winter commences, for the country is cold and damp. As soon as the game find cold weather setting in, they travel to some more agreeable climate for winter quarters. Being too late, and seeing that such was the case, we closed the hunt with the slaughter of five deer, and returned home.

To such as are not accustomed to a wilderness life, this fast of three days may seem to want some explanation; and in reference to it, I will only say that a man will live a long time under the stimulus of a high fever; and I know of no higher fever than that which may be excited by the prospect of a bear-fight, or of securing half a dozen fine fat bucks.

Sometime in September or October, I went to the "Blooming Rose" on business, and called at the house of Mr. Enlow, who, as I have before stated, married my wife's sister. I staid with him all night; during which time he told me that, a few days before, he had seen a place where bears had been feeding on chestnuts, and we agreed to give them a chase.

Accordingly, we made an early start next morning; but, on reaching the feeding-ground, we found we were too late, as the bears had already left it. We sent off the dogs after their trail, but by some means they became separated; and hearing one barking, we went to him, and found he had a small bear up a tree. We shot it, and hung it up, when the other dog returned to us, and we set out in search of deer.

We had hunted but a short time, when, seeing a fine buck feeding, Enlow agreed to keep the dogs quiet, and leave me to kill him. Before I approached near enough to shoot — for he was then moving off — I lost sight of him. Going to the spot where I had last seen him, I found that he had passed down through a narrow opening between two large rocks, and was then below the high ledge. I crept softly to the top of the ledge and looked down the hill, but could not see the buck, when, accidentally turning my eyes toward the base of the rock, there he stood, gazing up at me, and not more than twenty feet below the position I occupied; where he stood until I sent a ball through his back, when down he fell.

Enlow and the dogs at once came running to my assistance. My dog ran to the place where I still stood on the high cliff; and as soon as he saw the buck struggling at the foot of the rock, he jumped down, but in his fall lodged in the fork of a tall, slim sapling, and there stuck fast enough. He kicked and bawled to no purpose, and the longer he struggled the tighter he was pressed into the fork, until at last it split, and he dropped on the ground. Though he had fallen some eight or ten feet before he struck the fork, he was not in the least injured.

We skinned our buck, and, having split him, each took half; after which we set out for our respective homes. Having about four miles to go, and the river to cross, I traveled by short marches, until at length I came to the river, which, being high and muddy, looked dangerous. I sat down, and considered what I had better do. I must either wade through the river at this place, or travel a mile and a half, over a steep, rough road, to a canoe. As my load was heavy, and I was already tired, and as the worst that could occur in wading across at that point would be the loss of my gun and the venison, the first of which I could certainly find after the water fell, I determined to wade through.

I procured a strong cane, grasped the two legs of the deer with ray left hand, while the meat rested on the back of my neck, and, holding the legs with a tight grip before my face, I put my gun over the left shoulder, and struck out into the sweeping current.

I waded on until it began to come up to ray arm-pits; when, finding that all ray powder would be spoiled, I attempted to turn back, but could not; for when I raised my cane, and attempted to turn my body around, the swift current took me off my feet. Being convinced that my safety depended on proceeding, I kept on until the water ran nearly up to my shoulders; but, by taking very slow and careful steps, I waded between two and three hundred feet of that deep river, saving all that I carried except half a pound of powder, and got home unharmed.

I have no recollection of the events of the following autumn until about its close, when I was hunting at the Cherry-Tree Meadows. There fell a smart snow, and the weather had become cold and stormy, when I set out one morning before breakfast for a short hunt; and, knowing all the places where the deer would be hid from the pelting storm, that had been raging all the previous night, with a high gale, which was still blowing, I proceeded to one locality, and there discovered a trail, which took the direction of another good position.

I shifted my course, so as to bring the wind in my face; but on arriving at the place, I found the same trail had passed ther3 also, and proceeded on to still another good place. I again changed my direction, went round, and, with the wind once more in my favor, I went to the last place, and found the same trail had been there also A close examination in the deep, dry snow, now revealed the fact that it was not the trail of a big buck, as I had supposed, but that of a panther, which had been hunting on its own account; and I found that it understood how to find a deer as well as I did.

After discovering that it was a panther, I followed the track, to see where the animal took shelter, and traced it into a very large laurel-swamp. As my dog was keen for the chase, I let him off, when he dashed into the thicket, and in a few minutes I heard him fighting; then he started off in full cry, but presently stopped, and commenced barking.

Creeping through the brush, which was covered all over with snow, I came in sight of her ladyship, sitting in a tree. I took good aim at her head, fired, and tumbled her off her perch. I was so cold that I had a mind to leave her until I could return in more moderate weather; but on second consideration, I went to work, tore off the skin, cut off the head, and ran toward the house as fast as I could.

I had no more balls; but on taking off the scalp of the panther, I found in its head the ball which had caused its death, beat it into a round form, and put it into my gun again.

As I proceeded on my way home, I found a very large buck, lying down; and creeping up very near, I shot him, and the ball lodged as before. I found it a second time, again beat it round, put it in my gun once more, and, finding another deer between there and home, I was very near getting a close shot; and if it had laid still half a minute longer, I would have killed it with the same ball with which I had killed the panther and the buck. I was nearly frozen when I got to the fire.

Chapter Eleven

At that time, I had a steel-trap set for wolves, near the residence of a man named Little. He was a good man, and I sometimes lodged with him, as he lived in the lower part of the hunting-ground. After the snow before spoken of had melted off, I rose early, and went to Mr. Little's to attend to my trap.

I was walking fast along a road, when I saw an animal come into it and run along a considerable distance; but I could not tell whether it was a wolf or a panther. A little snow had fallen in the night, but not enough for me to tell by the tracks which of those beasts it was. As I was watching closely, I caught sight of the animal, standing by the side of the road, quite near me; and when he broke off into the thick laurel, I saw it was a small panther.

I went to my trap, and finding nothing in it, I returned I kept thinking about the panther; so when I came to where I first saw him, I turned aside, to try and find out what had been his business in that place. After searching round, I discovered that there had been two or three of them together, and that they had killed a large buck, of which they had eaten nearly half.

I went forthwith for ray steel-trap, brought it to the spot, made the buck fast to a tree, set my trap, and told Mr. Little to see to it. This occurred on Friday; and after setting the trap, I went home.

Being anxious to know how it would fare with the panthers, I went out to Mr. Little's on Saturday evening, in order to be ready; but, there being three or four ladies there, I remained till after breakfast on Sunday morning; when I started out to examine the trap. I had with me a fine dog, which was at home when I saw the small panther, or the matter would have been settled the first day.

When I came to the trap, there sat one of the panthers, fastened in it by one foot.

The ladies had begged me, if there was one in the trap, to let him remain until I could return for them, as they wished to accompany me and see the sport. So I left him there, and returned for the ladies; whereupon, there was a great hunt for bonnets and cloaks.

Mrs. Little told them that if they went out with me they might get a sight of the trap, but she expected that would be about all they would see; "For," said she, "he is forever playing tricks on some one or other, and I should be afraid to trust him."

But when I told them that I would not deceive them, they all, Mrs. Little included, accompanied me to see the fight.

When we arrived at the place, the panther was ready for a fight; but some of the ladies were afraid to come near enough to see the contest; though, on being assured that they should not be hurt, they ventured within a safe distance.

We slipped Mr. Little's two dogs at him, but tied mine back The panther, having one of his hind-feet in the trap, when the dogs sprang at him, boxed them with his sharp claws, seized, and bit them severely; whereupon the dogs would fly back; and whenever they advanced toward him, he hit them such terrible slaps with his paws that they began to be very careful how they approached. I suppose they had been fighting from a quarter to half an hour, when, as the dogs refused to risk their noses any more within reach of the panther's claws, we let out mine.

He made one spring on the panther, seized him by the neck, and holding on to him, kept him from biting; but the panther made the hair fly with his claws for a minute or two, and tore the dog very much with his nails. But at length the dog held his throat so tight that he began to grow weaker and weaker, until at last he surrendered, when the dog worried him to death.

The ladies became the friends of the panther when they saw him overpowered and unable to help himself any more, and their tender natures could not help but sympathize with the poor fellow in his forlorn condition. When he was dead, we took him to the house, and I staid all night to see if I could catch another; for I held them no good will, because they killed so many deer. That night, snow fell from four to six inches deep.

In the morning, when I saw such a beautiful snow on the ground, I told Mr. Little that I would try to find where the old panther had her residence; and after breakfast I took a scout around where the trap was set, for I was certain that the old one was in company with the young one when he got into the trap, and would come back to look for her cub again, I had not made more than half my circuit, when I found her track, where she had come out of a swamp, and was taking a straight course for the Savage river, which ran through a very mountainous country, covered with almost impenetrable thickets.

Traveling on with a light foot and a willing mind, I presently found a fine large doe, which she had killed, and sucked its blood. The body being still warm, I skinned it, took the track again, and followed it over the Meadow Mountain down to the Savage river, and on to the steep hills along its border, until at last I came to a very high, steep point; when, looking down to my left, in a little bottom, I saw that the snow over a large space was very bloody. I fixed my dint, in order that nothing should be wanting when the attack was made; and all being in prime order, bullets in my mouth and ramrod properly adjusted, I approached cautiously, and found another deer nearly eaten up, which had been killed before the snow fell — showing clearly that the old panther, when her young one got into the trap, becoming aware of danger, had taken her two remaining cubs down to that place, killed that deer for them to live on while she went in search of the lost one, and on her way back had killed the fine doe before mentioned.

When I came down to the bloody ground, they had that minute left their meat, and entered an almost impenetrable thicket. The dog was so keen that I pitied him, for I knew he loved sport just as well as I did; so telling him to try what he could do, off he went, when I began to be afraid that, if he caught one of the cubs, the old panther might make him, as Dr. Franklin says, "pay too dear for his whistle." Hearing the brush cracking, and expecting every moment to hear the dog yelp, I ran with all my speed to try to be in the fight; but away they went toward the top of the hill, over which the dog ran at full cry. I followed, and when I had gained the summit of the hill, I stood to see which course they would take next; but finding they had tacked, and were returning toward me, I remained quiet, and watched the panther running and dodging from one log to another, which gave the dog great trouble to keep the track. As they got on better ground, the dog gained fast on him; and as the panther was aware that the dog would soon be on him, he ran to a high tree, sprang up it, climbed to the top, and hid himself among the branches. Being concealed from both, I stood still, to see how the dog would find where the panther was. He came on at full speed, and passed the tree; but directly he turned back, took the track again, and came up to it a second time, when he reared up on his hind feet, smelled the tree, took his stand, and began to bark. I then shot the panther in the head, killing him instantly.

I called the dog off, and turning back into the thicket to hunt the other two, in a little time I heard him again running in full cry. I pursued them, and found by their tracks that he was pursuing the old one, which ran down a terribly steep hill toward the Savage river, and into a thicket of laurel, when the dog came to bay. I went to him, and found him looking up a tree; but there was nothing on it. I examined, and found the scratches of her nails where she had climbed the tree; but as she was not there, I concluded that she had jumped off the tree before the dog had come in sight, and ran off. I looked round to see in what direction she had gone, but could find no tracks in the snow. I then took a wider circle, and closed in; but still finding no track, I sat down on a log, and considered how it could be that she was gone, and no track left in the snow.

I reasoned with myself, that as she could not fly, she must have got on another tree; but there was no tree within her reach, though there were two large laurels standing in such a position that she could jump to them, and close by there were other laurels, so thick and strong that she might clamber on them. That was the last place I could see, on which she could go without coming to the ground. But on looking down the hill, I observed, about twenty feet below, a leaning birch, which was so crooked that the top came within ten or fifteen feet, while the middle of it was perhaps twenty feet, from the ground. It had been so long crooked, that two or three sprouts, about as thick as my thigh, had grown up on the main trunk; and between two of these limbs, or rather sprouts, there lay the panther lengthwise on the tree, with her long tail passed around one sprout, and crooked so as to lay on the trunk beyond the sprout next to her. I had passed directly under her, in circling round to find her tracks, and she was not more than fifteen or twenty feet over my head.

When I got my eyes on her, she was looking me in the face, and distant not more than five steps. I took a careful aim between her eyes, let her have the whole load in her brains, and down she dropped, without scarcely making a struggle. I skinned and scalped her as soon as possible, and returned to the thicket again, to look for the other young one; but it had hid so securely, that neither the dog nor myself could find it. As it was, I had killed three out of four of the family, and I went home satisfied with my success.

Having disposed of this family of panthers, I set my trap again for wolves; and in the course of a month or two, I again visited my friend Little, for the purpose of looking after my trap. He had an orphan boy living with him, who, having been out shooting pheasants, had found in the snow what he took to be a wolf's track, and told Mr. Little of it; but there was no notice taken of it, as it was a common thing to see the tracks of wolves. When I came over, the boy told me about the large track he had seen; so I went out to look at my trap, and when I came to the track, I found it was that of the largest description of panther. He had been gone two or three days, but as the weather was bad, and such as I knew would prevent him from travelling farther than he could find a shelter, I thought I would follow him, discover where he lodged, and in good weather I would watch his hiding-place, until he came out to hunt; then follow, catch him out of the swamp, and kill him.

TREEING AND SHOOTING A PANTHER.

I took his tracks, and was proceeding along rapidly, but as the dog all the time wanted to run before me, and I was afraid he would chase off the deer, I called him back two or three times; yet he was so anxious, that he would still get far ahead. At last, breaking from me, away he went. I got angry, and determined to give him a good whipping when he came back. As he began to bark, I supposed he had run an old buck too close, which, as they had not yet lost their horns, had turned to fight; and in that case the dog might get killed. I ran to see how things stood, when I found that the panther had killed a very large buck, and was lying by him eating him, when the dog winded him, put him to the best of his speed, and was barking at him. Hurrying after them, I soon came up, and found the panther standing on a limb of a pinetree; it then misting rain, and freezing as it fell. When I came up close, he looked at me so viciously, that I saw he had a mind to fight me; for he took no more notice of the dog, laid his ears back, bowed himself, and kept his tail wagging. As I understood his gestures too well to be mistaken, I left room enough between us to keep him from grappling with me — I suppose twenty steps — and then took my stand.

As my own gun had got out of order, I had borrowed my son's rifle, which had a percussion lock. He carried his caps in the box, in which there was a little pin, with one cap on it, to be handy in time of need. Having taken my stand, I levelled the rifle for a shot; but finding that the fore-sight was covered with ice, I wiped off the ice, and took aim again. As his head was turned down, looking at me, and in such a position that a ball fired between his eyes would pass directly to his brain, and seeing that he might become a bad customer, in case of any accident, I took a deliberate aim, and fired.

166

As the gun exploded, the panther sprang up the tree with the activity of a squirrel, and ran up to the top, where I could not see him for the numerous branches. Not knowing what the next moment might produce, I undertook to load quickly, when, on opening the box, out fell all the caps but the one on the pin. Then it was that good management was all important, and I thought if one more shot did not finish the fight, something serious might take place. I loaded carefully, placed the cap on right, so that it should not miss fire, and stepped off to a greater distance, so that I could see over the long limbs of the tree. At length I saw him lying in a fork of the tree, with his head covered by the limbs; but even if it had been a fair mark, I should have been afraid to shoot at it, having missed it before. His heart was my aim this time; and his position was such, that I had to direct my shot between the point of the shoulder and the neck-bone, so that the ball should pass to the heart without coming in contact with the large bones of the shoulder. Seeing my course clear, I took a good aim at my mark, and fired again, when he fell some fifteen or twenty feet, but caught hold of another limb with his sound fore-paw; for his left shoulder was broken by my last shot, after all ray caution in endeavoring to avoid those strong bones. There he hung to the limb, from which I expected every moment to see him fall; while I was unprovided with any means of discharging my rifle, and had no tomahawk, nor any weapon larger than a common pocket-knife.

He made many efforts to get on the limb, but could not accomplish his object, until at last he took hold with his hind foot, and commenced swinging himself sideways, when by a desperate effort he threw himself fairly on the limb. Finding himself upon it, he attempted to walk to the trunk of the tree, and not thinking of his lame leg, he went to bear his weight on it, when he again fell a distance of some ten or fifteen feet; but being well out from' the body of the tree, he caught on another limb, and tried the same plan to get on it. Being so far from the trunk of the tree, the limb bent under his weight, baffling every attempt he made, and at length, being brittle with the frost, it suddenly broke near the trunk, and down came the panther, holding fast to it, thus pulling it down top foremost, and with it stripping all the smaller limbs off.

The moment he touched the ground, the dog was on him, and then came what I had been so carefully trying to avoid. I ran to strike him with the gun; but knowing that it would be broken with the first stroke, and that I would have to pay for it, I threw it down, and set about hunting a club. I got hold of some that were too rotten, and others were so strong that I could not break them to a proper length. I was flying from place to place like a hen that had found a dog among her chickens, until at length I thought of the limb the panther had broken. I ran quickly, set my foot on it, and raised it up with all my strength, when it broke. I then snapped off the top, and having thus obtained a good weapon, I thought to steal up while the panther was busy with the dog, strike him on the hips and disable him, and keep at him until, somehow or other, I should get the mastery. I kept a tree between us, and drew near; but not being within striking distance, I made another step toward him, and struck as I stepped; but his quick eye catching the first glimpse of me as I came from behind the tree, he wheeled to catch me, and as he turned, the blow struck on his head, I aimed at his hips, but having turned himself entirely round it fell, by the greatest accident in the world, on his head, and brought him flat to the ground.

I stood perfectly astonished at the accident, thoughtlessly contemplating that strange as well as lucky circumstance, when I saw his eyes begin to snap, and he commenced to show signs of returning life. I took out my pocket-knife, and was going to stab him under the foreleg, at the point nearest his heart; but when I took hold of his leg to raise it, he snatched it from me with great power; and finding it no time to stay so near him, I flew from him as I would from a flame of fire.

When I looked back, the dog had caught him by the ear, and they seemed to be equally engaged. I again ran up with my club, and struck while they were both clinched. The dog was on the off side, and I struck so hard on the panther's head, that my club broke, when down went both the panther and the dog.

Finding that I had him down again, I was determined not to let him rise anymore; so I continued my blows until I found that he lay quiet, when I felt his head, and found it mashed soft. I saw my dog shaking his head, and finding that one eye was completely gone, I was much pained to know that the noble beast which had fought so bravely, should have experienced such a serious loss; and the more so, because I could not tell whether the panther had scratched it out with his claws, or I had inflicted the injury in striking the panther, when I knocked them both down. But no matter how or when it was done, he never uttered so much as a whine. In this fight, I think there was nearly a quarter of an acre of ground torn up, and the blood from the panther and the dog reddened the snow to such an extent, that it looked as if someone had been killing hogs. My poor dog spattered the road with his blood all the way home. This panther measured nine feet ten inches from the end of his nose to the tip of his tail.

Having had but two more panther hunts, I will relate them in this place. I had a friend named James Fitzwater, who resided on a fine hunting ground, convenient to the Glades, as also to the Meadow Mountain and the Savage hills. He was a kind, benevolent man, and his wife was also a kind woman. As I had often been invited to hunt with him, one of my sons went with me to Mr. Fitzwater's, to stay a week; and such was the good-will among the hunters, that they would not take any pay from each other, unless it would be in the way of a present, such as a sack of apples, or other small articles. We killed several deer; and on Saturday evening my son told me that he had wounded a fine doe, but had left her, and that he knew she would die, as several pieces of bone had fallen from her wound. As he was going home the next day, he told me that if I would go and catch her, I should have her; and it would save the deer much pain, as well as from dying by starvation.

So I concluded to go after the doe on Sunday morning Mr. and Mrs. Fitzwater were very strict Methodists, and of course could not make any allowance for breaking the Sabbath; but when I pointed out the misery and starving condition of the poor deer, and alleged that it would be a deed of mercy to put the creature out of its misery, the lady became reconciled, and off I started on my errand. I found the track where the young man had left it, and followed it but a short distance, when the tracks of a panther came in before me, and I found that he had pursued the deer until he had scared her up twice, after which he left her.

I kept his tracks instead of the doe's, and followed him with long, quick steps. When I came to level ground I trotted, uphill I walked fast, and downhill I ran with speed; and so I continued to travel from one place to another. The panther was hunting, and had jumped three times at deer, but had missed each time. I followed him quite up to the Yough. Glades, through many crooks and turns; and late in the afternoon he entered the State road, and followed it a mile or so; then left it, and commenced hunting again. Still, I pertinaciously pursued on his tracks; for I was bent on having his scalp, if I had to follow him next day also.

The chase continued until late in the evening, when I found a large buck which had been killed within two rods of the public road, where no one suspected a panther would dare come. The buck was covered over with snow and trash, and when I pulled him out he was quite warm. I let his carcass lay, and followed the panther's tracks with increased courage; for I was certain he could not escape me, I let slip the dog, and in a few minutes I heard him running at full cry toward a large glade. I ran until I had a full view of the glade, in hopes of seeing the dog catch the panther there, where all would have a fair chance to fight; but at the time when I expected to see him enter the open glade, all being again quiet, I concluded that the dog had lost him.

I stood listening, to hear when the dog would raise him again, and in a little while he opened behind me. I faced about, and found that the panther had tacked, and ran back to the place where he had killed the buck, as they often do, to dodge their pursuers; but his stratagem failed him, as the dog, taking no notice of the dead buck, pushed on after him at great speed. Finding the dog still after him, he then entered the public road, and ran along it until he came to Mr. Calmes's fence, when he jumped on it, and ran along it until, having gone a sufficient distance to tack, he turned back on the fence, ran about half way toward the place where he first got on it, when he sprang on a tree, and hid himself in a fork of the limbs. The dog in his hurry leaped the fence, and ran on, until, being unable to find the trail, he stopped. I was then in sight, and though I had a full view of the dog, yet I could see nothing of the panther. I became angry at him for losing the panther, as it was near night, and I began to fear he had dodged, and would escape me, after all my trouble.

I stood in the road, and watched the dog trying to find the trail. At last he turned to come back, and as he did so, I saw him throw his nose up in the air, and begin to wag his tail. I then knew that he winded the panther; and as he raised himself so high up to smell, I was also assured that my game was on a tree; so I began to look around among the trees, of which I could see all that were possibly within his reach. Still continuing in the same place, I again saw the dog rear up to smell, and wag his tail, as before; which making me still more certain, I looked at every tree, as I advanced nearer and nearer, and on the tree nearest the fence, within fifty feet of me, there sat the gentleman in a fork of the limbs, secreting himself behind a part of the tree, and peeping round at me. I remained quiet, to see if the dog would, find him; for I had not with me the dog which lost his eye in the last panther fight at Mr. Little's, but a young, unpractised, though very willing animal. The young dog could not find the panther, because the wind passed too high up above his head; when, seeing that he was becoming confused, I raised my gun, and sent the death-messenger through the panther's brains, as he was peeping round the tree at me.

As it was then getting dark, and I was nearly two miles from Mr. Calmes's farm, I at once set about skinning the panther. I cut off his head, which I intended to take before a justice of the peace, as an evidence that I had killed the panther within the limits of the county, and then draw on the county treasury for my premium. This was the prescribed legal mode for securing the premium allowed for the heads of wolves and panthers.

I did not finish my task until after dark, when I left his carcass lying in the road, and set out for Mr. Calmes's house. Mr. C. was well advanced in years, and had also become so corpulent that he could not hunt any more, but had been a good hunter in his time, and, like myself at present, was very fond of talking about what had been done in bygone days. I walked fast, and, although I had been traveling all day, from early breakfast until an hour after dark, and fully half that time on a run, yet I felt neither weakness nor fatigue. When I reached the gate, a negro boy ran into the house, and told his master that Mr. Browning was coming; and by the time I got into the house, he was up, had drawn on his pants, and, with every sign of satisfaction, was entering the room to meet me. He untied the skin, took out the head, and examined the great teeth, saying: "Them cursed teeth have been the death of many a fine deer, that might have been yet alive in the woods." Then he requested me to give him the details of my hunt. I told him where I started the trail in the morning, and that, fearing I should not overtake the panther until night, on level ground I ran at a moderate gait, and downhill I ran fast. After hearing my description, as he was well acquainted with all the ground I had passed over, he said that I had traveled from thirty-five to forty miles, and I was then fifteen miles from home.

We talked until ten o'clock, when we retired to the same room, as his lady being in Cumberland, there was not a white person about the house but he and myself. We continued our conversation after we went to bed; and about twelve o'clock the mail-boy came along, blowing his horn, to notify the old gentleman to attend to his papers. The latter made a great bustle, and attended to his business, after which there was but little of the night left for sleep. However, we laid in bed in the morning until the cook called us up to breakfast; and after disposing of that meal, the panther's skin was again reviewed, and the many mischievous acts recounted which his tribe, and perhaps himself, had done within the old gentleman's knowledge, such as killing deer, hogs, cattle, and sheep, and on one occasion a man.

Mr. Calmes then related the following thrilling story. He said that when he was a young man, and the Indians were very troublesome, a party of young men started from Virginia to travel to Kentucky. In passing through the wilderness, from the many trails they had seen of the Indians in those parts, they were one night afraid to keep a fire burning, for fear the prowling savages might see the light, and attack them by surprise; so they only let their fire burn until their supper was cooked, then smothered it, and laid down in the dark. After awhile, some of the party hearing an animal moving near them, they all seized their guns and rose up, when, as it ran off, they found that it was either a wolf or a panther. After the excitement subsided, they all laid down again to sleep; and one person lying with his head exposed to the outside of the camp, either a panther or a wolf, they could not tell which, crept up stealthily, and bit him so severely about the head, that he died before day-break, without speaking a word. In the morning the rest of the party sharpened sticks, dug a hole in the ground, laid the corpse in, threw some bark over it, covered it with what dirt they could get, on which they piled old logs, to keep the animals off, and so left their poor comrade. Mr. Calmes said he had no doubt, if that devil had been hungry, and found a man in the woods by himself, he would have fallen on him and killed him.

He then said to me, "Browning, your hunting is really of great service to this country; for, if you come on one of these sneaking devils, you spare no pains to kill him; and there is no knowing how many cattle, sheep, and hogs you thus save to the inhabitants. I was going to tell you to be always prepared for them; but I know you understand them, and will take care of yourself. But, whatever you do, never let one of the devils escape if you can help it."

After breakfast, the old gentleman and myself had a long talk, and he asked me to stay and take dinner with him; but, knowing that Mr. and Mrs. Fitzwater would he uneasy about me, for they expected me home the preceding night, I made an apology, bade my friend goodbye, and returned to Mr. Fitzwater's. They were much alarmed at my absence, but concluded that I had gone home, as the weather had become unfavorable for hunting. Concluding to return home, I bade them farewell, and entered the woods, to hunt along the route, or part of the way, at any rate.

On reaching Meadow Mountain, I began to ascend it, and had traveled some distance up, when I saw the tracks of an animal in the snow. There had been some soft days, and the snow on the south side of the mountain was covered with a strong crust; but, as the north side had not been affected by the heat, the snow did not there freeze into a crust. I made a close examination, and found that the animal had come out of a hollow tree. His feet being muddy, I was able to follow him by the colored tracks until I traced him to a deer which a hunter had killed, and there lay a man's hat.

I then saw that it was a panther of the largest kind; and, thinking of Mr. Calmes's advice, I determined to kill him if possible. It had found the hunter's deer, with the hat hung by it, to keep the beasts and birds away; but his panthership cared not if hat, coat, and pantaloons had all been there; he was determined to have the venison; and accordingly he made free to use nearly all the best pieces before I came along.

I took the track, which led to a terrible laurel-swamp; and, as I knew I was near his quarters, I sent in my inexperienced dog, and followed him as fast as possible. Presently I heard the dog in full chase; but in a short time he ceased his yelping, and returned to me. I sent him back, knowing that the panther had taken to a tree.

Reuben started off again, and I heard him once more in full cry; but after a little while he became quiet, and came back to me. I sent him off the third time, and he was such a fool that he would go as often as I told him; but I understood the panther too well to be put off that way; as his plan was, when he found the dog coming, to jump high up into a tree, and the foolish dog was unable to find where he went. As soon as the dog left the place, the panther would leap off and run; but when the dog came back, he would again jump into a tree.

Knowing what he was at, I kept getting still nearer to him every time he treed. The last time I sent the dog in, he took to a tree again; but having changed his course, to keep himself in the thickest of the laurel, and as I kept a good look-out, I saw him standing on a limb, just preparing to jump off. I called to him, to stop him from leaping, and fired in haste at his breast, though at a long range; but, being determined to fire at all risks, I brought (he panther down.

By this time, my foolish dog having come back to see if I was safe, I sent him off again; when, hearing a great bustle, I loaded, and hurrying forward, discovered his panthership, backed under some thick laurels, and his head the only part of him to be seen. Before he got into that safe place, however, ray young dog had fought him courageously, and the blood lay about in abundance. After I came up, wishing to ascertain what kind of material Reuben was made of, I let him see me, and then he became almost frantic with ambition. He flew at the panther, and, though beaten off, sprang at him again and again, until that animal's strong, sharp claws had cut him severely; when, thinking it was a pity to let him be torn to pieces by such a vicious brute, I called him off, and found him much worse hurt than I had supposed.

The panther made a blow at the shoulder of the dog; but only one claw — which was the middle one, and, I suppose, the strongest on the foot — entered his flesh. When he found that he had hold of the dog, he crooked the toe inwards; but, as the dog pulled back, the panther's leg was drawn out to its full length. He would draw the dog almost up to his head, when the latter would pull back; and thus the contest continued, until I shot the panther in the head and relieved the dog.

That was the last panther I ever saw; and I believe there has been but one other ever seen since, or even the tracks of any, in all our wilderness. Subsequently, I had a hard chase after one, but was completely defeated. I pursued him one whole day in January, then laid in the woods during a very cold night, took his tracks next morning, and ran him the whole of that day, until dark; meanwhile, having not a mouthful of anything to eat myself, or with which to feed my dogs. I camped out the second night, being determined to give him another day's chase; but the night was cold, and I was obliged to scrape away the snow and sleep on the ground, if sleep it can be called; for in that kind of abed a man does not sleep at all, as he is so chilly that it is only a state of stupor, and not sleep.

In the morning, when I straightened out my limbs, I felt stiff and hungry, and my dogs looked gaunt, and seemed unwilling to rise up. What was worse, I did not know where I was; for I ran the day before regardless of where I went, and when night came I was completely bewildered. So I parleyed with myself, whether I would again follow the panther's track, or steer for home; which must be between fifteen and twenty miles distant. I felt a little weak, and found that the panther fever was fast abating; and I knew that if it left me altogether I should be hungry, and unable to hold out another day. Added to all that, snow began to fall fast, obscuring the tracks. So I decided to steer for Mr. Little's, as his residence was seven miles nearer than my own.

I guessed at my position, and after traveling about five miles, I found I was right, and in the direct course for Little's farm. I took a straight line, regardless of laurel or any other thing, and succeeded in reaching Little's about twelve o'clock; but there was no one at home. As the door was not locked, I opened it, and found the house not only warm and comfortable, but in a cupboard a loaf of good bread, with crocks of sweet milk and butter; and sitting down, I made a good dinner.

The heat of the room, and my dinner, made me so sleepy that I was tempted to go to bed; but feeling certain that Mary was anxiously waiting to hear what had become of me, for she knew I had gone on a panther-hunt, and was always uneasy when I staid out overnight on such occasions, and as my poor dogs looked very hungry, I kept on, though I had seven miles still to travel. But I persevered until I reached home, and never went on a panther-hunt afterwards.

The business of my farm and my mill occupied me until the following autumn, when Hugh McMullen asked me to go with him to the head of the Potomac to hunt bears.

After having plenty of biscuits and rolls baked, we started off, carrying our provisions in our blankets, as we had thirty-odd miles to travel. Our course lay up the west side of the Big Yough. River, which rises within two or three miles of the head of the Potomac, until we reached that fine tract of country called "The Land flowing with Milk and Honey."

This place was so well stocked with deer, that I wanted to stop there, as it was not more than eight or ten miles from home; but Hugh wishing to see the Potomac, we kept on.

Presently I saw a tremendous buck, "hunting," as it is called, when, in mating season, bucks travel a great part of their time in search of does. This big fellow was traveling on this business; and as the ground was hard frozen, with no wind to drown the noise of his tread, I could hear every step he made. When he walked, I would walk too; and when he stopped, I would stop also. By this means I kept getting nearer and nearer; and after a while, finding a bush full of dry leaves, he went to it, and rushed his great horns into it; making such a noise round his own ears, that I took advantage of it, and while be was pleasing himself by fighting the bush, I ran up as near to him as I wished, took my stand, and waited until he had done amusing himself, when he walked a few steps and made a full stop, with his side fairly exposed to me. Then it was that my heavily-loaded rifle belched forth fire and brimstone, sending a heavy ball through his heart, killing him so quickly that he had not time to see who had done it.

This being one of the best kind of bucks, we took out his entrails, secured the carcass from animals and birds, and, pursuing our journey, reached the State Road at Mr. Johnson's tavern. As he was a pleasant man, we staid all night with him, and the next morning continued our journey toward the Potomac, until we crossed the great Back-Bone Mountain.

As it had clouded up thickly, and the wind and snow were beating against the tall hemlocks with great fury, we thought best to stop and prepare for a night's lodging in the snow, which was then nearly knee-deep. We moved into the piny ground for shelter against the wind; and aa we entered, seeing a large doe rise up out of the snow to look what occasioned the noise she heard, I shot her dead. We agreed to stay there all night; and, having an axe, we cut a spreading spruce-pine, it falling parallel with an old log, but leaving room sufficient for us to lay between the two trees. We then cut limbs, with which we constructed a shed on the windy side, made a strong fire in front, cut more limbs, laid them on the snow, and trampled them down with our feet. In falling, the tree broke another, which was very dry, and also rotten. This rotten wood we beat fine with our axe, covered our spruce limbs entirely over with it, and then laid our blanket over the whole. After roasting as much venison as we could eat, we laid ourselves down, and slept warm and comfortably until morning.

I enjoyed the best night's rest I ever had, considering the appearances when we began to cut down the spruce tree; the rotten wood, being dry and dusty, kept the cold out, while the limbs under us, being elastic, made an excellent wilderness-bed.

When daylight came, we almost hated to rise from our couch, where we had all night been sheltered so nicely from the storm; and although the snow had ceased to fall, the wind still blew almost a hurricane. But we got out of our nest at last, and roasted some more venison, basting it well with butter; for, not being as fat as we liked it. butter made it very palatable.

After breakfast was over, and Hugh had taken a sober, serious look at the snow on the laurels, and on the limbs of the tall pines which were drooping down under their heavy burdens, he turned to me, and said, "I wish we were back at 'Milk and Honey.'"

"Well, Hugh," said I, "under all the circumstances, I really think the best thing we can do is to go back and hunt nearer home; and I believe there are more deer about 'Milk and Honey' than there are here."

Having agreed to turn back, we took the hams of our deer, and all the other pieces that would make steaks, roasted and ate all we could, gave our dog as much as he wanted, tied up the balance, bade farewell to Back-Bone, and set out for "Milk and Honey."

We traveled till afternoon, when our dog winded a deer. We followed him, and soon saw a fine buck feeding quietly in open ground. It was so cold that we could not take time to creep up to him, so we agreed to shoot from where we stood. I fired, and broke his shoulder, when off he started for Yough. River, with the dog after him; and presently, hearing them fighting, we ran to help the dog, and found him in the water with the buck. As we could not shoot from the shore, lest we might hit the dog, we both went in the water close to the deer, shot him, brought his carcass to the shore, skinned it, hung it up, and started off again for Mr. Johnson's.

By this time it was night, and desperately cold. Our feet being wet, and beginning to suffer, we increased our speed, thinking to warm ourselves by running. At length Hugh said his feet were freezing; when I told him to stand in a little branch of water until they were thawed, and I jumped in up to my ankles; but he would not. As we traveled on, my feet became limber, while his got harder and tighter in his moccasins.

We pushed on as fast as we could; I wading every little stream, and filling my moccasins with water, which checked the frost and saved my feet, while his were freezing. At last we came to Johnson's; and when we took off our things, his feet were so much frozen that his toes rattled on the floor. All was done for him that was possible; still, he could not walk a step next day, while I was not frozen at all.

Next morning, Hugh and Johnson's son mounted two horses and went for the buck, and I turned my face toward "Milk and Honey."

I traveled on, but it was so cold that I could not hunt any that day. On getting to ray camp, I found a fire still there, which other hunters had left. I built

175

it up again, and contented myself by it that night. The next day, being more moderate, I killed two good deer, and brought them into the camp.

Day after day I killed more or less, every hour expecting Hugh to join me; but he did not come at all. I still continued to bring in meat, and hang it on a pole; but one morning one of my best saddles of venison was gone, and I could not tell what had taken it.

There was a small creek close by, which was covered with ice sufficiently strong to bear a man, and all round the camp the snow was so trampled down that no track of the thief could be seen.

Having a steel-trap not far distant, I brought it, set it immediately, and again went off hunting. When I returned in the evening, I commenced cooking my supper, and had seated myself to eat, when I thought of my trap, and went to the place where I had set it; but it was pone.

"Well," said I, "I expect your foot is in it; and if that is so, your scalp will pay me for the venison you stole last night."

Discovering where the trap had been drawn along down the creek, I followed the track until I found my gentleman thief which proved to be a huge catamount — in proportion to its size, I believe, the most savage creature in the world. Oh! but he did want to get at myself or the dog. But, not thinking proper to let him tear the eyes out of ray dog, I shot him; and after that I lost no more meat from the camp,

I staid here eight days; and on the eighth day, early in the morning, having shot a doe, and wounded her badly, I set my dog after her, when she ran for the river. I lived about seven miles down the river; and the doe, taking a straight course towards my residence, ran to the stream within a quarter of a mile of ray house; where the dog killed her, and went home, whither I soon followed him.

In this hunt I killed thirteen deer, and safely secured them all at the camp.

After this, the attention which my farm and family required occupied all my time until the following spring, which is the season for trapping bears; and, as I had caught some three or four, I had left one trap set.

A young man by the name of Wable had been boarding at my house; and, as he was anxious to fish for trout, on Saturday, two of my sons, together with Wable and myself, started toward Muddy Creek to fish; and in our way, we had to pass near the trap which had been left set. When we came near, as I proposed to examine it, we all went together to the trap, and, to our great delight, found a good-sized bear in it.

All hands wanted to see some fun, and no one more than Mr. Wable. My one-eyed dog was with us, and lie also eagerly raised his voice for sport. I concluded that the bear was not worth much, and that if he should escape it would be but a small loss; so we all agreed to let him come out and fight for his life.

Wable was much pleased with this arrangement; and when all was ready, every one knew where to take his stand except him. I went to the back part of the trap, and took hold of the lever to raise it, when, the moment it was opened, in rushed the dog, and he and the bear came rolling out directly towards Wable; who was taken so unexpectedly that he had no time to think what to do; but, seizing a big laurel that had been burnt half off, and which was barely strong enough to hold him up off the ground, up it he went, and, after succeeding in getting out of reach of the bear, was just beginning to see the fight, as the dog and the bear both rose upon their hind-feet, and accidentally fell against the bush upon which Wable was perched; when down it came, and the dog, the bear, and the man were all mixed up together among the laurel. Such screams as Wable uttered I never before heard; and such a frightened bear I never saw. The dog, hearing the horrible sounds, let the bear out of his grip; when off the latter ran, at full speed.

I gazed on Wable until the bear entered the thick laurel, and got out of sight. The dog, in following his track, ran with such force that he struck the blind side of his head against a tree, and as he fell he turned a somerset. He attempted to run back; but, quickly discovering his error, he took the track, and scampered out of sight.

Wable, by this time, had become more quiet; but continued pouring out curses on the bear and the laurel-bush. He cursed the bear for being too strong, and for breaking the bush; he cursed the bush because it did not grow bigger; and he cursed the fire, which had burned the bush, and made it so weak that the --- bear was able to break it down. He examined the burnt place, and then put whole blame on the fire, which had deprived him of the opportunity of seeing so much fun.

"But," said he, this is the last time any man shall see me in such a --- scrape as this; and those who like this kind of fun may freely have it all to themselves; for I want no more of it."

By this time, we heard the dog fighting the bear, and ran at the top of our speed to assist him. I was the first one there, and found the dog on the bear's back, in deep water. The dog had a firm grip of his head, and had so strangled him that he held him easily. I killed the bear with my knife; but Wable kept at a safe distance till all was over.

Chapter Twelve

Having mentioned something about the trapping season, I will here state one circumstance, which took place during the same spring, on an occasion when, with two of my sons, I went to attend to my traps.

We had taken two bears, and, as we approached another trap, we saw two cubs climbing a tree. We went to the trap, and found an old she-bear and one cub in it. One of the boys shot one cub from the tree; but, as I would not have either of the other two cubs killed, one of the boys climbed the tree and threw off the one remaining on it, and we caught him as he fell toward the ground.

We were then going to turn the old one out, to have a fight; but I concluded to try and get the cub from her before we did so. The mother, finding we
were trying to take her cub away, determined to keep us from it; so she took
it and put it under one of her fore-legs, and tamed the other side of her body
toward us, in order to keep the cub from our view as much as possible; but.
ai the little fellow would peep out at us, when she found him getting too
much back or forward, and thought he was becoming exposed, she would
place him in such other position as she thought would keep him safe.

When I saw how careful she was of her cub, I felt sorry for her, and told
the boys that we ought to turn her out, and let the poor thing enjoy the company of her little family; and, in order to enlist their sympathies, I took a pole
and tried to separate her from her cub; but she would not suffer it to leave
her grasp. We punched her with our pole, to make her give up the cub; but
she patiently bore all our insults, and would not fight us at all; being content
to suffer anything in order to secure her cub from harm.

My feelings were so completely in her favor, that a considerable debate
took place; and in the argument urged against her, I was reminded of the
number of hogs, sheep, and cattle which had been destroyed by bears in the
neighborhood. I was also told that a bear was no more to be pitied than one
of our hogs or sheep, which I did not hesitate to kill when it was necessary or
convenient to do so; and that there was never a more convenient time for
killing a bear than when we had one in a trap.

When the speeches were finished, it was agreed to take the vote on the
question; when it was decided that, as there had been a hostile disposition as
well on one side as on the other, and as no compromise had ever been made,
and no surety given to secure us from renewed grievances, the defendant
should be shot till she was dead.

No sooner had we executed the sentence on the old mother, and let the
cubs loose, than they claimed us for their protectors; and when we ran from
them, which we could easily do, as they were not larger than a half-grown
cat, they followed after us, crying as loud as they could until we stopped and
waited for them to come up with us; then they would make a kind of purring
noise, rubbing round our legs, hunting some place to nestle in and lay down I
put them in the bosom of my hunting-shirt, and carried them to our camp,
where I laid all night with them in my bosom; and in the morning we set out
for home, with the carcasses of three grown bears and the two live cubs.

When we got home, we fed the cubs with new milk, and were at no trouble
to raise them, until one broke his chain and ran away, and I never heard of
him again. When the other was about a year old, my sons took him to Funks-
town, in Washington County, and sold him to a Mr. Peters, who was a good
rifleman. He kept Cuffee until he was two years old, when he put him up at
shooting matches, and won him several times himself, until he made forty
dollars off him; after which, poor Cuffee was butchered and divided among
the sportsmen.

After the sports of that spring were over, I was closely engaged with my farming and milling, until September, when the leaves began to turn yellow. My little Mary, who was then perhaps forty or forty-five years old, and still retained her beauty, vigor, and cheerfulness, although the mother of eleven children, told me that I must kill either a sheep or a deer, for we had no fresh meat.

"Well, Mary," said I, "a deer killed is a sheep saved, and I will try my hand; but I have been so long without practice, that, if I see a deer, I shall scarcely know which end of the gun to put foremost."

"Well," said she, "as you hunt, when you come to good places, keep saying to yourself, ' Little end foremost, little end foremost; ' and when you see a deer, think of 'little end foremost,' and all will come to you again."

After this pleasant joke, I took my gun, and started off with my dog to the woods. I had about eight or ten miles to travel, to a place where I knew deer were plenty — the woods on which had been burned in the spring, and the deer loves to feed on this burned ground. I trudged on until I came to the outskirts of the burned ground, when, seeing a small deer feeding, I said, "little end foremost," and creeping up as near as I wished to be, I shot at and killed it. I then discovered the tracks of a very large buck; but as my dog could not follow him, I was so anxious to see him that I undertook to follow him by myself, and succeeded in trailing him to a thicket. I took one course through the thicket, but could not find the buck, when I took another course, with like success; and I had started on a third round, when, scenting my tracks below him, he came galloping directly toward me. Close to me laid a large tree, up to which the buck came, and made a full stop; when, without thinking about little end or big end, I fired at the distance of eight steps, and laid him dead.

When I viewed him after he was killed, I really thought him the most beautiful creature with four legs that I had ever seen. I took care of his carcass, and, proceeding on my course, did not hunt far before I saw another deer crossing my track. I fired again, and shot a doe, which, having never raised any fawns, was fine and fat. I took care of her, and again started off; when, within half a mile of the last deer, observing another one feeding, I crept near to it, and fired again, with the same result as before. I hung up this one also, and started again; when, taking a path made by the herd cattle, aid which led to my camp, as I walked rapidly along (for it was almost dark), there stood another deer. My gun again sent forth its unerring leaden messenger, by which time it was so dark that I could scarcely see to dress the carcass of my prize. After I had cleaned it, I cut off some good pieces, and stumbled on to my camp through the dark, made a fire, roasted some venison, and ate a good supper. Thus I put the "little end foremost" five times that afternoon, and got a good deer every time the little end (lashed fire and brimstone.

In the morning I started for home, arriving there about nine o'clock; and taking with me a boy and two horses, I went for my deer. I found all safe but one doe, which a gentleman bear had made free to tear to pieces, and what was left was as black as if hogs had been at it. I conveyed home my pretty buck and the other three, and thus saved my sheep. Since then I have often told Mary never to forget the "little end foremost."

After this extraordinarily lucky hunt, I traded my gun for a broken rifle, which was very finely finished, with silver mountings on every place that could add to its beauty. I took it to a gunsmith in Monongahela county, Virginia, about thirteen miles from my farm, and bargained with him to repair it by the last week in October. When the time came, I went on foot for it, intending to hunt as I returned home. When I arrived at the smith's, the gun was not done; and as it would take one day more to finish it, I agreed to wait there for it.

During the night there fell a light snow, when, as there was a rifle in the shop, which had been left there to be repaired, I took it, and went out to kill a deer for the gunsmith. As I had hunted in those woods before, and knew where to go, I went to a good place, where I discovered a fine buck, which, however, had started to run before I saw him. When I saw him running, I made the best guess I could for him, and fired, with but little hope of success; but when I came to his tracks, I found blood after him, and a short distance off I found him lying dead. Not being far from the smith's house, I dragged him thither, and was back in time for my breakfast.

I had desired Mary to have some bread in readiness for me when I returned home, in order that I might start at once to the Meadow Mountain, and begin my fall hunt. My gun not being finished before night, I staid until the next morning; and when day-light appeared, I rose, and started off with a most beautiful rifle on my shoulder. I went off with a light heart, as I had a fine day to travel; but though I hunted through good ground, I saw no game. When I got home, it being about eleven o'clock, I took my dinner with Mary, procured a sufficient quantity of bread, and got ready for a great hunt. I tied my provisions in my blanket, and started for the Meadow Mountain at a rapid pace, as I had to travel about fourteen miles to my camp, which I reached about sun-set. I made a fire, to be in readiness for me when I came in, and set off to a noted hill, which was known by the name of Browning's Bear Hill, on account of my having killed so many bears on it.

I had a laurel swamp to cross, and as I came out of it on to clear ground, I saw something in shape like a deer, though I thought it was too large to be one. It was then about dusk, and as I proceeded on, I looked at it again, when the deer turned his head to gaze at me, and I saw what I thought was the largest buck I had ever encountered. I turned my new gun on him, and took a fair aim, but missed him. He stood still until I had nearly reloaded, when he raised his tail, and galloped off before I could try him again. I had so clearly missed him, that I was greatly mortified; and with my gun in hand, I returned to camp, so mad and disappointed that I laid down without eating any supper. During the night I awoke, and found it snowing fast.

"Well," said I, "when day-light returns, I will show some of them that they will not all escape me as that old fellow did."

At daybreak I got up, ate a cold bite, and started off to the hunt; but the day was cold, the leaves frozen, and the snow not deep enough to deaden the noise of my footsteps. But on I went with all caution, and presently entering a large flat piece of land, covered with sugar maples, at a great distance I saw another very large buck coming directly towards me.

"Well, old fellow," said I, "I'll be bail you shall feel what my new gun can do, or it shall not be my fault;" for I had thought that, being in the dusk of the evening before, I had taken an erroneous aim, and missed; but I was determined this time to make good my former error. On came the buck until he was as near as I wished him, when I stopped him by speaking in a low voice. I took good aim, and fired at him, when he raised his tail and galloped off, while I stood astonished; for I had shot ai a distance of not more than thirty yards, and I knew that I could have shot his eye out if the gun had proved true. I had lost my old hunting dog, and had with me the slut from which I raised my good dogs. She was standing behind me when I fired, and as the buck ran around me, she took a straight course for him, and cut off the distance so much, that when I saw them last she was close behind him. I thought that the leaves had made so much noise, that the buck did not know she was near him; but when he found her so close, he turned to fight her off. Being partly a bull-dog breed, she seized him by the nose, and held on until she mashed his nose up to his eyes, and crushed both eyes entirely out. After firing my second shot, I was so confused and dismayed that I was longer than usual in loading again; but when I had nearly reloaded, hearing the dog make a surly growl, I was sure she was engaged in a fight with something. I hurried to the place, and there saw her hanging to the buck's nose. The buck made the most desperate lunges at her; but at every attempt she ran between his legs, when as quick as lightning he would throw his hind parts over her, and make at her with his great horns. In the meantime, I came close up, and shot him through the lungs.

On examination, I found my first ball had passed along his back, under the skin, without doing any injury; and then I felt certain that I had overshot my mark the evening before. I then put up a snow-ball about sixty yards distant, and shot at it, and found that my ball struck about eighteen inches above the mark. This gave me the fidgets; and putting the gun between the forks of a tree, I gave it a bend downward, which made it very crooked. I put it in again and again, until by frequent twisting I got it so that it would shoot a ball within six inches of a mark. I then concluded to try if I could kill with it in that condition.

I took some of that buck with me, fearing that I should not be able to kill any more, and that for want of meat I would have to come after the buck before I finished my hunt. So it turned out; for I hunted a whole week and got two deer, though I shot many times and missed. Towards the last of the week, one of the children came to me with two horses; when, being tired, angry, and discouraged, I took the two deer and went home, fully satisfied that beauty on the outside of anything was no proof that the inside was as it should be; and that, if a man has a good article, it is the height of folly to exchange it for another that he is unacquainted with, although it may look a great deal prettier than his own. This exchange of guns proved a considerable loss to me, not only during that hunt, but in the amount of time I lost in getting it in such a condition that it would shoot correctly. In all, I lost at least a week of the best time for hunting.

When I got my gun in order, I bought a dog because he was of the breed which I kept; but he was young and untaught I then made another trial at the same camp, though I got out late. I took with me my young dog in a string, and went to the places where I was most likely to find deer. I had to hold and control the dog; but when he began to take the wind, I saw he smelled game, though I had great trouble with him. Presently I came to where two very large bucks had been fighting a bitterly-contested battle. They had fought over nearly a quarter of an acre of ground, and when I came to the spot they were no more than out of sight. If I had not been troubled with the pup, I should have caught them while engaged fighting, and in all probability have killed both of them.

But be that as it may, I followed their tracks until they parted; and as I could not tell which was the largest, I pursued the one that took the clearest ground. I had followed him but a short distance, when I saw him walking slowly, with his head low, and as if sick. I had to be cautious how I approached him, as it was difficult to keep my pup quiet; but when at last the deer lay down, I had to be still more cautious, for then he had nothing to do but watch. However, I managed to get within sixty steps, and he knew nothing about my presence until my new rifle cracked, when over he turned, and never rose again.

When I examined him, I found his back was broken — showing that my gun still threw her ball a little higher than the sights. A fine fellow he was, but his shoulders and neck were so gored and bloodshot from the fight he had been engaged in, that they were not fit for use; so I fed them to the dog. After his saddle was considerably dried, it weighed eighty-seven pounds; and sixty pounds is a common buck's weight.

In a day or two my oldest son came to me, and, as another snow had fallen, we started off in the morning, after having previously go two or three dogs together, and it was not long before we found the tracks of a small bear. We let out all our dogs, and following them as fast as we could, heard them barking; but at last the noise ceased entirely. Proceeding onward, we found the bear had come down from his tree to run, when the dogs got hold of him, and had killed him; after which, two of the stoutest dogs had commenced to fight, and were then doing all they could to kill each other; but we separated them, and dogged them well for their bad behavior.

We carried our bear to camp, and the next day hunted for deer, with the snow falling fast. As we were crossing a little valley between two hills, we saw two fine does, and killed them both. In the afternoon, I was walking rapidly to get out of the heavy snow, when, in a clear piece of ground, I saw a fine doe close to me, eating chestnuts, and apparently unconscious of our presence. I pointed my gun at her, and sent a leaden messenger whizzing through her entrails that, in two or three minutes, laid her on the ground. We had three does, which it was hard to tell one from the other, they were so much alike; and as neither of them had raised fawns, they were exceedingly fat.

My cattle being out on the glades at hay, after a few days, I went, together with my oldest sons and the horses, to attend to their wants. The snow was very deep, and a shower of hail and sleet having fallen on the surface, had frozen into a crust; but in the piney region the trees had received the ice, and little or none came to the ground. The deer from the surrounding hills had gathered here to avoid the crusted surface; and as soon as I came to the outskirts of the pines, I sent the boys on to the camp to make a fire, while I hunted.

I had not gone more than half a mile, when, seeing a young buck busily feeding, I crept slily up to him, took a fair aim at him, and fired, when he ran a few yards and fell dead.

I hung his carcass up and went on, and soon found four more feeding. In a minute or two I discovered which was the leader of the flock. I determined to kill her first, and thus so confuse the others that they would not leave the place until I could kill some more of their number. I shot and killed her, when the others ran a short distance, and then stopped and waited for her. I again shot and killed another; and when the other two returned to see where the leader was, I shot a third. The fourth deer having ran off, I thought I had lost it entirely.

I dragged my prizes to one place; and while I was busy putting them away, I looked toward the spot where I had shot the rest, and there stood the fourth deer, which had come back to look for its companions. I shot and killed it; thus securing the whole four at four shots. I hung them all on one pole, and took some of the venison to the camp, where we passed a pleasant night.

The next morning being cold and windy, I left the boys in camp and went out to hunt. I killed four deer; but it was so cold that I could not hunt until night, and therefore returned to camp.

That night was bitter cold; but I turned out next morning, and found the fresh tracks of six wolves; to which I gave chase as fast as I could, and had not pursued them more than half a mile, when I saw them all enter a thicket. I let off my dog, which ran after them; but he had barely got into the thicket when I heard him coming back, with a very large wolf close to his heels. The dog, observing me, wheeled suddenly, met his foe, and, as they came together, seized him by the ear, and threw him flat on the ground. I saw him perform the feat, and ran with all speed toward him; but before I could reach the spot, the wolf was again on his feet and running into the thicket. I ran to the place and sent the dog in after him; but presently he came scampering out again, with the wolf close at his heels. They ran close by me; but, being fidgety, I shot without so much as cutting a hair off him, though I was not more than five steps distant; and thus, by my own bad conduct, lost fifteen dollars, which was the premium allowed on each wolf. I killed two more deer before I got into camp, which made the number secured, so far, eleven.

I had left my little Mary in a critical condition; and as, the night before, I had dreamed of seeing her in a deep, muddy river, I was so distressed by my vision that I could not stay any longer; and, cold as it was, I turned the cattle into the road, put the boys on the horses, and started for home. I wrapped the blankets round the boys, and drove the cattle as fast as they could travel, until I came to a creek; which being frozen, I attempted to break the ice, and in doing so, fell through to my knee in the water. I was sure I should freeze, as I had nearly eight miles still to travel; but, taking a towel which we had with us, I pulled off my stocking, wrapped up the foot that was wet, put on my moccasin, and got home safe.

Little Mary had presented me with a young son, and was doing finely, to my great satisfaction. After the weather moderated, I drove out with a sled and horses and brought the venison home safe.

Whilst I was writing this narrative, Mr. Enlow came into my room, and mentioned two bear-hunts in which he had been my companion, and we agreed to give their details according to his recollection. They had entirely escaped my memory.

"While I lived at the 'Blooming Rose,' wishing to have a bear-hunt, I took with me my rifle and a good dog, and started for Meshach Browning's; knowing that he was fond of hunting bears, and would know where to find them.

"We started off the following morning for the beech grounds, which we found completely upturned by the bears. With the greatest caution, we walked slowly on, looking in every place where a bear could be, and presently saw an old fellow feeding on beech-nuts. We attempted to creep toward him; but the leaves were so dry that the bear heard us, and rose up to reconnoitre. Browning shot at him, and off he went, at full speed. We let out our dogs, which pursued at full cry, and we after them, at our best speed, into a thick laurel-swamp. Both of us being young and strong, we made the brush fly as if a yoke of oxen was going through it; and when we had gained the clear ground, hearing our dogs at bay, we went to them, and found the bear upon a high tree.

"Browning, being the oldest hunter, took the first shot; but still the bear stuck to the tree. I then handed him my gun, and he again fired at his head, when the ball struck him on the ear, and passed through, without affecting the brain; but down he fell, and both dogs at once pitched into him. Then a hard fight ensued, and on a very small piece of ground. Browning, finding the bear would be too strong for the dogs, took his knife and made a heavy blow at its side; but the knife struck a bone, and the blade, being very long, bent in two places almost in the form of a letter S. I then handed him my knife, with which he made a second lunge, and the bear tumbled over very soon afterwards. He was a beast of the ordinary size, but very fat. We took out his entrails, hung him up high on a pine-tree, and proceeded on our hunt; and after killing several deer, the exact number of which I cannot recollect, we returned home in good spirits, full of sport, and keen for more.

"Being still inclined for bear-hunting, I went to Browning again; and as it was scarcely possible ever to find him in any other humor, so it was this time: he was both ready and willing for another hunt.

"In order to be on the ground early next day, we went that evening to the Cherry-Tree Meadows, and staid all night with Mr. Cunningham, who, though a sportsman, did not accompany us.

"The morning was cold and frosty, but we started into the woods again, taking our course nearly parallel with Meadow Mountain, and hunted until the weather became more moderate; when, on our left, at a great distance, we observed a bear feeding.

"I said to Browning, 'As you are an older hunter, and a better shot than I, you may have the pleasure of shooting him.'

"Off he started, but quickly returned to me, saying, 'Give me your gun too; and if the first shot should not kill him, I will repeat.'

"I gave him my rifle, and on he went; but the leaves were so dry that the bear heard his steps, and ran before he was within gunshot of him. I was left in charge of the dogs, with instructions to slip them when necessary. As soon as the bear started, I let both dogs go, and they scampered after him in full cry, and Browning followed at a pace at least half as fast as that of the dogs. I ran with all speed to where I saw him last, supposing that he had left ray gun there for me; but, as I could not find it, I ran first one way and then the other, until I heard the report of a gun, another following it in quick succession; when I knew that he had taken both rifles. I then went on, and arrived after all the sport was over, and the bear was dead. Browning told me that, notwithstanding both shots, the bear continued fighting until he stabbed him.

"After those hunts. Browning commenced trapping wolves, and caught one; when the wolf carried off his trap, and the hard rains washed out all traces of the trap, as well as those of the animal. As Browning had but one dog. and that one an untrained beast, and as I had one of his breed, which was acquainted with the woods, he came for myself and my dog. I accompanied him to the place where he had seen the last signs of the wolf, when we showed the trail to the dogs, which they were much puzzled to pursue; but at last my dog, winding the wolf, started off, and the young dog followed him.

"In a few minutes we heard them fighting, but before we got near the noise ceased. We searched about some time before we found them, when the wolf being nearly dead, we tied up my dog, in order to let the young dog have an opportunity of learning, by fighting the wolf alone. After the young dog had teased him a long time, the wolf recovered; and before we were aware, he broke from the trap, and ran off. As I had to untie my dog, by that time the wolf was so far away, that we both expected to lose him. However, we let my dog slip, and he and the wolf ran until they got beyond our hearing. We had great trouble to find the wolf; but when we did, the dogs had already killed him,

"Given according to the recollection and nearly in the words of

"Jeremiah Enlow."

On a beautiful morning in May, I took down my gun, called my dog, and with a cheerful heart and light foot took my course for my hunting ground. I went from one place to another, until, becoming tired of searching for bears, I turned my face toward home; when, as I was walking fast, and not thinking of game, I heard a strange noise, the like of which I had never heard before. Believing it to proceed from some kind of large bird, I turned to look what it could be, when I saw the two paws of a bear, her body being behind a tree which she was climbing, and sending her cubs up before her. As soon as her cubs were as high in the tree as she wished them, she descended to the ground on the off side of the tree, and ran away.

"Well, old lady," said I, "I shall not let you trick me in that way; for I know you intend to return."

I then hid myself at some distance, and in a few minutes I heard the bushes behind me rustle, and saw her passing by me toward the tree on which her cubs were hid. She went to the tree, raised her body up against it, and made a strange noise, when her cubs began to come down. I shot the old one as she stood on her hind feet, when she dashed into the bushes, and the cubs ran up the tree again. I let the old one go where she pleased, for I knew she was not able to give me any trouble in taking her cubs.

I shot one, and seeing that it was not larger than a cat, up the tree I went after the other cub, which, having gone as high as he could, I began to be afraid to look down, lest I should be scared; so I kept my face up The cub went out on a limb; and as I could not reach it, I tried to shake it off, but did not succeed; for it held on with its claws and teeth at the same time. At last, taking a long stick, I tied my moccasin to the end, made a noose of the string, and thus, after great difficulty, secured my little prisoner.

After I had hunted many years, and had become a very successful sportsman, I took it into my head to form a park in which to keep some deer. During the winter of 1836, there fell a deep snow; and after it had settled down, I made a pair of snow-shoes, in the manner here described. The front part of the shoe has a semi-circular shape, and it is two feet in length, terminating in a point at the back part. The outer margin, formed of one piece of very tough wood, is crossed about the centre by two strong ribs, placed at such a distance apart as will allow of the heel resting on one. and the ball of the foot on the other. Oak splits are then woven through these ribs from back to front, like the bottom of a chair. When used, the foot is placed on the two strong ribs, the ball of the foot on the front, and the heel on the rear cross-piece, where it is tied firmly with straps, that it cannot move one way or the other.

Thus equipped, I set off to the woods, to catch deer to put in my park. As I could not catch them myself, but was obliged to depend on a small dog, which I knew would tear and injure them, I took straps of leather and made a muzzle, leaving room enough for him to breathe, but not to open his mouth wide enough to bite the deer. So at it I went, and took several, but not one large buck among the number. I had seen the tracks of a very large buck, but he escaped for two or three days. At last, one morning I set out with the intention of catching him; and getting to the windward of his lair, I followed him up until I found in which direction he had run. I slipped the little dog, and kept on the trail until I heard him at bay, when I struck out at my best speed, which, with the wooden shoes, was about equal to an ordinary walking pace along a road; but when I came up, there stood the buck, bidding defiance to every trespasser on his rights and liberties.

I walked close up, bade him good morning, and told him that I had a summons for him to make his appearance forthwith at Browning's deer park. But the haughty animal raised his head high up, threw up his tail, his hair all standing out, and came boldly up to the attack. As he came he reared on his hind feet, and made a pass at my head; but as I saw what he intended, I stepped to one side, and seized him round the neck, when into it we went, round and round so fast, that it looked as if we were dancing Fisher's hornpipe. We danced and pranced till I threw him down in the snow; when, as he commenced kicking, my front underwent a complete raking. I bore it until I could endure it no longer, and was glad to let him up again; when we took another dance, and after two or three rounds I threw him again, and tried to tie him; but when I would relax my hold he would rise and lead me another dance. At last, becoming as mad as he was, and the fight becoming desperate, I got him down, and was determined to tie him at all hazards.

He continued to kick until he had so raked my front, that I felt as if covered with a blister plaster; after which he drew himself up, and with the points of his hinder hoofs caught my pants, and tore them from the seam of the waistband, taking one-half of my pants clear off to the ankle, leaving me half-naked, on a cold day and in the midst of snow.

Maddened at such an insult, I ran into him with desperation, and threw him down in the deep snow. By this time I was so worried and heated, that I felt no inconvenience from the snow and the cold; for I was smoking like a coal-pit. On my part, the fight had not been carried on with much vigor and determination, until I lost my pants; but after that happened, I became furious, and determined to conquer him, if it took me until the moon rose; and I did not thereafter suffer him to rise to his feet until the fight ceased. When he found that he could not rise, his whole aim was to get the rope off his neck, which by hard labor I had tied round it.

He would get his hind feet in the rope, and drag at it until he choked himself; and when I pulled them out, in a moment he would be in the same fix again. So it continued until he caught the points of his hoofs in a wrinkle of the loose hanging skin of his neck, and tore just half of it from his shoulder, as far up as the rope could go toward his ears. This looked so bad, that I loosened the rope, pulled the skin down again, and lot him rise to his feet. Finding that he was still inclined to fight, I told him that he was a brave fellow, but a big fool, for he might have known that I did not mean to take his life; but as he was so selfish, he might go and do as he pleased; whereupon he walked off slowly into a thick laurel, and I saw him no more.

I puffed and blowed awhile, until I had rested; when I took hold of the hanging leg of my pants, and, pulling it off, found it full of snow. I shook the snow out, and, though wet and frozen, I pulled it on again, and went in search of thorns. I was so lucky as to find some in a short time, and with them pinned the torn garment together, and thus got clear of holding it up with one hand.

Disappointed and angry at my defeat, I started with my little dog (which had seen all that was done, and, by-the-by, was very little better treated by the buck than his master) to look for more deer. In a short time, finding where a large drove had been running, I started the dog in pursuit; and as there was a well-beaten road, I threw off my snow-shoes, and ran after them; but presently meeting the dog coming back, I found the deer had all gone into the creek, and proceeded down the stream, I turned up the creek, and soon saw a young buck hid in a deep hole. I took care to keep below him, so that he could not get into the water below me, as then he could have run down the creek, when it would have been impossible for us to catch him. I went to the edge of the water, and as the buck was on the other side, I sent the dog over to rout him. As soon as the dog approached, the buck went and stood in the middle of the deep water; and I could neither get at him, nor would the dog go in to him. I then cut a long pole, tied my rope to it, and, making a noose, tried to slip it over his head; but he would not let the rope come near him. I continued trying to put it on him, until, while standing on the ice, over the deep water, and reaching after the buck, the ice gave way, and into the water I went, up to my hips.

Irritated at such bad luck, I pitched at him, when he bounded for the shore, whither I pursued him; and as he made a leap to rise the bank, I caught him by one hind leg, and then we had it; but, as he struggled up the bank, I drew his leg round a tree, and there held him until he tired himself, and laid still. I then tied him, and went to the woods, where I procured a pole, tied his hind legs to one end of it, and his fore legs to the other end, and then passed another cord around his kidneys and the pole, to keep him from straining his back. Then I took the end of the pole, and drew him to the big road, where I loosed him. In a little time he became quiet, when I turned him into the road, and drove him before me like a sheep, until he came in sight of the house; but, as he refused to proceed any farther, I had to throw him and tie him again, and draw him home, where I kept my deer five or six years.

Chapter Thirteen

In October of the year 1836, myself and my two oldest sons, John Lynn and William, went to my old hunting camp at Meadow Mountain to hunt. We got to the camp about four o'clock; when, having still time to hunt before night set in, we all turned out; and, as I knew where a bear had fed some days before, I went to see if he had left the ground; but, finding no traces of him, I was about to leave the place, when my dog winded game.

Thinking of nothing but the bear, I followed the dog until we came to a great thicket; into which I crept quietly, stepping carefully from place to place, and from one log to another, until I heard something walking among the dry leaves. I crept still nearer, until I found that I was close enough to see what it was if the brush was out of the way; when, by creeping a little farther on. I saw the tail of a deer, and expected to see him run off; but, as he again lowered his tail, I found that he was not aware of my presence. Venturing a step or two farther, I saw a tremendous pair of horns, and discovered that lie was feeding on chestnuts. At every mouthful he took, he would raise his head to see if there was any danger of an enemy approaching. I was then within thirty steps of him, but could see nothing to shoot at with certainty, on account of the thick brush. At last, however, I saw his back over a fallen tree; when, as I feared the wind would turn toward him, I took a good aim at him, and let fly Down he came, and as quick as possible I jumped on him, made a slash at his throat, cutting it to the bone, and after a few struggles he became my prize. I was a little unwell; but, calling for the boys, they came to me, and helped me carry him to the camp.

He was as fine a buck as any one could wish to see. We took off his skin, roasted some of the venison, which was of the best quality, and passed a merry night, as we had plenty of wild honey and apples, together with everything necessary to render us comfortable. We continued our hunt until a snow fell, which made fine sport for us.

On the following day, I went out early, and remained in the woods until after dark. Returning to my camp, I passed by one of my traps, and found a bear in it, which became furious as soon as I drew near; but, it being so dark that I could not see to shoot, I left it until the next day.

Early next morning I went to my trap, in which I found a large she-bear and a yearling; but the small one was dead. I then shot the old one, and, on examination, found that the old one had become so mad because she could not get at me the previous evening, that she fell on her own young one and tore it to pieces. It was so dirty and torn that I threw it away. We continued our hunt. killing a good lot of deer, until the close of the week; when we returned home, and sent our horses for our game.

The following week, myself and my oldest son, William, went out again; and the same evening there fell a new snow, which made fine hunting; but, as it was Sunday morning, we agreed to lay in camp until the next day. After our breakfast, William said he would go and spend the day with young Mr. Brooke, who was keeping bachelor's hall within three miles of our camp. I told him that I expected he only wanted to hunt, and made that an excuse to get into the woods, when he would go to hunting; but he declared he did not intend to hunt, and that if I would remain alone until evening he would join me. I agreed to his proposal, and off he started.

After he was gone, as I felt lonesome, I began to reason with myself whether it would be committing a sin to walk out and look for a deer by way of amusement; and the more I thought about it the more I felt inclined to go. It next occurred to me that my desire to go after the deer was equivalent to going; and that it would be no greater crime for me to go than to lay there all the time wishing to do so.

Reasoning thus, I took my gun, and started off with my dog. After a short hunt, I put up a fine buck, which ran but a short distance, and then stopped to look at me. I fired at him, when he sprang forward a few yards, and fell dead. I cleaned and hung his carcass up, and took to the woods again, where I found the tracks of a lot of deer, among which were those of one very large buck, which I was determined to secure.

I pursued the tracks with the utmost care, and at last came in sight of the deer; but, though I looked carefully for the big buck, I could see none with horns. I then shot at what I thought was a large doe, when off scampered the entire herd. When I reached the place where the deer I shot had stood, I found plenty of blood and hair in its tracks, and followed it until I was satisfied I could not get another shot at it, I then sent my dog after it again, which soon drove it into a creek; but when I drew near, and looked closely at the deer, I was astonished at its size, and thought it was the largest doe in the woods. I shot it, and got it out of the water, when it proved to be an enormous buck, without horns; which is a very uncommon thing. Being close to my camp, I carried him in; and William returned, according to promise, without having hunted at all.

We continued the hunt for six days, having good weather all the time, and as good a tracking snow as ever laid on the ground. But I never got another shot during the whole week, while William was killing deer almost every day.

As the season for hunting was nearly closed, William and I agreed to make a trial of our skill in that way; and for this purpose we went to Bear Creek Glades — the place where little Mary and I first settled in the woods.

We set out on Monday morning, and hunted from our home to the house where we intended to stop; there being no one living in it at the time. When we got there, in the evening, I had killed one deer, and William two.

On Tuesday we were out again, and in the evening I had two deer, while William had but one.

Wednesday we went out again. In the evening he had two, and I one.

On Thursday, I killed two and William one. On Friday, he killed two and I one.

On Saturday, as a snow which was knee-deep had fallen the previous night, we agreed to hunt as we returned home; and during the day I killed two. When I got near home, I discovered another in some laurel, and shot, him dead on the spot, which made the number three.

When William came home, he had two. We had each killed ten deer, making twenty in one week; and as the snow was very deep, we hunted no more that fall.

This winter was, as usual, very cold, with heavy snows; and in the spring, excepting some three or four bears, caught in traps, I do not recollect of any being killed.

In June, my wife, who was very partial to venison, asked me to go and try to procure a deer. I started off to our old residence, at Bear Creek Glades, and, after hunting the whole morning, found nothing to shoot at.

As I was returning home, I found that a haystack in the glades, which had been strongly salted, and had stood over winter, was resorted to by the deer for the sake of the salt, and it seemed as if they were at it every evening and morning.

I went home without any venison, but told Mary that I could secure a deer the first time I would go out and watch that haystack, and that I had never seen more service-berries in any one place than there were there. She immediately proposed to ride out with me and gather berries, and after dinner we set off for the glades.

We had a pleasant ride, and got there about four or five o'clock. There was hay in the house, and we carried blankets with us to keep us comfortable. I made a fire for her, and told her to keep my dog there until she heard my rifle crack, and then to send him out to me.

When I reached the stack, I could see no place to hide myself from the deer when they came; so I climbed up on the stack, rolled up a large bundle of hay, hid myself behind it, with the exception of my head, and laid my gun on the roll of hay, with the muzzle pointing in the direction I expected the deer to come.

As I did not think they would come before sundown, I was sitting quietly in my place, when, raising my eyes, there stood a beautiful buck, with a pair of velveted horns, looking me in the face, apparently afraid to approach. As the breech of my gun was lying in my lap, I had to raise it in order to level it at my game, which I commenced slowly to do; but, being over anxious to secure the deer, I suppose that I did not arrange my sights properly; and, though I fired at a distance of only thirty steps, the ball never touched a hair of his hide, and he ran off, leaving me to seek venison elsewhere.

We staid overnight, and I helped Mary to gather as many berries as she wanted, and had the comfort of riding home without being encumbered with anything but the berries.

The affairs of my farm occupied my attention, with the exception of killing a few deer in the glades during the haying season, until the latter part of September.

My old uncle Spurgin had removed his residence to Preston County, Virginia; and having some business in that quarter, Mary proposed to accompany me on a visit to the old people. I had been to see the old man a short time before, when he told me that he knew of three large bucks which frequented a great thicket, though he could never see them.

Taking with me Mary, my rifle, and my dog, I set out for Virginia, and travelled on until I arrived in the neighborhood of the thicket; when I told Mary to continue along the road to the old people's house, while I would bunt through the woods, and join her before dark. So we parted, and I went into the woods and found the thicket of which the old man had spoken.

A light shower of rain fell a short time before I approached the thicket, which made it as good an evening to hunt a buck as could be desired. I entered the thicket with all possible caution, and in the midst of the worst place in it I took my stand; knowing that if they still harbored there I would see them before sundown.

I stood, perhaps, twenty minutes, when I discovered something which looked like the point of a buck's horn. I gazed at it for some time without being able to decide what it was, but still could not take my eyes from it. Presently, down it went, and I could see nothing more of it. There was a fallen tree within one step of me, upon which I mounted, and thus was able to see over the bushes, when there stood a buck, within close range.

I took a good aim at him, although he was fully half covered by bushes; but fearing the wind should turn toward him, I made the best I could of it, fired at, and shot him; when as quick as possible I jumped on him, and had his throat cut in a twinkling. Looking up, I saw two more running slowly, whereupon I rammed down a naked ball, and by the time they had reached the other side of a little stream, I was ready. As they stopped to look back, I let fly again, and popped over another. The dog, seeing that one kicking, started after, and ran the other one clear off. I dressed their carcasses, hung them up, and reached my uncle's by dark. When I took the venison to market, one saddle weighed eighty-six pounds, and the other eighty-four pounds.

A week or two subsequently I went into the same woods to hunt, on a very rainy day. When a hard shower fell, I sought the shelter of a hollow tree, or of some projecting rock; or else I would take three pieces of bark, lay them on poles, and sit under them until the showers passed over, when I would move on again. So I continued to do until evening, in the meantime seeing nothing to shoot; but as I was hunting with the greatest care, looking and listening intently, I heard a stick break. I remained quietly in my place until I heard a second crack, when I observed the highest limbs of a chestnut tree, and, looking up, Haw a bear breaking off the limbs, and throwing them to the ground, with the intention of coming down and eating the nuts, when he had enough for a full meal.

I stepped toward the tree very cautiously, and had got within shooting distance, when the wind shifted from me. The bear proved to be a female, with three cubs, which were eating the nuts under the tree, as their dam threw them down. The moment the old one caught my scent, she came down on the off side of the tree, ran away through the bushes with her cubs after her, and was out of sight in a few moments, leaving me the lot of chestnuts as the only consolation for being so completely outwitted. I sat down, and gathered the old lady bear's nuts without the least remorse of conscience for robbing the widow and orphans of the food which had been collected with such care.

In my next hunt I had to depend on myself alone, having neither my dog nor my own gun, as, the lock having given way, I had sent it to the gunsmith's to be repaired. John McMullen, Mary's brother, had left a small gun with me until he wished to use it, which I took, and went into the hunting ground of the Glades, on a mountain called the Roman Nose. The day turned out to be cold, with snow falling slowly; and as I knew the deer were all hid in the thickets, I got on the windward side of the mountain, in a patch of high weeds, and was standing there, looking carefully about me, when I saw the tall weeds shaking, and something approaching me. I kept my place until I saw a bear running at full gallop, and as he was passing me, I called to him to stop. He obeyed the call, and did stop at a good distance, say sixty or eighty steps, when I fired, and off he ran at full speed.

Going to his tracks, I saw blood after him, and therefore followed him until I arrived at the steep side of the mountain, down which he went. Having on a strong pair of moccasins, which were soled with stout leather, they were frozen so hard and stiff, that I could not travel down the steep places, except by holding on to a bush, and running from that down to another, which I would seize hold of, and thence take another start. In this manner I followed his tracks down the mountain, until at last I saw him lying in a sink, and to all appearances dead; but as I watched him carefully, I discovered that he breathed; and when I spoke to him, he merely shuddered, and then became motionless again. I frequently shouted at him, but could not rouse him to anything like sensibility.

Taking my gun in my hand, I let go the bush I was holding by, when down I went into the sink, within one step of the bear, which sprang to his feet as he heard me rushing down the bank. We were so close to each other that I had neither room nor time to loose; and as I entered the sink, I wheeled toward him, with the intention of firing and jumping down the steep bank, when, if he followed me, I determined to run down the hill as far as he might be inclined to pursue me. But, by good luck, as I entered the sink I fired, without taking any sight, and the ball accidentally striking him in the head, he fell. Before he had time to recover, I attacked him with my knife, and gave him two fatal stabs, which laid him dead at my feet. I then rolled his carcass down the mountain to the level ground, dressed it, hung it up, and returned home.

In a few days there fell another snow, and the weather became exceedingly cold. A very large buck which ranged along the western side of the river, was so cunning that the hunters could never get a shot at him; and though I had tried him several times, yet by some sly manoeuvre he always contrived to frustrate my plans, and make his escape.

On the morning spoken of above, I was going to give him another trial; and as the river must be forded, I rode across, and sent the horse back; after which I entered the woods. I had gone but a short distance, when I discovered his tracks in the snow, which I followed until they crossed a flat piece of ground, and ascended a steep hill on the other side. At the top of the hill was a high ledge of rocks, forming a curve; and in a thicket below the rock I knew the buck lay, watching for the approach of danger.

As soon as I saw what he purposed by going into that place, I left his tracks, went round on the other side, and mounted a high rock behind him; when, being much higher than he was, and there being a steep hill below, I could see everything around me. I stood on the rock, and looked about me with the utmost care, but could see nothing of the buck, until, casting my eyes down at the base of the rock, directly below where I stood, there lay the buck, contentedly chewing his cud, apparently considering himself perfectly secure. He was watching the ground in front, not thinking that an enemy could approach on the side which the rock so completely covered. This rock being fully twenty feet high, I was obliged to shoot nearly straight down; but when I saw what a complete advantage I had, it greatly marred my pleasure to think that such a noble animal, possessing all the beauty bestowed by a

BEAR LISTENING AND TWO CUBS.

194

pair of fine large horns, a well-formed body, and tapering limbs, whose life had been innocently spent, never having committed an injury against either man or beast, — should be thus sacrificed. My desire of killing him was so weakened, that I really had thoughts of letting him escape the death that was then hanging over him; but, again, it occurred to me that he was one of the creatures placed here for the use of man; that, if I let him go, probably the next hunter who caught him In his power would surely kill him; and that it would be as well for me to take him as to let any other person have him.

So taking a good aim, I fired at him, when the poor fellow gave a few jumps, and fell dead; and I declare that the death of that deer gave me more real pain than pleasure. He was a large, old fellow, his head and face being quite grey with age. I took his skin and returned, having the river to wade, and at least a mile to travel before I could reach home. The winter being then near, I believe that buck ended the fall hunt.

The following spring, all the delightful thoughts of a pleasant summer's near approach, with anticipations of stirring sport and early game, were beginning to revive, when two friends of mine, one a Pennsylvanian, came to my house, with the view of hunting for bears. All being ready, off we started for Pleasant Valley, taking with us three dogs, and hunted with great care, but to no purpose, as apparently the bears had left the place. We were about to return home, when I saw a bear standing on her hind feet, looking for us, as she had heard our footsteps.

As quick as thought I drew my sights on her, and fired, when she fell. I ran to her as soon as possible, but by the time the bear was on her feet again, the dogs were all tearing away at her for life. I found one dog down, and the bear biting him badly; when, seeing that the knife was the only thing to decide the matter, I drove it into her twice, and ended the fight. Her cubs were then shot from a tree on which they had climbed for safety; after which we skinned her, quartered her, and carried her home on our shoulders.

The summer passed off with the usual pleasant occupations and amusements, such as mowing hay in the glades, killing deer, catching trout, and shooting wild turkeys, until about the tenth of October, when, taking with me my gun and dog, I set out by myself for the Negro Mountain, to hunt. The day, though clear, was desperately windy; so much so, that I was afraid the trees would fall on me. On I went, however, until I was within a mile of the mountain, the bushes reeling and twisting through and round each other with the wind, when suddenly the body of a large buck became visible quite near to me. As he had no knowledge of my presence, I turned my gun on him as quick as possible, and fired; after which he went but a few yards, and fell dead. When he ran I saw two more, as large as he was, also running; and when he fell the other two stopped for him to come up with them. I loaded again, and sent a second ball whizzing through one of these two; when the third buck stood looking at those that were down and kicking their last, until I loaded the third time, shot again, and killed this one also — all within a few steps of each other. I dragged them together, hung them all up, and turned my steps homeward; but the next day I sent out the boys and horses, and brought them all home without damage.

I then commenced gathering my corn, having Thomas McMullen, Mary's youngest brother, helping me. We had great quantities of all kinds of pumpkins among the corn, and as Thomas and I were both fond of stewed pumpkins, on Saturday we hauled them to the house, and told Mary to stew as many of them as she thought we could eat with cream, on Sunday morning.

At breakfast next morning, the pumpkins and cream being set out, young McMullen bantered me as to who could eat the most. At it we went; and we ate until Mary, laughing, left the table. She was standing in the door, when we heard a dog running in full cry; and Mary called to us that there was a bear coming, with a dog after him. We both sprang to our rifles, and started out; when the bear passed us at his best speed, with a dog dost behind him. Calling my dog, I sent him off; and as soon as he began to open on the track, McMullen and I followed; but our best speed was very slow, as we had eaten so much pumpkin and cream, that, in running up hill, we were so short of wind, that we could not make headway at all; and when the bear turned to go downhill, we were so clumsy that we dare not take long steps. So we walked along after the bear and dog, until we heard the latter bark, when we knew that the bear was treed; and proceeding on, puffing and blowing, we presently saw the bear sitting on a tree.

We walked slowly on, trying to regain our lost breath, until we were within good shooting distance, when I levelled my rifle, and sending a ball through his brains, he fell helpless to the ground. After resting ourselves, we carried his carcass home, where we found Mary and her children laughing immoderately at our race up and down the hill; for as it was only distant two hundred yards, and within view from the door, they could see plainly the helpless situation in which our enormous breakfast of pumpkins and cream had placed us.

My next hunt took place at the Little Crossings and the Meadow Mountain; and the very evening I arrived there, I commenced my sport. The wind was very high, and blowing almost a hurricane, which is the life of a hunting day; for while the wind is blowing so hard, the game cannot hear the footsteps of the hunter. I pushed on, until I saw a buck eating acorns, which I immediately shot through the lungs, when he ran but a few yards, and fell. I took care of him, carrying his saddle with me to the camp. I staid out the whole week, and on Saturday morning, after killing four or five deer, I started for home. Traveling two or three hours, I came to a thicket, where my dog showing signs of game being near, I stopped, and present? I saw a tremendous buck walking leisurely along.

As he turned and began to walk from me, I became so much afraid that I should lose him, that I was taken with such a trembling, that I could scarcely hold my gun at an aim. However, I did the best I could, and fired, when off ran the buck at full speed. Proceeding to the place where he stood when I shot at him, and finding by the hair and blood left behind that he was considerably wounded, I started the dog on the track before me, and followed the buck more than a mile; but could not get a sight of him. However, I directed the dog to try his luck with him, which he was very willing and even anxious to do. I had to follow the footprints of the buck, which were very dim, as he had taken his course along the Negro Mountain, where the ground was so hard that he made but little impression on it.

After a long and tedious trailing, I found that the buck had turned his course from the mountain, and was making for Bear Creek, which is a tolerably large stream; and I could see that the deer was traveling at his best speed, to keep clear of the dog. His tracks soon became much plainer, on account of the softness of the ground, when the buck was forced to take long jumps, at each one his feet sinking deep in the soft ground, and enabling me to follow at a rapid walk.

After traveling four or five miles, hearing the dog at full bay, I looked no more for the track, but ran to him the shortest way I could; and soon found him and the buck standing in the creek. The latter had stabbed the dog so severely with his sharp horns, that he would not go within his reach any more, but stood at a safe distance, and barked at him; and if the buck attempted to run away, he would seize him by the hams, whereupon he would turn and horn the dog off. In that way the dog kept him there until I came to his assistance, when I shot the buck in the head, and killed him. He was the largest deer I believe I ever killed — the two hams, not including the loin, or what is called the saddle, weighed ninety-four pounds; and if the loin had been attached, the whole would have weighed nearly a hundred and twenty pounds.

After this hunt, I again went to the same grounds, and spent a week, with but small success; though, while returning home, I saw a fine buck lying down, with nothing but his head visible. I walked softly up, until I was within close shooting distance, when, taking good aim at the side of his head, I sent a ball from my big rifle through the middle of it, and settled his account. I skinned him, hung him up and continued my course toward home, stopping on the way at the house of Mr. James Cunningham, who was a hunter, and whose lady was extremely fond of honey in the combs.

Mr. Cunningham asked me if there were any bee-trees yet standing in the woods. I told him there was one, and only one, that I knew of, which was at least two miles from his house, on the route to my home; but that I thought we would not have time to cut the tree down that evening. Indeed, I did not like to lose the time necessary to fell it, for I was anxious to get home, as it was a cold evening, and there was a little snow fluttering through the air. But no excuse would serve; the honey must be obtained at all risks.

Recollecting that there was a small tree standing close to the one in which the bees swarmed, I told Mr. C. that if he would take with him a long rope and his tomahawk, I thought I could climb the tree and cut the honey out — thus dispensing with the trouble of felling it. He procured a bed-cord, a bucket, and a tomahawk, and was soon ready for this honey hunting expedition. Off we started in all haste, and easily found the tree. I climbed the small tree until I was opposite the hole through which the bees entered, when I pounded on the tree, and finding that it was hollow, I began to cut into it. But on making an opening, I discovered that it was not in the place where the honey lay; so I went lower, cut another hole, and reached the honey. Although it was cold and snow falling, the bees poured out on me, and stung my face, hands, bosom, and wherever they could touch my skin, until I was forced to leave the hive, descend, and make a fire; when up I went again, put some fire into the hole, and blew the hot smoke in among the bees, until they were strangled. The poor little creatures had to yield, and let their long hard-earned store be taken from them. I then commenced taking out the honey, and letting it down to the ground by the rope; but when I got at it, I thought I might as well take the whole out at once; though the question arose as to what I could put the honey in until I should send for it.

Telling Mr. C. to spread down my buck's skin in a hollow of the ground, and stack the combs of honey on that, I let down one bucketful after another, until the skin would hold no more; when I was obliged to stop taking it out, and leave the balance in the tree until the following day. Mr. Cunningham having obtained a bucketful of choice combs for his wife, which was all she desired, each of us went home.

The following day I sent the boys out with a horse for the combs; and when the honey was pressed we had eight gallons of a clean, pure article, exclusive of what was sent to Mrs. Cunningham. This tree was among the best I ever found in the woods. At different times I found three other trees which yielded eight gallons and a half each, and one which yielded twelve gallons; but it must be remembered that, in those days, a bee-hunter could seldom find a tree containing such quantities, as the average was generally from two to three gallons, and the quantity has much diminished of late years. I am certain that this statement will apply as a general rule; for I have often discovered two and three bee-trees, and on one occasion five, in one day.

While I lived in the Glades, honey was no object; and if a bee-hunter found a tree near a neighbor's house, all the family would be invited to take a share of the honey, be it little or much; and the same rule applied to venison or wild turkeys, as seldom any charge was made between neighbors. But this generous and hospitable practice has been entirely set aside by the younger class of people who have taken the place of those who resided there from twenty to forty years ago.

The season for hunting closed shortly after the bee hunt just described, and winter put a stop to my sporting in the woods. A cold winter confined my pleasures entirely to my home circle, comprising my wife and children; and several of the latter, who had then reached the age of puberty, were passionately fond of music and dancing. Myself and wife being no less fond of seeing our children enjoying a dance, the young people would often collect at my house, and there spend an evening in merriment; and at other times they would join a dancing party at different places in the neighborhood.

We thus spent our time agreeably until spring; but when the birds began to warble their sweet notes among the trees, the trap, the dog, and the gun, came freshly into memory. I set the boys at the ploughs, while I traversed the woods; but it appeared as if bad luck met me at every step I took. I had several fights, and was defeated every time; and as my dogs were much discouraged, I concluded to depend on my traps. I had caught one bear, and going to another trap a short time after, I found a large fellow in it. In order to raise the ambition for fighting in my twice or thrice whipped and discouraged dog, I shot the bear through the mouth, breaking all his dangerous teeth, so that, if he got the advantage of the dog, he could not do him any serious injury. Having, as I thought, everything ready, I took hold of the lever, and raised the trap, when the bear sprang out at the side next to the laurel, which was very thick. I saw the bear running into the thicket; but as two of the best dogs had not seen him depart, and were sure he was still in the trap, they obstinately refused to leave it, and it was a considerable time before I could make them sensible of their mistake. Even after I got them to take the trail, they ran but a short distance, and returned to the trap, still believing that he was there. That was the last I ever saw of the bear.

The following week I again went to examine the traps, one of which was large, and made of steel; but when I reached the place where this trap was set, I found that it was gone. I took the trail, and followed the bear until he entered a thick laurel swamp. As there was a heavy log-chain to the trap, which made it easy to follow him, I went on until I heard the laurel breaking, when, knowing that a bear was running off, I sent the dogs after him. They were soon out of hearing, when I took the trail of the trap again, being determined to find it; for I knew that the bear which the dogs were running had no trap about him.

I followed the trail until I came to a very large bear, which was not only dead, but nearly eaten up. Another uncommonly large bear, having found him in the trap, had fallen on him; and of all the fights I have ever seen the signs of in my life, that beat them. The log-chain was wrapped around the laurels, some of which had been pulled out by the roots, while others had been smashed down. Heaps of brush had been rolled up, logs turned over, and rocks moved out of their places; indeed, it looked much as if a yoke of wild, strong oxen had been turned out with the yoke on. Then imagine two infuriated bears; for no man can believe what immense strength there is in one of these animals, until he sees with his own eyes what they can do, when properly tested.

Having lost this bear, which was entirely destroyed, and summer coming on, I abandoned the sport, with the exception of killing some deer in hay-time, and catching trout, which was always a matter of course at that time. So things went on until the hunting season returned again.

During November, I went into Deep Creek Glades and hunted one day to no purpose; but late in the evening I saw a deer at a great distance. While I was creeping to where I last observed it, the deer moved off, and I was compelled to put the dog on his track; after which, I followed him until I got sight of him, when I shot at him, but only broke one of his hind-legs. He ran for the creek, but the dog caught him before he got to the water. He whipped the dog off, but I came up directly, and gave him a shot in the head which laid him out dead on the spot. My son Will having joined me, we took a side of the ribs, and started for Meadow Mountain, which was in sight of us, though it was two miles to where we knew some bears had been feeding a day or two before.

We fixed up a little camp with such slabs as we could find among the broken timber, built up a good fire to come to at night, and then turned out to look for bears.

We went to the place where they had been feeding, and were looking and listening with all possible care, when suddenly an exceedingly large buck came walking very fast toward me. I let him come until I was sure of him, when I called to him to stop. He did so, and gazed all around to see whence the noise came, when I took a deliberate shot at him; after which he made a few jumps, and fell. We cleaned him, hung him up, and directed our course toward the camp, which we reached after dark, where we enjoyed our buck's ribs when roasted, and spent a pleasant night.

The next morning we turned out, and, after hunting nearly all day without success, in the evening we lost ourselves; when, finding night stealing on us, we selected a large fallen tree, built up a fire against the side of it, making it large and long enough to throw its heat on both of us, then scraped together leaves in abundance, and laid down on them. My son laid his feet in my bosom, and I laid mine in his, each hugging the other's feet close. When one turned the other turned also, and thus we spent the night in tolerable comfort.

The next day, being again unsuccessful, and not getting any game, we went home, and subsequently sent for our bucks, which we found safe from beasts and birds, and brought home.

The following spring brought with it many of my old delights, such as the sweet chirping of birds, and the gobbling of wild as well as tame turkeys. I told Mary that while the boys done the plowing, if she would attend the mill, she should have all the tolls she could make, while I would go and hunt at the Little Crossings, which was fifteen miles from home, and kill some bears. I knew she would do so, for she frequently tended the mill while I was absent;

and, indeed, she was the best miller on the place; for she knew how flour should be ground to make good bread.

She agreed to take charge of the mill until I returned, and off I went to the hunting-ground, which I reached by four o'clock, and soon found there were no bears in those woods. In the evening I was still looking from place to place for bears, when I observed three deer at a great distance; and as I saw no chance of getting a bear, I concluded to shoot the smallest deer So, creeping as near as I could, I picked out and shot the smallest deer, believing it to be the most tender, and the best venison. It turned out to be a very large buck, and in better plight than I expected to see them so early in the spring, it being then about the first week in May. I skinned the fore-part, but left the hind-part whole in the skin; after which I carefully cut all the flesh off the fore-part, and taking a small cord, I sewed up the skin, and putting all the meat into it, tied it up, and started for home.

Night coming on, I heard a wild gobbler making a great noise as he was seated on his roost. I let him brag and gobble until it was so dark that he could not see me on the ground, though I could still see him on the tree, when I crept softly on until I was near enough to be sure of my game. I then fired at and secured him. After taking out his entrails, I packed him in the buck's skin with my venison, and continued my course for a short distance toward home; when I made a fire, and lay down for the night.

As soon as daylight appeared I heard gobblers in all directions; but thinking I had enough for one man to carry, I went on, and left them to gobble as much as they pleased.

Becoming tired, I sat down to rest; when, hearing a turkey gobble close to me, I spoke a few words in the turkey language. In a minute he came to see, as he thought, a new sweetheart; but the crack of my gun convinced him of his error. I took out his entrails, and put him also in my buckskin sack, which then contained the whole saddle of the buck, all the flesh of the fore-part, and the two turkey gobblers.

I went on with my load for half a mile, when I arrived at Dr. Brooke's. He weighed my burden, and found it to be eighty-seven pounds; and, as I had yet eight miles to travel to my home, I was satisfied for that spring.

I was just getting to be desirous for another hunt, when two of my neighbors proposed that we should go to the "Land flowing with Milk and Honey;" though there were such quantities of rattlesnakes in that region that I was somewhat afraid to venture there. However, concluding to go with them, we set out for the land of rattlesnakes, and arrived at the ground in time to make an evening hunt.

I took long grass, and, making a long rope of it, I wrapped it round my legs to my knees, which made it impossible for the teeth of the snakes to reach the skin, and out I started, and found that deer were very numerous.

I had hunted but a short time, when, seeing a small buck, I cracked away at him. He ran but a few rods, and fell dead. I dressed him, left him on the ground, and continued my hunt; and after traveling less than a mile, observing a doe among some thick bushes, I let fly at her, and broke her back.

By the time I had cleaned her, it was evening, and getting dark. I was then a mile or two from camp; and, being very much afraid of the snakes, I took a shoulder from the doe, which was in fine order, as she had no fawns, and started for that place.

As I went on, walking fast, I came to some shelly rocks, when the snakes began to rattle; the weeds seemed to be shaking all around me, and I could see them twisting themselves in every direction. I did not stop to look, but took to my heels for life, and ran for some distance. I began to take it a little more coolly as I drew near the camp; and looking to my right, toward the top of a steep bluff, I observed the body and head of a deer within close range. I could not then distinguish the sights on my rifle; but making the best guess possible, I fired, and down it fell. I ran to it, cut its throat, soon had it cleaned, and set off to camp; having three good deer, which, though small, were the best of venison.

My friends had killed nothing, though they had fired several shots. We took a hunt next morning, when one of them killed a deer; and after taking breakfast, we saddled our horses, gathered up our venison, and started for home.

Chapter Fourteen

It is an old proverb that "after the sweet comes the bitter;" and it seemed to be so with me. I had lived a long time in the full enjoyment of health and domestic happiness, but the time had arrived for me to experience a reverse in my career.

My wife expressed a wish to visit our second daughter, who lived six miles distant. We had one horse that was wild and scary; but as he was a fine pacer, and she was an excellent rider, and afraid of nothing, she selected him to convey her to her destination. I felt afraid when I saw her take her seat in the saddle; but off she went, at a sweeping pace, and arrived safely at her journey's end.

After a stay of two nights, Mary took a small granddaughter before her on the saddle, and started to return home. But on her way, a little boy, who observed her coming, not wishing to be seen by her, stepped behind a tree, and, as she came opposite to it, turned round to escape. The horse, however, catching a glimpse of the boy, made a quick bound, and threw Mary flat on the road. The sudden fall, with the little girl in her lap, dislocated her backbone a little above the hips, and made a complete cripple of her.

She survived the accident three years, during which time she enjoyed not one day of good health. In the early part of her sickness she would not let even myself know her true situation, nor until her case became hopeless, and she was confined to her bed; when my hopes of happiness became more and more gloomy.

Such was her disposition, that she could not remain Idle, but would sit propped up in her bed, and sew and knit until her weakness overcame her, and she was forced to continue in a lying posture all the time.

If ever there was a true penitent, Mary surely was one. After a long-continued illness, she became every day weaker, until the twenty-ninth day of January, 1839, when she breathed her last.

Oh! heavens, what a stroke! The dearest friend of my bosom, the earliest love of my boyhood, the kind and affectionate mother of eleven of my children, taken from us for ever! All that I could say then, and even now, is, "Father, thy will be done." Now let her soul rest in peace.

The following verses have been composed to her memory:

I've heard that first and early love
   Outlives all after dreams;
But memory of my first great grief
   To me more lasting seems.

How oft my mind recalls the day
   When to my peaceful home
Death came, a dread, unwelcome guest,
   And beckoned to the tomb!

He left his seal upon her face;
   I shuddered at the sight;
And shudder still, to think upon
   The anguish of that night.

That gracious brow and kindling cheek
   Were cold as sculptured stone;
Those eyes were closed, that once had beam
   As bright as ever shone.

Yes; cold the cheek, and cold the brow;
   The eye was fixed and dim;
A husband mourned a loving wife.
   Who'd lived alone for him.

I knew not if 'twas summer then,
   I knew not when 'twas spring;
And if the birds sang in the trees,
   I did not hear them sing.

If flowers came forth to deck the earth,
   Their bloom I did not see;
I thought but on one withered flower,
   The last that bloomed for me.

A sad and solemn time it was
  Within that house of woe;
All eyes were dim, all hearts cast down.
  And every voice was low.

Softly we trod, as if afraid
  To break that tranquil sleep;
And took last looks at her pale face,
  Remembrance long to keep.

And when, at last, she was borne afar
  From this world's weary strife,
Often in thought I lived again
  With that kind and loving wife.

Her every look, her every word.
  Her varied voice's tone,
Came back to me, like things of worthy
  Most truly prized when gone.

Our sweetest hours glide swiftly by,
  And leave the faintest trace;
But that deep mark that sorrow wears
  No time can e'er efface.

My pen is powerless. I will not attempt to give anything; like an adequate description of that period of affliction, as it is easier far to judge of than to describe.

With returning spring I could see nothing that afforded me any delight; and I could not think of going to Mie hunting-grounds, as my spirit for sporting was entirely gone; and from that date — January 29th, 1839 — my career as a hunter and a woodsman ended. There was nothing done at hunting that spring; and during the entire summer there was neither bear-meat, venison, nor trout used in my family. It was to me a summer long and gloomy in the extreme.

When autumn arrived, and a little snow fell, my third son, James, who was married, and lived four miles west of me, came to my house, as he was going to Meadow Mountain to hunt for bears, and desired some of the family to accompany him to the hunting-grounds. As the rest of my sons were otherwise engaged, I told James that I had been thinking of going myself, as a relief to my feelings, but that I had not sufficient courage to undertake it. He asked me if I had become afraid of a bear. I told him that I would accompany him; when, if we could find one, after I had taken a good look at him, I would tell him more about it. Speedily equipping myself, we set out for the Little Crossings and Meadow Mountain.

We traveled on until, finding ourselves on the hunting ground, we became more and more cautious, and were looking and listening with the greatest care, when I saw the head of a fine-looking deer, which was peeping round a tree at us. I told James to try to kill her, as that would be the only chance we would have, and the distance was over a hundred steps. He took fair aim at her head, and fired, when off she ran, with one ear hanging down, and holding her bead sideways. But she succeeded in getting off and we saw no more of her.

We continued our course after bears, going from one place to another, and at last saw the tracks of one, which we traced into a laurel-swamp. We sent our dogs in after him; but, as they could make nothing of him, they returned to us, and we continued our course to another beech-ground, which seldom failed.

As we were drawing near to that place, which was our last hope of seeing a bear, for the evening had become warm, and the snow began to thaw and fall from the tall hemlocks, I told James that as we approached the outskirts of the beech ground we should be very careful and watch closely; for every bear in the woods would feed that evening, and I expected to see one there.

We proceeded with all care, and presently saw a large boar gathering beech-nuts, as if not aware of our presence. I told James to keep the two dogs quiet, while I would draw near and shoot the bear; but he asked me to let him have the shot; to which I agreed.

He started towards the bear, and had gone some distance, when he made a noise, which the animal heard. I saw the bear starting to run off, and called to James to shoot, when he fired at him. Off went the dogs, and myself after them.

I soon came up to the fight, but, shooting in too great a hurry, I hit the bear so far back that I did not kill him. As the combat became close, our dogs being in danger every moment of being crippled, if not killed, seeing a good chance for the use of my knife, I took advantage of it, and made a stroke at him, followed by another in quick succession, which ended the last bear-fight I ever had

That occurred in October, 1839. In company with my youngest son, Jeremiah, I then went to Bear Creek Glades to hunt; and the first morning I found the tracks of a buck, which I pursued a long time, until at last he entered a prodigious bleak place, where the wind was so cold that I had determined to leave him, and go home out of it, when, as I moved a few feet more on his tracks, I saw his head within ten steps of me; the wind having been blowing so hard that he had not heard me approach.

I carefully took my gun from my shoulder, turned it slowly until I brought it to bear on his head, and sent my ball through the middle of it. I laid hold of and drew him to a place where the wind could not strike me, skinned him, and hung him up; thus, working hard, I soon became warm; after which I went to the house, where Jeremiah was to be at noon

After dinner, we agreed to hunt through the woods home, as the deer therein were few, and very wild. As we proceeded on our way, we found the tracks of four deer, which we pursued, as their traces were very fresh; and, taking the leeward side of them, we would run round to get before them; but they always managed to be before us. The third time, seeing them passing again, I fired quickly, and killed a very fine doe, of which we each took half, and carried her home with us; but in doing so, suffered much from the cold.

My time was passing heavily away, and, having three of my youngest sons and one daughter, Sally, still with me, I determined to keep them together; but, not being content to work at home, I put the farm into the hands of the boys, and hired a girl to help Sally.

The following winter, some friends having recommended me as a suitable person, I was appointed, together with two other gentlemen, to assess the taxable property of Allegany County.

Experience had taught me that my children were not equally competent to carry on the business of my farm; and I also remembered the advice of my departed Mary, who, on the day before her death, had counselled me to seek some good woman as a companion, so that the property which she and I had gathered by means of hard labor should not be squandered and lost to the children. She had further directed my attention to a certain widow, who had never been the mother of any children, and recommended me to marry her if I could. But at that time I really thought I never could love another woman enough to wed her, and so I told Mary; to which she replied that she knew me too well to think so; and that after I had forgotten her I would love another.

And so it turned out; for, after I saw that it was absolutely necessary for me to have a housekeeper, and the more so as Sally had married, and had notified me that she was going to leave me, I began to make advances toward the little widow, and had reason to believe that she was favorably inclined toward me. But before any engagement was entered into, she was seized with a violent fever, and survived its attacks but a few days.

I met with this disappointment at a time when I was busily engaged with the assessment, and residing in a hotel, or rather a boarding-house, in Cumberland. The landlord, a man of perhaps forty years of age, had married a beautiful girl of seventeen or eighteen, whose situation making it necessary for her to remain in her room, her mother, a widow, forty-four years of age, who had no other child, was residing with her daughter, and attending to the business of the house. Thinking she was the wife of the landlord, I had taken no further notice of her than to see that she was a sprightly as well as excellent landlady, and I had boarded one week in the house before I knew that she was a widow.

At supper one evening, I happened to call her by the name of her son-in-law; when she replied that she was not the wife of the landlord, but the mother of his wife.

An old Yankee neighbor of mine then remarked, "A widow, I suppose?" to which she replied that she was, when he presently whispered to me, "That's your chance. Browning."

As I had made up my mind to procure a wife as soon as I could suit myself, I began to look at her with more interest than I had before taken, and discovered that she understood all about housekeeping. Being urged on by my Yankee neighbor to seek an interview with her, I watched my opportunity; and when I found her in the ladies' parlor, in a rocking-chair, I took the liberty to walk in, offering as my apology that the bar-room had become so noisy that I had ventured to come in there in hopes of escaping the disagreeable noise; and, if I was not trespassing, I would like very much to spend a little time in peace in her company.

She said there was nothing amiss in my doing so; that, having just got through with the business of the kitchen, she had left the girls to clear up the things, and being tired, had seated herself there to rest a while.

I remained perhaps an hour with her, and, being pleased with her manners, continued my visits to that room each night, as my business engagements permitted. She seemed to be interested in my company, and to make me equally so with hers.

Matters went on in this way for three or four days, when I was compelled to leave for the lower part of the county; and after the assessments were made, we hired a competent clerk to make out our books for the Levy Court; after which I went home. Subsequently, being summoned on the jury, I felt somewhat more willing to attend, on account of my little widow; and when the time came, and my name was called, I was not missing. I took lodgings at the same place, of course, with a full purpose of blowing up the old coal with Mrs. Mary M. Smith, which was the name of the little widow. She was slightly under the medium height, with a finely proportioned person and a well-formed face; indeed, she was considered by all to be as fine-looking a lady as any of equal age.

When I renewed my visits, I found her as agreeable as usual, and spent some pleasant hours with her. But a squall was gathering. I did not see her for three days, when, apprehending that some mischief-maker had been at work, and not knowing but that opposition was coming from the landlord and his wife, I asked him what had become of Mrs, Smith, as her place at the table was filled by a young woman. He said that Mrs. Smith and himself had had a little family dispute, which he did not wish to make public. So it went on until the evening of the third day, when, observing her standing at one of the front doors, I went to her, and inquired what had been the cause of her absence. She said that she did not wish the landlord to see her down stairs, for she had not left her room before for three days. I asked her if she would meet me that evening in the ladies' parlor, as I was anxious to hear what was going on. She replied that she would; that she was her own mistress, and would do as she pleased; and that she would inform me as to what we had to depend on.

When the time arrived, I went to the parlor, and found her there. She told me that her son-in-law had scolded her for keeping my company, and had threatened her with trouble if she continued to do so; to which she replied that she would do what she thought was for her best interest, and that she would not stay in Cumberland if she was to be treated like a servant.

We then agreed to marry, and ask nobody's consent about it; but in about half-an-hour in came her daughter, very angry, and ordered her mother to walk out of that room. I told her not to be in a passion, as I was only trying to persuade her mother to become my housekeeper; that I wanted a wife, and would like to secure her mother; and that I thought I should do so some day or other. She was very angry, and left us in short order. We kept on with our discourse for a short time, when I left the house, and engaged boarding in another tavern; after which I could only see my affianced wife when I passed up or down the street, while she was at the door, or with some others in the entry.

Thus matters continued until the following summer, when I took it in my head to visit the little widow again, though I had nearly fifty miles to travel to Cumberland. When I arrived at the place, I learned that the landlord and his lady had gone on a long journey. This suited my purpose exactly; and as the little widow was in full charge of the whole house, we had a pleasant opportunity to prepare plans for our marriage.

We knew full well that we should meet with the fiercest opposition from her son-in-law and daughter; and the pastor of the church had been made to believe that Mrs. Smith's husband was still living in the West. Objection being made on that ground, I was told by the clergyman that I should never speak to her again on the subject; and she was placed under a like restriction. Subsequently she removed from Cumberland to the eastern part of Pennsylvania, and I visited the western part of Virginia.

I had a friend living in Natchez, where it was said that John Smith, her husband, was still living; and being in a small county town in Western Virginia, and seeing letters mailed for Natchez, I went to my lodgings, sat down, and wrote to my friend in that town, to make inquiries for me regarding the whereabouts of John Smith, and to ascertain whether he was dead or alive. My friend wrote me, in answer, that he was dead, beyond any possible doubt. Still, the prejudice was so strongly rooted, that the minister would not solemnize the marriage; nor could we have anything done in our behalf until I consulted the bishop, and made him acquainted with the whole matter. He ordered the ceremony to be performed, and we were married on the 23d day of April, 1841; and I obtained as kind and industrious a wife as any man ever had, and, in a word, one who suited me to admiration. We were married in Cumberland, and I took her home to my farm, where I put her in possession of all my property.

We soon had everything in good order, and I began once more to feel myself contented and happy. I continued my fanning to good advantage, finding my second Mary M. not inferior to my dear little Irish Mary, whose memory was still cherished in my heart, and now lives afresh every time I visit the places where we sported, and passed our early loves together. It was only yesterday that I passed by the farm where, in our youthful days, we combatted with the wild beasts and rattlesnakes. In my now lonely situation, having lost my second wife, and weighed down with years, whenever I view those places where I experienced so much pleasure, my heart is rent with anguish, and the blood almost chilled in my veins, at the thought that all those pleasures are at an end. But I will leave my feelings to be judged of, rather than attempt to describe them.

But to proceed. My second marriage was solemnized; though it really seemed impossible for me, at any stage of my life, to marry a wife without the bitterest objections. But having outlived all those difficulties, I came to the conclusion that, though fifteen years younger than myself, I had obtained a fine, active wife. Irish Mary's words became true, in part, so far as loving my second Mary was concerned; for I really loved her to admiration. After my mind was thus set at rest, and I had settled down once more, the hunting fever began to rise again; so I took my horse, and went into the laurels of Meadow Mountain, where I set two large traps, and caught one bear; but in consequence of a wedding to which my wife and myself had an invitation, I neglected the traps so long, that the bear gnawed off a log, and escaped.

The spring following, I set my traps again; and while attending to them, I found there was a den of wolves not far distant. One day I told my wife that I would visit my traps, and at the same time would look for the wolves; but she, like my first wife, was fearful that, when the old wolves found me meddling with their whelps, they would turn on me and tear me to pieces. I reasoned with her, and told her that my other wife used to entertain the same fears; but that, after a long experience, she got entirely cured of them; and that she must not be uneasy on my account, for I had lived almost a lifetime among such animals, and never yet received a wound from any of them. After she had heard my reasons, she became less afraid; so, taking with me my horse, dog, and an orphan boy who lived with us, off I started for my traps and the wolf den.

There being a deer lick in the neighborhood of the traps, I made a fire, and directed the boy to stay by it, and keep the dog quiet, while I went to the deer lick to watch. I there climbed high up in a tree. I expected to hear the old wolves howl when it was dark; for they never carry their food to the den, but take it within a hundred steps or so, and then howl for the young ones to come and feed on what they bring. It is supposed that the old wolves will not take any prey near their dens, because they are afraid that other animals, such as bears and panthers, will smell the place, come to their den, and destroy their whelps. I do not know why it is, but it is certainly true that they never carry their meat to the den, but keep at a good distance, where their pups feed; and it is my opinion that the above supposition is correct, for a wolf is, beyond all other animals, the most cunning.

After having sat some time in the tree, as still as possible, I heard a rustling noise behind me; but though I turned round, and looked with great care, I could see nothing, I seated myself again, and heard a stone knock, as if some animal, having trod on one end of it, when the weight was taken off, the stone had again fallen back to its place. This time I was sure there was either a bear, wolf, or panther near; and was expecting to see it every moment, when a man spoke to me, and asked: "Why don't you shoot?" It was my son William, who had also come to watch the deer lick. He came up to me, and sat down a little while, when two pretty little red deer made their appearance. He shot at the foremost one, and then asked me for my gun; but I modestly declined to let him kill both, telling him that I would try a hand myself. I fired, and down dropped mine, while his was dying; and by the time we reached them, they were both dead; so we picked them up, and carried them to my fire.

There we found two men, who had come thither to hunt the wolves. One of them had been out the night before, and had heard the wolves howling; but being afraid to attack them by himself, he had induced William and another to help him to hunt them. On their way out they found my horse's tracks, and followed me until they found the boy at the fire, who told William where I was gone, whereupon he came to me at the lick. The night being warm and pleasant, we all enjoyed ourselves finely, roasting venison, and planning how to take advantage of the wolves the following morning. After all had expressed their views as to the best mode of attack, we lay down and slept until daylight next morning. After breakfast, we were all ready for the attack; and as each scalp of the old wolves was worth thirty dollars, and those of the young ones fifteen dollars each, it was necessary that the best means should be taken to secure the whole pack.

We therefore went on until we came in sight of the steep hollow, which was covered with pine and laurel trees, and rocks. Some of the party wanted to go round to the north side of the supposed den; but I objected to that mode of attack, because I knew that the wolves would smell us when we were far from the den, and make their escape with their whelps.

"Now," said I, "there being four of us, let us separate, and take a straight course through the hollow, keeping sufficiently close together to enable us to see from one to the other; and as our dogs will be on the leeward side of them, we will come on them by surprise, and they will have no time to carry off their young ones, but will attack us immediately, to keep us from the den."

This plan was agreed to at once; William Browning and Joshua Mason taking the left, whilst John Dewitt and myself took the right side, at a good distance apart, and remained perfectly silent. It was agreed that if anything should take place which would make it necessary to consult each other, one should whistle like a bird, and all would then meet to advise together. We started off among the rocks, and had gone but a short distance when Dewitt and myself, finding a road over which the old wolves had carried food to their young ones, I gave a long whistle, like a young turkey, and we all assembled together. While we were examining the road, one of the dogs came running toward us, with a frightened look; and when we sent him back, two old wolves immediately came dashing toward us, snapping and tearing after the dog. As the other three men were in front of me, I stood in my place, to watch the effect of the guns; but the wolves, on getting a good sight of the men, wheeled back, when both dogs made an assault on the den. The wolves cut so keen, however, that the dogs retreated again to within five steps of the men. I asked, in a low tone, why my companions did not shoot; but obtaining no reply, I determined, if I again got sight of the wolves, to shoot, running or standing; for I knew that, as soon as the wolves found they could not maintain their ground, they would leave the den, and clear out.

The third attack the dogs made, they were again beaten back — the wolves, as before, following them closely; but as they turned very quickly towards their den, I fired at the hindmost one, and broke one of its thighs; and immediately after a ball from William's rifle broke its back. As soon as the old male wolf found that his mate was gone, he gave a loud growl, and left the battle-ground in our possession.

It was hard to find where the young wolves were in the den, there being numbers of holes which had been used as inlets to the main den. As we could not find them without tools, we sent a hand for those that we wanted, and another to take care of our venison. Dewitt and I remained at the den, to keep the old wolf from carrying off the pups, and, if possible, to find out where they had concealed themselves. While the two men were gone, everything being quiet, the young wolves began to whine, when we found they were in a different place entirely from where we had supposed them to be. But as our venison had to be taken home, it fell to the lot of myself and my boy to carry it thither. We left the battle-ground for this purpose, and late the same evening the other hunters re turned with the heads of five young wolves, which, together with that of the old one, were worth one hundred and five dollars.

After this hunt, I attended to my farm and mill, which kept my family in comfortable circumstances. During the summer, my fifth son, Meshach A. Browning, gave me an invitation to visit him, saying that there was in his neighborhood a deer-lick which was much used by a large buck.

I went to see him, according to promise; and when the proper time in the evening arrived, we started for the deer-lick. As we were proceeding thither, we encountered a huge rattlesnake, with which we soon settled accounts. After fulfilling the prediction made in the Scriptures, that "the seed of the woman should bruise the serpent's head," we then went to the lick, and took our seats on a high rock, where we remained until dark without seeing any deer. Withdrawing to a short distance, we made a fire, and slept until the birds began to sing their sweet notes among the trees.

Rousing up my son, we walked lightly to the high rock, took our seats, and kept a close look-out for our buck, even after the sun was shining and drying up the dew; when I proposed that we should eat our breakfast and go home. At the base of the rock ran a fine spring of water, on the border of which I suggested that we should take our meal. As my son, however, objected to us leaving our seats, saying that it was possible a deer would yet come, we continued in our places, and had nearly finished our breakfast, when he saw two bucks at a distance, coming toward us in a great hurry. They were sometimes galloping, and sometimes trotting; which paces they held until they were nearly within rifle-shot.

My son rose to his feet too soon, and was preparing to shoot at too great a distance, when I took him by the arm, and begged him to hold his fire until the bucks came quite near, as they could not smell us, for we were on the leeward side.

But I could not prevail on him to sit down until, seeing that he was trembling with the buck fever, I told him that he would miss, and we should lose a fine buck

He said that if he missed he would pay me the price of a buck.

I replied that it was not the price I wanted, but the buck.

I then seized his gun, and told him to sit down, for he was trembling so much that he would shake the acorns off a tree if he were sitting in one.

He sat down, laughing, and said that I might take my own way.

By this time the two bucks were within range, and still approaching. My son insisted that I should then fire; but as I was determined to make sure work, I let them come on until they were within thirty steps, when they both stopped to examine whether any danger was near. Bang went my gun, or rather my son's gun, in my hands, and the big buck dropped on the spot. My son loaded the gun again, and ran after the smaller one; but it made its escape.

While the young man was gone after the little buck, I went to the large one, and found that he was so badly wounded he could not rise to his feet. He became furious as I approached him; and, although his horns were soft, and covered with what is called velvet, he seemed willing, if he could, to put them to any use by which they could do him service. But the poor fellow was deprived of all power to do anything in his own defence, and left to abide his fate; which occasioned me little pleasure, but rather aroused in me a feeling of pity for him.

Thus was the last deer killed; and in all probability, it was the last I ever shall kill; although I have since watched licks, and tried many times to kill another. Yet it is not impossible that I may someday kill one, though it seems very unlikely.

On account of the scarcity of game, my hunting was becoming laborious; and, as all other hunters were not governed by the kind and fair feelings which used to regulate their actions in bygone years, they began to take my traps, use them, and keep the game caught in them; thus greatly interfering with my sport. So I concluded to leave hunting, and enjoy myself with my wife at home on my little property.

Although, at times, I felt a strong desire to be in the woods, yet, finding myself unable to undergo the fatigue, I gave up the idea of being a hunter any longer, closed my business, and sold my farm, reserving twenty acres to myself and wife during our lives. I built a comfortable house on my reservation, and lived therein peacefully and pleasantly until the 14th day of February, 1855; when my wife was attacked with a severe stroke of palsy, which left her a complete cripple. She survived the first stroke; but on the 8th day of September, 1857, she was again stricken, on the other side of her body, and died in twenty-five minutes.

Thus was I a second time left alone in gloom, and almost despair, to wander from place to place in search of comfort, and to find but little. That little, however, I hope will be the means of keeping my feet in the paths of rectitude, that, when I am called to meet the common destiny of all flesh, I may be able to do so in the full hope of a glorious immortality.

My acquaintance with this lady originated about eighteen years before her death; and whilst living with me, hers was a life of continuous peace and harmony. The following verses have been dedicated to her memory:

> We lived together sixteen years
> In quiet, love and peace;
> And then misfortune dire decreed
> Our happiness should cease:
>
> Death came between us, to divide.
> And struck the fatal blow
> Which took from me one loved full well
> Since eighteen years ago.
>
> The last look that I gave, she lay
> With hands crossed on her breast;
> I kissed the lovely, placid face,
> Which spoke her spirit's rest.
> And now she dwells beyond the sun.
> And I am left below,
> To mourn for her I've loved so well
> Since eighteen years ago.

Chapter Fifteen

Having said something about the glades, I think it will not be amiss in this place to give a brief description of what was then a most beautiful country; together with that of a few settlers, at the time when I first became acquainted with them.

This delightful valley lies between the great Back-Bone Mountain and the

213

western hills of the Youghiogheny River, and covers an area of ten or twelve miles. This mountain commences at the Savage River, one of the tributaries of the Potomac, and runs from north-east to south-west, while the Hoop-Pole Ridge begins at the narrows of Deep Creek, and runs nearly parallel with the Back-Bone. All the waters on the eastern side of this mountain fall into the Potomac, and all those on the western side into the Youghiogheny, which empties into the Ohio River.

The glades are, or then were, clear, level meadows, covered with high grass, which was altogether different from what is there produced now, being of a much better character, growing nearly as high as rye, with a blue tassel at the top. The blades were set very thick on the stalk, to the height of three or four feet, I have often seen that grass tied in a knot over a horse's withers while his rider was sitting on him; and when it was cut in good season, it wintered cattle equally as well as timothy, though it was not so good for horses.

There were then hundreds, if not thousands, of acres of this grass growing where there is now nothing but bushes, and a rough and very inferior kind of grass, which serves very well for early pasture, but is of little worth for hay.

My mind cannot imagine a more beautiful sight than could then be obtained from the highest grounds of the Hoop-Pole Ridge, which commanded a view of the valley between that and the great Back-bone — a distance of from six to eight miles. It was a grand sight to watch the tall grass, rolling in beautiful waves with every breeze which passed over its smooth surface, as well as the herds of deer, skipping and playing with each other. It was not a strange thing to see a great lubberly-looking bear forcing his way through the grass, when every deer which got a sight or a scent of him would bound off, with tail erect, toward the nearest thicket. Sometimes a wolf could be seen prowling among the high grass, endeavoring to sneak on a fawn, or, if possible, even on a grown deer.

I used to think the months of April, May, and June were the best for a visit to these natural and beautiful meadows, as during those months there was not such a high growth of grass as would hide the turkeys from the traveler. From fifty to one hundred young turkeys, in one large glade of perhaps a hundred or more acres, all engaged in catching grasshoppers, flying, running, and in every sort of action, was a sight pleasant to the eye of the beholder.

Men of other States, but first those of Virginia, becoming acquainted with our glades, they were so much delighted with these unbounded pasture-lands, that they prevailed on some of the settlers to herd large quantities of cattle in them, for which they paid from fifty or seventy-five cents per head. This being soon discovered by Pennsylvanians, they followed the example of Virginia; and from April to September they crowded the glades with hundreds and thousands of cattle, eating, tramping, and running over every place in the glade country.

Meantime, the herders were at all times in the glades, calling to and whooping at the cattle, besides shooting at the deer and other game, until the animals became alarmed, and all the best of those that were not suckling fawns abandoned the glades and hid in the mountains; when the deer, owing to this constant slaughter, became scarce. Those herders would bleat like a fawn, and when the distressed mother would come, they would shoot her down, and leave the poor little fawn to starve.

This cruel practice was carried on until the neighboring settlers became so much annoyed at it that they petitioned the Legislature to pass some law, or laws, for their relief. But, unhappily, no law was ever enacted which could prevent the practice; and the people, seeing themselves still imposed on, and the laws made for their benefit and relief entirely disregarded, rose, went to the glades in the night, and there attacked and shot numbers of the cattle; and no doubt they would have shot the herders also if they had attempted to rescue their flocks.

This, in a great measure, put a stop for some years to the herding of foreign cattle, but not until the game was seriously thinned by these and other means, no less disgraceful; such as chasing the deer in deep snows, when they could not help themselves, and when neither meat nor skin was fit for use. Hundreds were destroyed in this way; and, between the one and the other practice, the breed of deer in Allegany has become very scarce.

After the lapse of a few years, the same plan of herding was again put in operation, with more ruinous consequences than before; and it has resulted in the almost entire destruction of all the grass and game in the country, and the loss of many cattle, which have been driven off with the foreign stock. Nobody was benefited by the operation but the owners of the herded cattle, and great injury has been done to the settlers in the glade country.

The early settlers, being but few in number, had a hard time to maintain themselves; and had they not used the greatest economy, they could not have lived in the wilderness at all. But they all made their own clothes: they raised flax and wool, which the women spun and wove into linen and linsey for the men, and flannel for their own wear. This was certainly better for females in winter, and not liable to half the danger from fire that cotton is at this time.

If any man wished to hire help, the parties would have an understanding as to what the wages were to be paid in. Sometimes linsey, pork, beef, honey, or corn, and at others, a calf, pig, sheep, deer-skin, bear-skin, coon-skin, or a wolf's scalp, together with many other articles, were used as substitutes for money. But if any man was so lucky as to have money, the wages he paid would surely be lower; and a day's work ranged from thirty-three to fifty cents — differing according to the length of the day. No difference, however, was made between harvesting and digging potatoes. If a man wore a pair of boots, he was considered a gentleman; and if a single lady had on a pair of calfskin shoes, or, by chance, a pair made of morocco, she was at once declared a belle.

All the settlers lived in cabins, and fed their children on bread, meat, butter, honey, and milk; coffee and tea were almost out of the question, being only used by a very few old ladies who had been raised in other parts of the country. Meat was generally plenty; for if the farmers could only keep the wild animals away from their hogs, the nuts and acorns would make thorn very fat. Pork, beef, bear meat, and venison were easily obtained, and on fair terms; but wild meat was not thought so much of, on account of its being so plenty in every place.

In those times, politics were but little understood; and all the voters in the glade country were Federalists, except one, old Mr. George Rhinehart. [1] We always held an election on the first Monday in October; when would be seen a goodly array of bunting-shirts and moccasins, and almost every man with a big knife in his belt. A foreigner would have supposed that the voters were really some military party going to oppose a threatened invasion; and if a quarrel occurred, they would take off perhaps both coat and shirt, and fight until one or the other acknowledged that he had as much of a beating as he was willing to receive. Then their friends, if they did not get into a scrape among themselves, would take the combatants to the nearest water, and wash off the blood. If no serious injury was done, which was seldom the case, that would, in nine fights out of ten, be the last of the quarrel.

The people in the country west of Cumberland were exceedingly generous, and particularly so to strangers traveling through their territory. If there was danger apprehended of a stranger losing his way, a hunter would pilot him five, six, or even ten miles, until he was out of danger of being lost; and then would not receive any compensation for his services

Although my feelings have been much harrowed by the recital of my recent afflictions, yet I will relate a story for the amusement of some of my readers who are yet in the enjoyment of youth and high spirits. It is a funny tale, and exhibits *one mode at least* of training a bear dog.

About twenty miles from my place lived a man named Steward, who had a son called James. They were not considered hunters, though they killed some bears, hunting in the moonlight. The old man, being very industrious, would not take time to hunt in daylight, but would go after dark; and sometimes, by shooting in the dark, he would miss his aim, and kill a dog. It so happened that, having but one of his old dogs left, he had raised a fine, large young one, which was big enough to be used in the chase, but had never seen a bear.

They had caught a bear; and the old man, taking the skin, wrapped it round his body, arms, and legs, and with a needle and thread sewed it in many places, to prevent it being pulled off in a scuffle. Then calling Rover, the bred dog, and tying him with an old cord to the porch, he told the old lady to see that he did not bite the rope, and come after him. Steward then went into the meadow, which had been mown, but had again grown up full of green grass, to try the courage of his young dog. Down he dropped on his hands and feet, to act the bear among the apple-trees; while James hissed the young dog on.

The pup, half mad and half afraid, made a great noise, and snapped at the supposed bear's hams; but when the old man would jump at him, strike his hands on the ground, Und snort like a bear, the pup would fly off, and return again to the fight, thus affording much amusement to both the father and the son.

But Rover, also eager for the fight, and seeing the Dear in full view, made several efforts to go, but was checked by hill mistress for some time. Seeing such fine fun, however, he could boar it no longer, and making a furious bound, he broke the cord, and started full drive toward the supposed bear, the old lady screaming, with all her strength: "Run, daddy! run, daddy! Rover is coming! Rover is coming!"

The old man, seeing his danger, made haste to an apple tree, and, springing up, caught the limbs; but before he was sufficiently high in the tree, Rover caught him by the leg, and began to tug away; while the pup, being thus encouraged, began to snap too. James, being pleased with the spirit of the pup, did not think, or perhaps was not aware, of his father's danger, but stood looking on until the old man roared out: "— the dogs! Beat them off, Jim I beat them off, Jim!"

Jim replied: "Hold tight, daddy. Grin and bear it a little longer; for this will surely be the making of the young dog."

By this time Mrs. Steward came up with her stick, and succeeded in relieving the old man from his dangerous situation; but not until he was so badly bitten, that he was confined to the house for several weeks.

As many persons are not conversant with the different characteristics of the wild animals, I will here give a short account of the most dangerous and mischievous beasts common to these forests. Bears, when they first come into existence, are not larger than a full-grown mole, or a half-grown rat, and entirely devoid of hair, being as naked as a young mouse. Their eyes are closed for the space of nine days, and they are generally brought forth about the middle of February. The young ones are nursed by their dam with great care, and suckled in the den until about the tenth of May, when, being then about the size of a cat, their dam leads them out to the feeding ground, and teaches them to eat nuts, acorns, berries, bugs, worms, little animals, ground-hogs, rabbits, squirrels, bird's nests, hogs and sheep, and sometimes cattle.

The bear, when full grown, weighs about four hundred pounds, and is exceedingly strong, far beyond what is warranted by its appearance. It can seize a large hog in its grasp, and walk on its hind feet a hundred yards, without resting its burden on the ground.

The bear becomes exceedingly fat when well supplied with nuts; and, strange to say, when well covered with fat, it eats sand, and the rosin which comes out of pine trees. These substances pass down to within two or three inches of the end of the last intestine, where they form a hard mass, to which the intestine adheres so firmly, that it cannot be separated from it without tearing the inner coating of the bowels. In this condition the bear enters its hole, lays and sleeps from about Christmas until the last week in April, and, if the weather be unfavorable, until the first day of May, neither eating a particle of food nor drinking any water. When the weeds and grass have attained a sufficient growth, the bear comes out, and eats weeds, which so purge him that he is speedily relieved of this obstruction; after which he can eat what he pleases.

The bear climbs trees with great facility, and procures honey from the wild bees, as well as acorns and chestnuts from the highest trees. It frequently cuts, or rather gnaws, its way out of log traps made for the purpose of catching it — the logs in which are frequently a foot in diameter. It is a bold, undaunted beast, though not apt to pick quarrels with other animals; but if any others trespass on its rights, it then becomes furious and vindictive. I love and admire the bear, because it desires to insult neither man nor beast, nor will it suffer any to insult it.

The bear is not at all particular in its feeding, nor dainty in its appetite. It appears, however, to have a preference for vegetables, green corn, nuts, berries, and acorns; but scarcely anything comes amiss, when pressed by hunger, and worms, slugs, all kinds of eggs, small quadrupeds, and even carrion, often tempt it to allay the cravings of hunger. When other food fails, a straggling hog or a sheep is almost certain to become its prey; and, to secure the former, the bear will often venture so near a house as to be within reach of the rifle. Bear meat is considered a delicacy by those accustomed to it, and the hunter always deems it a prize worthy of much effort to obtain.

Next comes the panther, which is altogether of a different disposition. Although possessed of great strength, perhaps fully equal to that of the bear, it is a most dastardly coward; and will suffer itself to be driven into a tree by a half-grown dog, when one snap of its teeth, or a single blow from its paw, would forever silence the dog. The panther seeks its victim in the dark, and, springing on it, — whether it be the largest-sized buck, a hog or a sheep, a cow or a two-year old colt, — it will throw whatever it seizes to the ground, and kill it without a seeming struggle.

I once saw where a panther had killed a four-year old cow for Col. Lynn. Two young men and the Colonel were traveling in company; but the Colonel left them, and hurried on to have dinner ready, leaving his companions to follow at their leisure. The Colonel saw the cow in the road as he passed along, and the young men, who were not more than a quarter of a mile behind the Colonel, and traveling in open day, found the cow dead in the road. More than twenty minutes could not have elapsed between the Colonel's departure and the discovery of the dead cow. The panther had broken her neck in two places, and her back-bone in one.

The panther is a great sneak. If it meets a hunter in day-light, it will slink off, but will not run if it can help it; and if the least noise like the barking of a dog striken its ears, it is ready to climb a tree. In that way I have killed many of them. During day-light they will not fight until wounded, but in the night they are bold and dangerous. I believe the reason that I have at all times escaped them, was, because I always kept at least one, and mostly two good dogs with me; and their cowardice deterred them from making an attack on me.

The wolf is next in strength and size, but far more cunning and mischievous than the panther, like which, it is seldom seen during day-light, but in the night it is mischievous, as well as impudent. It will come very near a house, and chase away the sheep to a safe distance, when it will kill them as long as it can find a victim, fill itself with the blood, and, in all likelihood, not return again to the same place for a month, fearing to be caught in a trap.

Wolves always seek the most hidden places in the wilderness in which to make their den, where they raise their young. They sometimes penetrate to a great distance underground, but they always go under far enough to shelter themselves from all storms. While the female is unable to seek food for herself, and even after she brings forth her litter, the male attends to her wants, and will travel ten or fifteen miles in search of food for her and her whelps. If the distance is great, he will swallow large pieces, until he is stuffed full; when he will return home, and disgorge it for the use of his family.

If he takes a small sheep at a distance of from two to five miles (I have known a wolf to carry a yearling sheep at least six miles), he manages to get the sheep on his back, holding it firmly by the neck, and thus conveys it to the young ones, until they are of sufficient strength to go out and provide for themselves. When they are able to chase the deer, they all hunt together until they start up one, when they chase it in company till they become tired. Then one keeps the deer all the time at full speed, while the others watch; and if the deer makes a turn, they strike in before the one that is pushing the deer, and continued the chase, while the others watch the wind for the scent. The deer, thus pursued alternately by a fresh wolf, soon becomes tired, and takes to some stream to escape its pursuers. As soon as they find the deer takes to the water, they separate, some going on one side of the stream, and some on the other; and as they can run faster on land than the deer can travel through the water, they soon tire it, and it becomes an easy prey to its ravenous pursuers, which in a few moments tear it in fragments, and devour every morsel of it.

At the request of many persons, I will endeavor to explain the character of the most dangerous reptiles which inhabit the mountains of the Alleganies.

The first, and most dangerous, is the rattlesnake; which lives by its cunning, and can charm birds, squirrels, rabbits, mice, chickens, etc. I have seen a rattlesnake with a full-grown rabbit in its stomach.

I was once riding in the woods, when, seeing a jay-bird making strange movements, flying back and forward, and crying piteously, it occurred to me that a snake was at work decoying the poor bird within its reach. I tied my horse, and went to see what was the matter with the bird; but when I arrived on the ground, I could see nothing move of it; neither could I hear its cries any longer. Observing the weeds shaking where I supposed it was, I hurried to the place, and there saw a rattlesnake with the bird in its mouth, and not more than half of it visible. The snake was lying on its back, with its tail

wrapped round a small bush; and, supposing the bird to be dead, I waited to see what the reptile would do with its prey.

The snake's mouth was spread out of its usual shape, but with its upper jaw it held the bird fast until the under jaw, by little and little, was pushed forward to meet the upper one, when the corners of its mouth were stretched out, while the snake, drawing itself up, and holding fast to the bush with its tail, slid the bird down, though apparently in great pain while so doing. Then it would move its jaws as before, first one and then the other, until it again bad a good hold; when, drawing itself up, it would elide the bird down still farther. After seeing thus much of its way of making its living, I took a club and gave the snake a heavy blow a little below the bird, which made it so sick at the stomach that it pushed the bird out sooner than it had swallowed it. It then let go of the bush and died.

In addition to the foregoing, which was the only case I witnessed of a snake charming a bird, I will here relate an instance which was seen by my son, Thomas Browning, of the operations of a rattlesnake upon a flock of birds. He says,

"My father once sent me to the woods to give salt to some young horses. On my way, I saw a great number of birds of different kinds collected in one place; and they all seemed in distress, as if they had discovered an enemy robbing their nests. As their attention appeared to be drawn to one spot, I went to the place; but as I approached it, all the birds flew off to the trees except one, which we call a flicker, or yellow-hammer, a bird one size larger than a robin. It was sitting on a small stick, very near the mouth of a rattle-snake, apparently insensible of danger; the snake looking at the bird, and the bird looking as earnestly at the snake.

"I stood still, to see what would be done. The bird seemed to be in great distress, and sent forth most pitiful cries. They both kept their places for a minute or two, when the snake commenced moving very slowly towards the bird, until it was near enough; gently opening its mouth, it took the bird by the breast, slily and easily burying its jaws in the feathers, and then it clenched them with a strong hold that its victim could not resist. The bird then seemed fully sensible of its danger, and made great efforts to fly off; but the serpent held on, the bird raising him several times partly from the ground. The snake, however, cared not for the fluttering of the bird, some-times lying on its back, and making no effort beyond holding on securely, and the bird soon yielded.

"I felt so provoked, and my feelings became so much enlisted for the inno-cent bird, that I struck a heavy blow with a club across the snake's neck, which soon relieved the poor thing, and it hopped off a short distance. I went on to do my errand, and on my return in the evening the bird was dead. I suppose that, when I struck the snake, the blow caused its poisoned teeth to enter into the bird's flesh, which occasioned its death." [2]

I have never seen a snake swallow either a rabbit or a squirrel; but I have taken them out of their bodies, and therefore say they do prey upon them. I have killed thousands, and seen them under nearly all circumstances; and although, as before remarked, I have never seen the rattlesnake swallowing his larger prey, I will state one instance, which occurred in my own neigh-borhood, and was related to me by Mr. James Barnard, and other eye-witnesses, for whose credibility I can vouch.

Mr. Barnard states that himself and other hands, when mowing in his fa-ther's meadow, discovered a large rattlesnake, which had a ground-hog in its mouth, and partly down its throat. The hog was about half grown, or possibly a little more, and the body was fully as large as that of a rabbit. The young men saw the reptile striving hard to swallow its prey, and waited to witness the result; but being unable to spare any more time, they were compelled to leave it until evening.

Visiting the place late in the evening, and finding the snake had done but little more towards swallowing the hog, they concluded to leave it for a morning visit.

In the morning, finding the ground-hog a little farther down, they left the snake undisturbed, and visited it alternately three times each day, for seven days, before the ground-hog was swallowed; and at the end of that time they found the snake with that animal in its body. The serpent, however, was quite helpless, being unable to crawl away with so large a burden, — probably three times its own weight, — which it could not drag over the sticks and rocks in its way.

I am sure this is all true.

The rattlesnake is by far the largest and most dangerous of all the reptiles in these regions; and I have sometimes killed those that were five feet six inches long, and ten inches in circumference below where the prey was deposited. It is not spiteful, however, unless provoked.

These snakes are of three different colors: one is almost black; another, which generally grows larger than the black, is beautifully spotted with yellow diamonds; and the third is of a dirty brown, nearly the color of the ground, and never grows to a large size; but it is so very wicked that it will run at a man, and bite as soon as it comes near enough to reach him.

I was once making wild hay in a glade in which there were hundreds of snakes, and one of my sons-in-law was assisting me. I was so much afraid of the serpents that I did not like to be out after night; but after we had shocked our hay, and were about to start home, seeing some young horses coming toward our shocks, we staid long enough to drive them off. We then left for home, which we reached without coming in contact with any snakes.

Next morning, being Sunday, after breakfast we went to the glades to see if our hay was safe from the cattle, which would throw it down if they came there. When we arrived at our destination, seeing the same horses, we went to them, and found one, a young mare, bitten on the nose by a snake. I think she was four years old, and a very fine animal belonging to the young man's father. Before we got her home she was entirely blind, and the blood was dropping from hundreds of places where the veins had burst through the skin.

We got the mare home, and applied some remedies; but to no purpose, as the swelling increased continually. In the evening, the old man and his wife came over to try and save their favorite colt; but all in vain. The swelling increased until the head was entirely out of shape; and I am confident, if the head had been put out of the stable door, no one could have told what it was. The eyes were entirely closed, and there was nothing to show that eyes had been there but a very small wrinkle in the skin. The mare lived until about eight o'clock; and I am sure that every breath she drew could have been heard a quarter of a mile; such was the difficulty in her breathing. At length the windpipe seemed to be altogether closed up, and she died in the greatest agony.

The next day, the young man, myself, and daughter again went to making hay, as we had some grass in swath which required to be spread out. We had been but a short time at it when I heard a kind of scream, while I was at one end of the swath and they at the other, and I saw my daughter laughing at her husband, while he stood almost speechless.

As I drew near, I heard a snake rattling at them, and saw that it was one of those dirty colored fellows, which, being determined on biting somebody, would jump first at one, then at another; but we kept him at good distance. After the young man got over a little of his fright, — for the snake had been under the swath which he was spreading, and jumped at him two or three times, — I made a pass at it with an iron fork, and one of the points entered the skin of its neck.

When the evil serpent found it could not loosen itself, it twisted around in all sorts of ways. I turned its head toward its body, and invited it to try a bite upon its own hide; which it did as quick as possible, sinking its fangs deep into its own flesh. I made it bite itself deeply several times, and then let it go, in hopes it would do something that would show us how to cure the bite; but we were disappointed, for it became so sick in a few minutes that it could barely crawl under the hay to shelter itself from the sun; though as often as it would cover itself up I would throw the hay off again. By this time it got quite uneasy, and tried to bury itself in the mud; rolling over, and over, and over again, and turning different shades of color. Its scales would rise up, and it would look white; after which it would again assume its usual hue. It thus continued changing its color, until at length, turning suddenly on its back, it died; and there was not the least sign of life after it turned over.

In all cases, after they are apparently killed, there will always be signs of life remaining in the tail for many hours, even after they have their heads cut off. But I feel certain that their poison is as fatal to them as it is to men or other animals; and I know that in this case the poison killed the snake, and that it was in great agony while it lived.

On another occasion, previous to the one just mentioned, I was traveling in company with two other gentlemen, Mr. John House and Mr. Jacob Clemmer; and on our way we encountered a very large rattlesnake stretched across the road. Mr. House, who was a famous hunter, and, like myself, had a great aversion to snakes, particularly dangerous ones, immediately said, "I will take that rascal's hide off him."

The other gentleman and myself opposed the dangerous attack on his snakeship. But Mr. House was firm in his purpose; and, taking out his knife, he cut a forked stick, sharpened both of the prongs, and going cautiously up to the snake, he poised the stick over its neck, about four inches behind its head, and drove the forks into the ground across the serpent's neck; which held him so tight that he could not get out. Having on a strong pair of boots, he set his heel on the snake's head, keeping his whole weight on it, and then took hold of it with his left hand, when his thumb and fingers could not meet round its body.

Holding the snake fast. House kept slipping his hand up, until it was near the tail; the serpent, meantime, turning, flouncing, and rattling, while my companion screamed at him to let it alone. But he was not to be turned from his purpose; and, stretching the snake up (it was nearly as tall as the man), he then took the knife, and, cutting round the reptile's neck near to the head, ran the knife from the stick, up the snake's belly nearly to his hand, thus ripping it from stem to stem. Then, throwing down the knife, with the thumb and finger of his right hand he picked at the skin, and starting it up a few inches, he took hold of it, and at one pull took the whole skin off, rattles and all. Every part of the snake's body was laid as bare as a skinned eel. The snake, as soon as its skin was off, and House had removed his foot and the forked stick, coiled itself, and dared us to come again, by poking out its forked tongue at us. I took a stick and held it to its head, and it bit it every time I put it within reach.

We let it alone for some time, to see what it would do; and when it found we had ceased to trouble it, it crawled away from the road at least a rod, and coiled itself up under some leaves; when I put the stick toward it again, which it struck several times. We then left it in that condition; but when we returned the next day, the snake was nowhere to be seen. Whether it crawled off, or some animal or bird devoured it, I do not know; but I saw no sign of its having been eaten there. When it crawled away after losing its skin, it moved by means of its ribs, like those large worms which frequent old stables.

I was once on the Yough. River with Mr. Jeremiah Casteel, when, seeing something crossing the stream above us, being in a canoe, we paddled up to it, and found it to be a rattlesnake. We pushed our canoe close to its snake-ship; but when it discovered that it was our intention to assault it, it prepared for battle, and gave notice that it was as good on water as on land. It coiled itself up on the water, inflated its body with air, and there laid, as light as a bubble, holding its rattles high up from the water, and rattling as well as if it had been on land. Not thinking it could jump on the water, I was in the fore-part of the canoe, holding the paddle in my hand to strike with, when, just as I was drawing off to give the snake a blow, it made a pitch at the canoe; but as it came I struck it with a paddle, barely checking it. I then made another blow at it, disabling it slightly, caught it with the end of the paddle, and pushed it down to the bottom of the stream.

I held it under the water long enough, as I thought, to drown anything; but when I allowed it to rise again, it was as fresh as when I first put it down. I held it under another term; but to no purpose; for it was the same thing still, and I could not see that my strokes of the paddle were doing it any harm: it seemed as if the water had restored the snake to its former strength and vigor. When I found that it could not be drowned, I took my paddle edgewise and aimed a heavy blow across its neck, which put an end to its resistance.

It would appear that rattlesnakes can neither be readily choked to death nor drowned. Once, when a boy, I was going on an errand to a place about two miles distant, and near my home I found a rattler. Quickly procuring a piece of hickory bark, I made a noose, tied the bark to » long switch, snared the snake by the neck, dragged it to a tree, tied my bark to a limb, and went my way.

After staying two or three hours, I returned; when I found the snake hanging as limber as a string. "Well," said I, "my fellow, you'll never bite anybody after this."

I then took my pole and loosened the bark; but, to my great surprise, the snake was as fresh, and as full of life, and fight also, as he was when first hung up. I am in doubt whether or not they breathe at all — certainly not like other inhabitants of the land.

Rattlesnakes are brought into existence in the following manner:

The female snake deposits twenty or thirty eggs in the ground, where the warm earth gives them life, and at the proper time the old one comes and receives them into her body, where they remain until she enters her den in October. In April and May they all come out together, when the young ones are usually from six to nine inches long, and can shift for themselves.

On one occasion, about the last of April, William Browning, a brother-in-law, Mr. Enlow, and myself, went to a rattlesnake den which was within a quarter of a mile of William Browning's house.

The evening was cool, and, entering the den, we commenced our search, and soon found several large snakes, which were so chilly that they could make no resistance. We continued killing them until we could find no more on the ground; when we commenced turning up the flat stones, under which we discovered many little snakes, not more than six inches long. Where we found the small ones there were no old snakes near. When we could discover no more, we counted the dead ones, which were eighty-four in number.

Having found three small ones by themselves, together with the fact that I have seen the eggs in the snakes' bodies in July, in October discovered the young snakes in their bodies when they entered their dens, and in April found the young ones entirely by themselves, the conclusion above stated has been forced upon me. It must be remembered, however, that I have never seen the old snake deposit her eggs; nor have I ever seen her swallow her young; but I only drew my conclusions from the facts just set forth. Certain it is, however, that the young of the garter-snake (which is a common and well-known species, by no means dangerous, of which I shall say but a few words, as little notice is generally taken of them), when in danger, run to the mother, which receives them into her mouth and swallows them, thus shielding them from harm.

225

But to return to the rattlesnake. It has large teeth in the upper jaw, and some have two long fangs, while others possess four. Those with four fangs have two on each side, directly behind which stand two others, so that when they strike at an enemy they make four cuts. These teeth are exceedingly sharp and strong, with crooked points; and about an eighth of an inch from the sharp point a small hole is perceptible in each tooth as soon as it grows to any size. That little hole passes up the tooth, and connects with a larger hollow in the hind-part of the tooth, which cavity, in a large snake, is about the size of a common straw; beneath which, at the base of the tooth, lies a little bag, containing the poison. As the snake strikes, he elevates his upper jaw, drives his teeth in, and then presses his jaw down. This pressure, acting upon the base of the tooth, forces the poison out of the bag, through the tooth, into the gashes made by the sharp points, and the wound is completed.

Having shown how they make the wound, it will not be amiss, perhaps, to mention some of the remedies used. If the bite be in a place that will admit of it, cut out the part bitten; when, the blood flowing out freely, by rubbing the wound downward, the poison will run out with it. Another remedy is, to gather the weed called boneset, or St. Anthony's cross, boil a handful of it in new milk, drink the milk, and bind the weed on the wound. This I have never known to fail in effecting a cure in a few hours when applied promptly. Also, drink from a pint to a quart of whiskey; which will not intoxicate the patient, but will neutralize the poison. It is likewise commonly reported that spirits of turpentine, applied plentifully to the wound, will draw out the poison and effect a cure. Lastly, take common yellow clay, mix it in a mortar, and apply it to the wound, supplying fresh clay as soon as that on the part gets warm, until the poison is drawn out; which will be in twelve hours. The best preventive, however, is to wear strong boots, or coarse leggins, through which the snakes cannot sink their teeth into the flesh.

As there are no other dangerous snakes in the hunting ground which I frequented, and as I have never seen more than two or three copper-heads during my life, I will finish with the snakes after making a few more remarks.

From the vast numbers of these reptiles which formerly abounded in this region, it is surprising that so few persons have been bitten by them; and I account for it from the fact that they nearly always give warning by rattling before they strike. They are now, however, greatly diminished in numbers, as they are always destroyed when Been; and it is, or has been, the practice of those visiting their dens to go there late in April or early in May, before they stir abroad, expressly to kill them. In this way, and by the frequent burning of the forests, after they leave, and before they return to their dens, vast numbers are annually destroyed. They are now (1859) comparatively rarely seen, except in a few localities difficult of access, of near their dens.

A word or two regarding the best mode of raising and training good hunting-dogs; which is one of the essentials for a hunter to know:

Take a half-blooded pup, a cross between the bulldog and the greyhound, **feed him well,** — for a starved pup will surely be a thief, — and when he is able to follow you to the field, make him lie down at your feet, and do not allow him to rise until he is told. When he gets a rod or two from you, either make him return, or wait till you come ap with him, and then make him lie down again. In all cases where he does his duty caress him, and he will soon learn to love his master; after which he will not be afraid, and mil away to avoid correction. Whip but lightly, until you have so trained the dog that you can depend on his obedience to your command to stop, or to return at your order. When you have taught him this, you may venture a little more severity, according to the offence; and when he is taken to the woods he must be first taught to trail his game; for if a deer is wounded he should trail it carefully, going but a step or two before his master, until the game is killed. When the master can see the deer which he has killed, he should let the pup go towards the carcass, and then call him back; then, advancing a little nearer, he should let him go to the deer a second time, and call him back again; then let the master accompany him to the deer, and flatter him as much as possible. By this means, when he is sufficiently instructed, and is sent to catch a wounded deer, he will kill it, return to his master, and guide him to the spot where it is lying. And he must never leave his master more than two or three steps, lest a deer bound off, and he run after it, and be spoiled.

When in the woods, and your dog seems to desire to run after deer, pretend you see some, and take the gun in your hand as you would if you were creeping toward a deer; when, if the dog misbehaves, you can chastise him. By treating a dog this way every time he becomes unruly, he may be entirely cured of his faults.

I have had some very fine dogs which were a cross between the bulldog, the greyhound, and the fox-hound; but the only objection to them is, they are so noisy that you can never steal on the game, but keep it always on the lookout.

A hint or two concerning trout-fishing may not be amiss.

It is generally considered that the trout are the most beautiful as well as the most delicious fish that swim. They will not live in any but the purest waters; consequently they are only to be found in mountainous regions and cool climates. The Alleganies have been famous for trout, and there are great numbers there at this time; although they have been much reduced by residents from other states, who, with seines, catch them in great quantities, and leave on the ground all that are considered too small for use.

The trout is a beautiful fish, and varies from the smallest size to twenty-two inches in length. When in good condition, they are blue, with two rows of small red spots along the sides. The time for catching them is from the first of May until the last of July, and the bait used in the early part of the season, while the trout are running up the streams, is the common red worm; but in June and July, when they settle in deep, still water, the tail of the crawfish is preferred by all skillful fishermen. After they settle in deep water, from the first peep of day until nine o'clock is the best time to fish for them with a hook; but the evening also, from five o'clock until eight, is a good time to take them. A small, rough-looking white worm, found in rotten wood, excels all other bait I have ever tried; but the small grub-worm also makes good bait.

After the middle of August, the trout begin to decline in quality, become poor, and the meat is dry. In September they commence spawning; when they ascend the small streams to sandy places, where they may be seen in great numbers, depositing their eggs in the sand; but in October they return to the deep water, at the mouths of the warm branches or springs, where they remain until the following spring. In February, the young trout, scarcely an inch long, can be seen in squads of a hundred together in those warm streams. They remain there until they are sufficiently strong to keep out of the way of the larger ones, when they swim down to the deep water and take care of themselves.

[1] This old Mr. Rhinehart was a Frederick county man, and a Democrat, or rather a Republican, as they were called in the days of Thomas Jefferson's Administration. At every election he would deposit his vote, and it was the only Republican vote polled in the entire District. I speak of this merely to show the firmness of one man, in contending against ninety or a hundred, as a circumstance which does not often occur among voters.

[2] I am aware that, among the incredulous portion of the community, some of my statements may, and probably will be, rejected as fabrications. I can excuse such, for the reason that, had I been brought up in a city, I suppose I should, like them, be an unbeliever; but I can assure all that I have not written one word that is not as strictly true as if I had been under oath; and in this country these accounts are not only not disputed, but they are confirmed by many old settlers.

Chapter Sixteen

With a short chapter on the mode of trapping some of the animals which I have been so long engaged in hunting, and a brief notice of the soil, productions, etc., of portions of Allegany County, I shall conclude my narrative.

I have been asked to describe the wooden trap used in catching bears, which is built as follows:

First, a floor of split trees is laid on the spot whereon the pen or trap is to be constructed, which should be selected between two trees, standing from eight to twelve feet apart, so tha.t a pole may be laid across, to serve as a lever for raising the upper part of the trap. Two end logs are then laid down close to the floor, which must be five feet long, and two side logs notched closely down on the end ones. Another end log is then notched on to the side one at the front end of the pen, and all securely pinned together; after which a second end log is laid on the rear end, and a round notch made in both the side logs to receive it. This end log must roll as the top of the trap raises. Then, beginning at one side of the pen, cover it over with half-trees, split in two pieces, leaving no crack through which a bear can put his nose, or he will tear off slabs until he makes a hole large enough to escape through.

C. S FASLER. DEL

HUNTERS' CAMP ON MEADOW MOUNTAIN.

Thus, having the body of the trap completed, and all pinned down to the end logs, the next thing is to set it. Behind the trap drive two stakes into the earth, and about two feet from the ground bore a hole through each of the stakes, through which put a pin of strong wood. On this pin place a piece of flat wood, about two feet long, with a hole bored through it about six inches from one end, and a notch cut in the short end; thus making the lower end of the trigger, as it is called, eighteen inches, and the upper end, six inches long. Take a pole, say eighteen or twenty feet in length, and lay it on the cross-pole which rests against the trees. This pole projects about three feet over the cross-pole, and a strong withe, made of long, thin hickory switches, is fastened to a pin in the fore-part of the trap, and looped round the end of the pole, to raise the upper half of the trap. Then, by taking hold of the long end of the pole, and pressing it down, the upper half of the trap may be raised up sufficiently to let the bear go in. Take fresh meat, lay it in the pen, and tie it fast to the trigger by a string passed through a crack of the trap. One end of the string being fastened to the meat, and the other end to the trigger, bear down on the back end of the pole, and put the end of it into the notch on the upper end of the trigger, and the trap is set.

When a bear enters, he takes hold of the meat and pulls it forward; when the string, being tied to the lower end of the trigger, draws the top of the trigger oft' the pole, and allows the upper half of the trap to fall, when all the notches drop into their places. The bear is then compelled either to remain in the pen until the trapper comes, or to gnaw a hole large enough to escape through; which they often do when the logs have become decayed by age.

BEAR-TRAP.

To entice the bears, I used to roast the leg of a deer, and while the meat was roasting, rub honey over it, so that it would smell strong of the latter. Then I would cut off pieces, tie them under my moccasins, walk through the grounds the bears frequented, and return to the trap; when every bear which smelled my tracks would follow the trail to the trap, and generally get caught.

To catch wolves, I used to take the carcass of a cow or a horse, and lay it in a small stream of water; then I would go off some distance, so that the wolf would not see where, cut bushes, and stick the ends in the mud so thick that the wolf could get at the meat only in one place, which was left open and clear. The carcass was so laid that the wolf could eat at either side.

A wolf will never jump over the carcass, but will hunt some place at which he can cross the stream, and go round to the other side to eat. Then, about six or eight steps above the place, and the same distance below, leave a passage open for him to cross the water, and set bushes in so thick that he can't get through at any other place. Widen the stream where he crosses, so that he can't step over it; put a flat stone in the middle of the stream to step on, and lay green moss on the stone, to make it look as if it had never been moved; then cut meat into small pieces, and strew them on both sides of those cross-ing-places, both above and below the carcass.

When a gang of wolves come to the meat, the larger ones drive the smaller off, which run about, seeking food; and, soon finding the small pieces strewed round the crossing-places, they run across, stepping on the moss-covered stone, and every time they return they are sure to go over at those places, setting their feet precisely in the same place on the stone.

When I find they have made tracks on the stone by wearing away the moss with their feet, I remove the stone, and put my steel-trap in its place; covering it in the same manner as I had previously covered the stone. When the wolves again return, the little ones run immediately to the crossing-place to seek food, and putting their feet in the very place they should, the trap takes such a fair hold of one foot that they cannot escape.

The old ones being at the meat when a young one is taken in the trap, they are not afraid to return to the meat again, as there was nothing there to scare them. After all become afraid of the crossing-places, I take my trap, and set it in the mud where they stand to eat the meat, and catch one there, after which they will come no more to that place.

After trapping them that way for several years, they became so cunning that they would not touch any bait I offered them. Then I adopted another plan, which is as follows:

I found that they would pick up any fragments of old bones that lay on the land; but if they lay in water, or close to it, they would not touch them. So I saved all the large bones from the table, particularly the joint-ends of the beef bones, beat them to pieces, put them in a basket, mounted a horse, so that my tracks could not be scented, and scattered the bones over a piece of ground as large as a small garden, and around that place stuck some bushes, through which they would have to pass.

When they had eaten all the little bones, I gave them a second mess, and placed my trap between the bushes, cutting the ground precisely the size of the trap, but carefully carrying away every particle of the dirt taken out. Sinking the trap about one inch below the surface, I then laid old leaves over it, and covered these about one inch deep with buckwheat-bran, which keeps the wolf from smelling the trap. Then I took some of the grass which grew about the spot, and laid it so carefully over the trap that no eye could discern the difference between that place and the surrounding ground. This done, early in the morning, or before a shower of rain, which destroys all smell, has never failed to catch a wolf as they are running about in search of the little bones.

The method used for trapping bears and wolves will answer also for panthers, catamounts, wildcats, and even foxes. Care must, however, be used with foxes, as they are about as cunning as the wolf, and of course the same precautions should be observed in trapping them.

Trapping the otter is an easy task, compared with the wolf and the fox. The otter lives in the rivers and larger creeks, and eats the cray, and all other kinds of fish that it can catch, as well as insects living in the water. Like the beaver, it builds a house, commencing the mouth of it, or door, in the water, to avoid giving the scent to its pursuers. It digs or scratches into the bank, rising higher and higher, until the dwelling is placed above the highest stage of water, and the opening is deep enough below the surface to escape the notice of its enemy. It then makes a large place in its hole to hold leaves, grass, moss, etc., which serve to keep it warm in winter, and in which it sleeps during cold weather.

During the warm days in winter, the otter comes out on the ice to play; diving under the water and catching fish while they are stiff with the cold, and can't escape. Where the fish are collected in great numbers, in deep water, it dashes suddenly among them, and thus makes sure of catching some. In playing, the otter seeks steep banks, and, sitting on its hind-parts, and supported by its fore-feet, it slides down a bank; climbing up again and again, until it is tired of the fun, when it leaves some of its musk on the place as a token that it has been sliding there. Every otter which comes to that place and smelled the odor, will roll over, and cut all kinds of capers upon the bank and in the water, till they get tired; after which they deposit their musk in like manner.

To catch them, I set a small, common steel-trap, about two inches under the water, at the place where they slide down the banks, and exactly where they enter the water, by which means they are forced to tread on the trap, when they are caught by one foot, or both. The chain must be long enough to allow the otter to enter into the water, in order that the trap may sink with it to the bottom and drown it, or it will bite its foot off above the trap, and escape.

The following is the mode of shooting deer by firelight:

If the deer come to a lake or river to drink, and eat the moss which grows beneath the water, a canoe must be prepared, with a piece of bark peeled from a tree, bent in the middle till it forms a half-square, and secured in this position by a forked stick, the lower end of which is fastened to the bottom of the canoe. One side of the bark thus forms a screen for the canoe, while the other side serves as a shed over the gunner sitting in the bottom of the vessel. A candle with a large wick, placed in the middle of the bark, will give sufficient light to render objects visible at the distance of thirty or forty steps.

The canoe is started in search of game with a boy to pole it quietly along the stream. He must never raise his pole out of the water; for the dropping of the water which falls from the pole when raised would frighten the deer. As the canoe glides noiselessly along the stream, nothing but the candle can be seen by the deer; and they stand watching it in amazement, till the canoe comes within eight or ten steps. The reflection of the candle at a good distance makes the eyes of the deer appear like balls of lire, and their bodies look as white as those of sheep. They will not move till shot down, as they are unaware of danger till the gun is fired; when perhaps a dozen will dash out of the water, making a great splashing, and rush through the bushes and weeds along the banks.

Hunting by candle or torchlight furnishes great amusement, as during the night all wild animals seek their food. In moving along the stream, the canoe will glide into the midst of a family of otters, which, being blinded by the glare of the candle, have no fears till they find themselves so near a hunter, whom they are exceedingly afraid of. Then they will flounce about and dive under the water, though it seems as if they could not leave the place until it again becomes dark.

Perhaps you will next encounter a flock of ducks, which will take the same kind of frolic until the light passes beyond their position. They are all perfectly crazy as long as their eyes are blinded by the glare of the candle, which affords much amusement for the night-hunter engaged in shooting deer.

Shooting deer at a lick differs but little from the mode just related, if the lick be a natural one. The plan is to climb a tree, to the distance of thirty or forty feet, and there make a nest of limbs to shade the hunter. Then either a few coals of fire and some fine splinters, or a large candle, is tied to a pole like those used in fishing, and a place is fixed to lay the pole on after the candle is lighted. When the deer come to the lick, the candle is laid as near over it as the length of the pole will admit, when the light will display the entire body of the deer and the sights of the gun as plain as they could be seen by daylight. The deer will sometimes stand until they receive a second and a third shot; so perfectly astonished are they at the blaze of the candle and the thunder of the heavily-loaded rifle. They become confused, and seem to lose their senses for a time.

The way to make a deer-lick with common salt, is to select a place where the deer have found a crossing, and near which is a tree, on which a convenient seat can be arranged at a considerable elevation. Then take a small stake, drive it into the ground to the depth of eighteen inches or two feet, and fill the hole made by it with clean alum-salt. Make three or four such holes, fill them all, and sprinkle a little salt over the ground around them. The deer will soon find the place, and come often to lick the salt, while the hunter, sitting high up in the tree, has every chance for obtaining a fair shot at them.

It is a strange thing that a buck has to wait from the first of April till the last of September for the growth of his horns; and they seldom use them in their own defence until the middle of October. It does seem to me as if nature has prepared their horns only for the purpose of fighting each other during the time they are making love to the does; for if those horns had been intended for the defence of the deer, why should the doe be without them, or why do they fall off so soon?

The wild buck is a most beautiful animal; and when he first comes into existence, he is red, with two rows of beautiful white spots on bis sides. His mother suckles him with great care, hiding him in the most secret places, to elude the search of all his and her enemies.

He is thus raised in all innocence till the following spring, when he is one year old; at which time a pair of little horns commence growing straight up, like those of a goat. Those little horns fall off during the succeeding winter, and when he is two years old a crooked branch grows out, with one spike on it. He is then called a forked-horned or spiked buck. At three years old, he has three prongs on his horns, and is then termed a three-pronged buck. Every year that he lives after this period, until he arrives at the age of five or seven years, his horns increase, and become very large, until they finally contain as many as twelve or fifteen points.

In the winter, when they become tired of carrying those heavy, useless weapons, they lay in the bleakest and coldest spots they can find till their horns freeze, and, in a week or two after, become loose at the head. I have many times seen where they have lain all night, rose, and shook themselves, and there would sometimes lay both horns, and at others, one horn, with a quantity of hair attached to it. This generally occurs in February, and in April their horns start out to grow again. At this time they meet in the same feeding-grounds, become acquainted, and form such strong attachments to each other, that if a hunter shoots one, the others will frequently remain with it till some of them are also killed.

This friendly feeling seems to continue all the time their horns are soft, and covered with a skin called velvet, on account of its softness. In September the horns are fully grown, and about the last of that month they seek the highest and warmest places, where they lay for their horns to dry and harden, still keeping the same company.

About the last of October, they become jealous of each other, fight among themselves, and separate until the mating season is over; when they return to their old feeding-ground, come together again, and so live till the following fall.

In the spring they are poor and shabby, and the venison is of little worth until June, when they lose their winter coat, and assume a deep red color. Their hair is then very thin, and they appear as if they were almost naked.

At this time they come to the licks, when their meat is excellent and juicy; and they frequent the low lands, to avoid the hot sun and flies, till the time arrives for them to harden their horns, when they again take to the high lands.

Having said many things in relation to the game and their habits, I think it may be well to say something concerning the country in which those animals live. Their haunts have been altogether in that part of Allegany County west of Cumberland, where the lots were laid off for the soldiers of the Revolution.

Allegany County is bounded on the east by Fifteen-Mile Creek and the great Sideling Hill from Mason and Dixon's line south to the Potomac River; thence up said river, on the south bank of the same, at high-water mark, to its source, where there is a stone planted, called Fairfax's Stone; thence, by a due north line, to Mason and Dixon's line; and thence, along said line east, to the aforementioned Sideling Hill.

The eastern part of this county, between Green Ridge and Town Hill, between Town Hill and Warrior Mountain, and between Warrior Mountain and Martin's Mountain, is divided into valleys. In these valleys the soil and climate seem much the same; the former producing fine wheat, corn, tobacco, oats, and rye, as also fruit, which grows luxuriantly; and decidedly the best peaches I ever met with were grown there. The people residing in these valleys seem to be in the full enjoyment of peace and plenty.

The western part of this county differs much from the lower part; the face of the country being more elevated, the climate colder, the water clear and cold, and in all the considerable streams trout are found in abundance. This part of the county is divided by mountains: first, there is Dan Mountain, which runs from north to south, parallel with the Potomac; then the Savage Mountain, running much the same course, and the Meadow and Negro Mountains, also taking the same direction.

The Dan Mountain obtained its name from the fact that old Mr. Daniel Cresap was the first settler on those fine bottoms along the Potomac; there he hunted bears, and had some encounters with the hostile Indians residing on that mountain. The Meadow Mountain owes its title to the once beautiful glade on its western slope. The Negro Mountain is so called because, after Braddock's defeat on the Monongahela, a scouting party, traveling Braddock's Road, came in contact with a like party of Indians, when a skirmish ensued, in which one Indian was killed, and a very large negro mortally wounded. The negro was laid under a rock until the party should return from their expedition; and I have been told by one of them that when they returned the following night, the negro was still groaning under the rock; but their fear of the Indians was so great, that, not daring to go to his assistance, they left him to die in the woods on the mountain.

Between the Savage Mountain and the Meadow and Negro Mountains, is a country abounding in the finest pine timber, together with oak, curled maple, birch, and chestnut timber. Wheat, rye, oats, and potatoes are the principal productions, and timothy grows admirably in this region.

From Negro Mountain we come to Selby's-Port, on the Yough. River, or, as it is commonly called, "The Crossings." This part of the county is much broken up by abrupt hills. The land, in places, is well adapted to the growth of Indian corn, wheat, rye, oats, and tobacco; and there are in this locality some fine farms, with excellent orchards of delightful fruit.

We next come to the cove and town of Accident. This is decidedly the best part of the county; it has but lately engaged attention, is now a fine grain-growing neighborhood, and is settled by an industrious and enterprising class of farmers. The land is of good quality, level, well-watered, and healthy. It is among the best wheat-growing sections in Maryland. Indian corn is raised there; rye, oats, tobacco, and Irish potatoes all grow abundantly; and grass flourishes remarkably well.

But the most striking feature of this county is the glades, which are large, level bodies of land, a part of which are open, natural, wild meadows, with a wet, marshy soil. The ridges between those meadows are timbered with white oak, are generally clear of stone, lay well for farming purposes, and no doubt, when properly cultivated, will form a good grain-growing country. The land has mostly been in the possession of men who knew but little of the proper mode of farming, and who probably never entertained a thought about doing anything to increase the fertility of the soil; and consequently the land has not been, nor is it now, near so productive as it can readily be made.

In many sections through the county, limestone abounds, is easy of access, of the finest quality, and inexhaustible in quantity. It is supposed, by those familiar with its use for agricultural purposes, and who have examined this soil, that in no portion of the State would the application of lime produce more marked and beneficial results.

It is my opinion that at one time these glades have been large lakes, which have been gradually filled up by the washings from the surrounding mountains, and by the decay of great masses of grass and leaves — both those grown on the soil, and what have been blown down upon them from the mountains.

This glady region abounds with thousands and hundreds of thousands of the finest kinds of trees, comprising all descriptions of pine, both white and yellow, curled maple, wild cherry, curled white oak, and curled birch, as also black and white walnut, wild cucumber, and chestnut

There have been a few farmers in these glades who had the means of giving the land a fair trial, and they have succeeded in raising excellent wheat and rye. Oats never have been known to fail there till the last summer, when the crop was an entire failure there as well as elsewhere.

This glade country is celebrated as a potatoe-raising region, producing from eighty to one hundred bushels on a single acre. It also abounds in coal and iron-ore, and has ample water-power to propel all kinds of machinery. I will here insert the opinion of the Agricultural Chemist of the State of Maryland, who visited and examined this region.

In speaking of the various coal-beds, and of the quantities in other places, he says, "By far the largest quantity of iron-ore is found, however, in the coal-fields of the Yough. River and in its tributaries, which lie in the coal-basin. This river cuts through the coal-seams and exposes the raw edges of the coal-beds, and thus makes natural sections of them, which offer great facilities for the examination of this section of the county. These natural sections show the coal-beds which I have mentioned above as existing here, and disclose at the same time very rich and abundant beds of clay iron-stone (carbonate of iron.)

"I have examined and determined here five distinct beds of this ore; the thinnest being about one foot, the thickest five feet in thickness, lying parallel to each other and to the coal-veins which accompany them. These veins I found not in one place, nor in one neighborhood only; but in all the tributaries of these streams which lie in that coal-basin, extending from Selby's-Port to beyond Oakland, on the Baltimore and Ohio railroad.

"I cannot but believe this to be one of the richest ore regions in the United States; and, with its facilities for coal and water-power, it offers inducements for investments rarely equalled. This country has been very little explored; its merits are not known, and consequently unappreciated. Its iron wealth by far exceeds that of any other part of Maryland, and lands here are selling for only nominal prices. I earnestly advised the owners of lands here not to part with them at anything like their present prices, but to wait for the advance which is sure to arise as soon as they become perfectly known. Iron is now the great necessity of the age. Its use is increasing an hundredfold for all the purposes for which it formerly was sought, and it is daily being applied to many novel purposes. Iron boats, houses, and bridges will use a large quantity. The wear and tear of the railroads now in use demand a large quantity, whilst those under construction and in contemplation will consume a great deal more than is now used. There will be a constant demand, at high prices, and this region, with other parts of Allegany, will furnish work for a large number of furnaces for almost illimitable periods.

"These remarks are induced by what I myself saw and examined in this region, and fall short instead of exceeding the real state of the case."

These remarks of the State Chemist, together with my own personal observations, leave no doubt in my mind that Allegany County only wants to be better known to raise it to an equality with its sister counties — particularly when its healthfulness, the fine, buoyant atmosphere, and pure water, all seem to contribute to the happiness of its inhabitants. If it were possible that I should be here twenty years longer, perhaps I would be as much astonished at its progress as I would have been thirty years ago, if at that time a man had stated in my neighborhood that an engine would be constructed to transport as great a burden as fifty or an hundred horses could draw on wagons. Every man would either have pronounced such a person entirely crazy, or else would have thought he was trifling with their good understanding. But when the good soil, and all those resources of coal-ore, with the immense quantity of timber, and unsurpassed water-power, shall be brought into use, Allegany will then not only be a very different country, but unequalled by any portion of the State in her natural productions, resources, and enterprise.

www.ingramcontent.com/pod-product-compliance
Lightning Source LLC
Chambersburg PA
CBHW030530100426

42813CB00001B/200